BLOWING THE WHISTLE

The Psychology of Football Refereeing

Stuart Carrington

DARK
RIVER

For Charlie

About the Author

Stuart Carrington is a Lecturer in Sports Coaching Science at St. Mary's University, Twickenham, London. He holds an MSc in Applied Sport Psychology from Staffordshire University, a BSc (Hons) in Sport & Exercise Science from the University of Gloucestershire, and holds the Primary Certificate of Rational Emotive Behaviour Therapy (REBT), accredited by New York University.

His areas of interest include the influence of emotions in sport, learning styles and coaching preferences, the impact of society on behaviour, and the relationship between philosophy and psychology.

Stuart has worked as a football coach, representing two Premier League football clubs, and has coached football to players of all ages in the UK, France, Italy, and Australia.

An avid football fan and follower of all sports, he lives in Berkshire with his wife, Louisa, and son, Charlie.

Also by the author

Turner, M., Carrington, S., & Miller, A. (2018). Psychological distress across sport participation groups: The mediating effects of secondary irrational beliefs on the relationship between primary irrational beliefs and symptoms of anxiety, anger, and depression. *Journal of Clinical Sport Psychology*, 1-38.

Acknowledgements

I would like to thank James Lumsden-Cook at Bennion Kearny for not only agreeing that this was a worthwhile project, but for the valued guidance, feedback and criticism needed to make this book happen.

Many thanks to Dr Tom Webb, who was especially helpful and gracious in sharing his expertise, Dr Martin Turner, Dr Lee Moore and Keith Hackett who agreed to be interviewed for this book; your knowledge and experience is most appreciated. I would like to extend my appreciation to Lee Markwick from the Referees' Association for his invaluable input.

Additionally, sincere thanks to all the referees and referee mentors interviewed (of which there are too many to mention) who shared their views with total honesty, without which I would not have been able to gain such insight into the world of refereeing.

I owe much to the teachers and lecturers who have influenced me over my life and have fuelled my passion for the subject. Most notably Neil Harvey, Dr Abbe Brady and Dr Martin Turner. You made an impact. Many thanks for all the researchers whose work I have drawn upon and don't get the attention they deserve.

Finally, it goes without saying that not only would I have not completed this book without the support of my family, I would not even have started it. Thank you to my parents who gave me everything, especially the best advice a person can receive: that one's best is always good enough. As always, thank you to my wife and best friend, Louisa, who was happy to be a 'book widow' while I wrote this and for your constant encouragement. Most importantly, thank you for giving me the best give gift a man can ask for. All of me loves all of you. Thank you to Charlie, for being Charlie. The taste of love is sweet, when hearts like ours meet.

Table of Contents

"The point I'm making is that he makes a decision in five seconds, or two seconds, or one second or whatever it is, in the heat of the moment with 22 players, with 30,000 people shouting and bellowing. All I'm saying is you don't make that point strongly enough. It should be over-emphasised how hard it is to referee a match."

Brian Clough, 1979

Introduction

The FIFA World Cup Final on July 15th 2018, between France and Croatia, attracted 163 million viewers worldwide. For years, people will remember the names of the goal scorers, 19-year-old Kylian Mbappe's wonderful performance, and Hugo Lloris of France lifting the trophy. A tiny fraction, at best, will remember that Nestor Pitana of Argentina was the referee and his compatriots Hernan Maidana and Juan Belatti were the assistant referees.[i] Despite football drawing such incredible attention, analysis, and fandom, the officials are often forgotten. Examination will typically come only in the form of criticism.

There are a number of possible explanations for criticism. One is that the tribalistic nature of football fans dictates that their team could not possibly have been second best and, consequently, failure was the referee's fault. Another is that the echoes of Muscular Christianity, the 'Corinthian Spirit', and the amateur ideal, still resonate so loudly that neutral referees have never really been trusted or respected in the UK; an area that will be discussed later in this book. A third reason may be that spectators and media pundits do not fully understand the Laws of the Game, while a fourth explanation could be that, sometimes, referees just make massive mistakes.

Besides criticism, there is also a lack of interest in referees and their role. One explanation for this may be that match day officials in England have only been professional since 2001. When it is considered that most professional clubs in the UK were formed over 100 years prior to this date, it may be natural that our interest in referees is still in its infancy.

Another key reason for the apparent lack of interest may be attributable to the nature of the game. The sports philosopher Graham McFee discussed the work of David Best in order to differentiate between two types of sport, and sports officiating.[1]

---

[i] For the record, Dutchman Bjorn Kuipers was the fourth official.

1

The first is 'purposive sports' which are characterised by the end goal being independent of the means. In other words, how a team or individual completes their objective is irrelevant, provided it was done within the rules of the game. Football, therefore, is a purposive sport as 'how' a goal is scored is neither here nor there (provided no violations occurred); a goal has the same outcome and value regardless of how it was achieved. Hence football is objective, as the team with the greater number of goals scored, within the time frame of the contest, wins the game.

Purposive sports are in contrast to 'aesthetic sports' which are characterised by the end goal being dependent on the means. For example, the end goal of figure skating is to achieve the highest score from a set number of officials. But a high score cannot be achieved without the routine being performed in a specific manner and without the officials *seeing* it.

It seems logical to assume from these descriptions that the performance of the officials in aesthetic sports is more significant than in purposive sports. However, despite football having many objective judgments (e.g., the ball either crosses the goal-line or not), there are also many subjective assessments that an official must make.

On average, an official makes 245 decisions per game. 60 of them will be 'technical', such as awarding goal kicks or throw-ins when the ball goes out of play. These are objective judgments. However, 185 decisions are judgments that the official must interpret, such as fouls, advantage, or disciplinary action.[2] Therefore, although the sport of football may be 'purposive', the performance of the official is of great importance. In fact, the role of the official in football may be more important than in other purposive sports, such as basketball or netball, as a game of football may be won – and often is – with only one goal being scored whereas in most other purposive sports many points are scored *en route* to victory. Therefore an official's decision to award a penalty, or not, may be decisive.

It is for these reasons that the psychological influences on the performance of matchday officials are of interest. In order to examine them, it is necessary to clarify what exactly a referee is responsible for, and what constitutes 'good performance'. The FA[3] state the referee must do the following:

- Enforce the Laws of the Game
- Control the match in cooperation with the other match officials
- Act as timekeeper, keep a record of the match, and provide the appropriate authorities with a match report, including the information on disciplinary action and any other incidents that occurred before, during, or after the match
- Supervises and/or indicates the restart of play

From these statements, it can be concluded that, in order to perform well, an official must interpret and apply the Laws of the Game correctly while keeping control of the players in order to ensure a safe playing environment, whilst maintaining a number of administrative duties that start before (and extend beyond the conclusion of) the match. It appears a fair assumption that a 'good performance' is a challenge for a match official but one that is important to meet.

If we were to remove variables such as fitness and viewpoint, a spectator might believe that they are equally as capable as a referee regarding decision making. This assumption is wrong. When the decision-making skills of national level footballers are pitted against those of national level referees, the referees are the clear victors with an accuracy rate of 80.6% compared to the players' 55.1%.[4]

Maybe it is not quite as easy as it looks.

This book aims to do three things. The first is to reveal the psychological influences on the performance of referees. The second is to use practical and real-life examples to show how these theories translate into real-life situations and *why* they influence behaviour. It is this aim that separates this book from common popular discussion about referees; they may highlight difficulties such as 'aggressive players' but often fail to explain the effect this has on performance. The final aim is to consider these psychological influences and reflect on recommendations to improve the performance of officials.

To meet these aims, the book is presented in three parts.

In part one, we shall uncover the possible influences on a referee's performance. In the first three chapters, we will establish the impact of match location: does a game's position sway the referee regarding playing time and discipline? Additionally, when football matches are played at the home ground of any given club, it has long been assumed (or feared) that referees will favour the home side. For example, in 2013, West Ham United manager Sam Allardyce was charged by the FA for misconduct following an FA Cup tie with Manchester United at Old Trafford, during which the referee awarded the home side a penalty shortly after West Ham United felt they should have received one. Allardyce said:

> *"There's no doubt the difference between Rafael's [Manchester United player] handball and Spence's [West Ham United player]. Spence plays for West Ham and the away team, while Rafael plays for the home side at Old Trafford. You see it time and time again at Old Trafford."*[5]

This chapter will investigate whether or not Allardyce's claims have any foundation in truth and, if so, what it is about home advantage that influences the referee?

In chapter four, we extend the investigation of crowd effects to the impact of appeals. Referees are not only subject to 22 competitive players trying to persuade them to make a call in their favour, but also to the appeals of the crowd. Could it be that referees actually use these appeals to help them make decisions?

Of course, protests can sometimes go too far and a player, coach, or team may get a reputation for being aggressive or abusive. Does this intimidate a referee or influence them in some way? We'll find out. By doing so, we'll answer the question posed in chapter six that asks whether or not referees have pre-conceived ideas about individuals. For instance, if a referee believes a player to be a 'diver', how does this affect their ability to remain impartial and to judge events on what they have seen and not what they expect? This question is looked at in more detail in chapter seven.

We will conclude Part One by looking at the other end of this spectrum: do referees show favouritism towards some players? If you think that referees are easily persuaded by the actions of a successful player – an international captain or the dazzling foreign superstar – then this is the chapter for you.

We'll then move on to Part Two, which looks at the individual differences amongst referees and how they are even more important than the factors discussed in Part One.

In chapter nine, we shall attempt to answer the question, 'why would anyone want to be a referee'? Officiating in football is an often thankless task; as a fan, if your team wins, the discussion and focus are on the players or coach and the referee is merely a footnote. If your team loses, the referee makes a convenient fall guy or was simply another element that conspired against your team.

Additionally, and importantly, we shall investigate the effect that motivation has on performance and why it is an important predictor of performance.

Chapter ten looks at a personality trait often attributed to referees: arrogance. Are referees the arrogant control freaks they are often portrayed as? Perhaps the more important question is (regarding their performance) does it matter? We'll answer both here.

Of course, the most important aspect of any individual is the emotions they experience. This, after all, is what makes us individual. In chapter twelve, the emotions a referee experiences will be explored and their significant influence on performance. It is therefore advisable that a referee controls their emotions. As former FIFA referee Keith Hackett stated in an interview for this book, losing one's temper "would be a sign of defeat." This area, along with an explanation of *how* to control emotions when officiating, is discussed in chapter thirteen.

The final part of Part Two is spread over chapters fourteen and fifteen and looks at an often neglected feature of being a matchday official: mental health. Recently, mental health in sport and football has received a great amount of media attention.

However, this attention is not extended to those who, as it will be shown, suffer from the same stressors as players and coaches. So are referees suffering from poor mental health? And why is there such little focus on this area? Finally, chapter sixteen will reveal the coping strategies used by referees to deal with their increasingly difficult demands.

Part Three will meet the final aim of the book, and chapters seventeen and eighteen will set out practical applications that referees can implement in order to minimise the influences revealed and maximise performance. However, responsibility to help referees goes beyond them helping themselves. Therefore chapter nineteen will establish what governing bodies, fans and the media can do to improve working conditions for officials.

It is hoped that this book will be enjoyed by everyone, from those with a particular interest in sport psychology, to fans of football in general, and especially the community of officials that I have begun to learn more and more about. Some of the psychological influences may be more relevant to elite referees whereas some may be of more importance to amateur officials. I hope everyone can take something from the book.

Referees face an unenviable task but, as the saying goes, without them *there would be no game*. Why would anyone want to do it? Let's find out!

PART ONE

THE PSYCHOLOGICAL INFLUENCES ON A REFEREE

1: When in Rome: Are Referees Influenced by the Location?

A referee hones their skill over a long time. They pay their dues, climb the ladder and – once they make it – nothing will stop them from being the best referee the world has ever seen. They will be respected by fans and loved by the players because their desire to be the best will ultimately mean they are the fairest arbiter in the game. Sounds good, right? It's a nice dream, and an honourable desire, but one that ignores the many psychological influences that a referee is vulnerable to.

As we will discover, there are many factors that can make a referee do things they may never have thought of doing. For instance, how would *you* react if 40,000 people were not only trying to direct your attention and behaviour in a very specific way, but happy to personally abuse you if you don't succumb to their will? That's what we're going to look at in this chapter. We will review evidence regarding the influence of the matchday location and establish if there is any truth in the long-running theory that referees are biased towards the home team.

Home advantage, in sport, is one of the most-supported truths, particularly in football. In fact, home advantage is more commonly found in football than in other team sports, such as hockey, basketball and baseball.[6] This phenomenon is not only very real, but it is also found across different levels and nations in the game. To put a figure on it, approximately 60% of points gained are from home matches.[7]

Why is this? There are a number of possible reasons, many of which have been discussed by fans.

The most common explanation concerns player performance, implying that players simply perform better at home. Perhaps they feel more comfortable in their surroundings?[8] But it is possible that there is more to it than that. Indeed, players will often discuss the importance of the crowd, referencing the crowd's enthusiasm as instrumental in a team's success. Former Stoke City striker, Mamady Sidibé, stated:

"There was a real intimidation factor. I'll always remember our first home game against Aston Villa in August 2008, we won 3-2 and I got the winner in stoppage time. The fans' role in getting that result can't be underestimated. They made us believe and we wanted to get the win for them. The whole place went mad when I scored."[9]

This statement suggests that the crowd plays a part, but does so because they motivate the players. While this is not disputed, particularly as 'verbal persuasion' can increase a person's self-belief (see chapter ten), it is plausible that the crowd influences referees too. Questions have long been asked by fans on this effect. For example, are officials intimidated by home fans? Does the number of home fans have a psychological effect on refereeing decisions? Do home fans influence the amount of stoppage time played (or not played)?

One way of answering these questions is to ask the referees themselves, but anecdotal evidence regarding the home crowd effect is ambiguous at best. Former referee Jeff Winter stated in his book, *Who's the B*****d in the Black*, that "…I never, ever felt I was influenced by the crowd… but subconsciously, who knows?"

The quote is telling as it reveals that referees often *don't know* if they are being influenced or not. This is not a slight on a referee but an acknowledgement that human beings can be naïve at best, or ignorant at worst, to the social influences that surround us.

Let's get to the bottom of this. First, we must investigate whether or not there is an influence. If there is, then we can ask *why* this is the case.

'The 12th Man' and the Referee

Does the crowd influence the referee? Yes. There is ample evidence to suggest that referees are influenced by the environment around them. This influence manifests itself in two ways: first, officials are more likely to play more stoppage time at the end of game should it be beneficial to the home team[10] and, second, referees issue fewer yellow and red cards to players on the home team as well as awarding fewer penalty kicks to the away team.[11] We shall call the first claim (regarding stoppage time) 'influence on opportunity' and the second claim (regarding punishment of players and the awarding of penalty kicks) 'influence on discipline'. Let's investigate these claims further.

Influence on Opportunity

In 2009, Manchester United beat Manchester City 4-3 at Old Trafford. The decisive goal was scored by Michael Owen in the sixth minute of injury time. This was not the first time that Manchester United had benefitted from, what many believed to have been, excessive time added on.

In the inaugural Premier League season (1992/93), Sir Alex Ferguson's Manchester United were being held by Sheffield Wednesday with one goal apiece before Steve Bruce scored a winning goal in the seventh minute of injury time. It gave Manchester United three valuable points, and they went on to win the title. The concept that Manchester United received excessive injury time, when it benefitted them, became known as 'Fergie time'. An interesting perspective on this comes from ex-Premiership referee Graham Poll who said:

> *"You dispel it [that referees favour 'big sides' at home] as popular myth that other teams are jealous of Manchester United's success. But when you take a step back you realise there could be something in it. I think it would be too easy to say it's rubbish. When you stop and think psychologically what happens, the pressure that's on you at Old Trafford or the Emirates or Stamford Bridge, the pressure that is implied on you must have an effect, even if subconsciously."*[12]

The first part of the above quote is what gives people doubt regarding the influence of the crowd on a referee. It is possible, after all, that teams who win (more than they lose) do so because they are good at scoring late goals. This could be attributable to a number of reasons. For example, maybe stronger sides tend to have more possession and therefore weaker sides may tire more as the game goes on, leading to more mistakes being made. Or it could be that we simply remember late goals more because of their dramatic nature. Many will remember, for example, Sergio Aguero's 94th-minute winner against QPR at the Etihad Stadium in 2012 primarily because it meant that Manchester City won the Premier League as a result. Aguero himself stated that whenever he hears about last-minute goals, he thinks of that particular one.[13] This is because, as the authors of *The Numbers Game: Why Everything You Know About Football is Wrong*, inform us:

> *"Our brains are wired to remember and overvalue those events that are most startling and vivid."*[14]

In other words, we remember 'stand-out' events, such as the obvious error a referee made that led to a goal, but ignore the good decisions or the mistakes that were inconsequential. For instance, how many other injury time goals did Manchester City score that year and are they remembered as well as Aguero's?[ii] And did referees play more time when they were losing at home compared to when they were losing away? Our aim for this chapter, therefore, is to establish whether referees show a home team bias when deciding how much stoppage time to play at the end of a match.

To do this, three things must be established. First, are referees responsible for the amount of injury time played? Second, what evidence is there (besides a few high profile cases that will always attract attention) that there is a case to answer? Finally, what are the justifiable reasons for a referee to play more (or less) injury time?

Are referees responsible for deciding how much injury time is played?

In 2012, BBC Sport published an insightful report relating to a question and answer session they had with the PGMOL.[iii] The most significant aspects of this report were:

[ii] Manchester City scored 9 goals in injury time that season, including another injury time goal in their title winning game against QPR.

[iii] Professional Game Match Officials Limited – the board responsible for providing officials for the Premier League.

1. There is no set criteria for how much time should be added on, only 'rules of thumb' (for example approximately 30 seconds per substitute or goal scored)[iv]
2. All timekeeping issues (such as deliberate time wasting) are dealt with at the referee's discretion
3. One of the assistant referees, and the fourth official, are charged with monitoring how long a physio is on the pitch for (although their watches are never stopped)
4. They advise the referee how long the minimum amount of injury time should be
5. The fourth official notes down every stoppage in play and can present this list to the management of any club if requested
6. Despite discussion at the PGMOL committee (which meets quarterly) and endorsement from many current and former Premier League managers (including Sir Alex Ferguson), the PGMOL have never submitted a request to the International Football Association Board (IFAB) to have the responsibility of timekeeping taken away from referees. The PGMOL state that, in order to do this, evidence must be shown that it would be a worthwhile change to make.

These facts lead us to the conclusion that the referee is in charge of time added on, answering our first question.

What evidence is there that referees play more injury time when the home team is losing?

To answer this question, let's look at some data.

[iv] Interestingly, there is no such guidance by FIFA, demonstrating a discrepancy between the governing bodies.

Figure 1.1 reveals playing time difference for the 'big six clubs'.

Club	Average playing time when team is winning	Average playing time when team is losing	Time difference (when team is losing)
Manchester United	93:18	94.37	79 seconds extra
Liverpool	93:27	94.23	56 seconds extra
Manchester City	93:22	94.12	50 seconds extra
Tottenham Hotspur	94:12	94.37	25 seconds extra
Arsenal	94:17	94.35	18 seconds extra
Chelsea	93:12	92.41	31 seconds less

Figure 1.1: Premier League added time research adapted from Opta Sports (2010 – 2012). Cited from Pritchard, 2012.[v]

Although Figure 1.1 shows that referees *do tend* to play more time when the home team is losing, it does not provide adequate evidence that IFAB should change their policy on timekeeping as the difference does not seem particularly significant.

In turn, by only giving us the information for the 'top six' clubs, how do we know whether all clubs receive a similar amount of time or not? Frankly, these statistics (and the sample used) are not enough to prove that officials are influenced by the home crowd, but they don't dispel it either. There is, then, a need to look into this area further. To do this, we must establish the legitimate reasons for time added on.

---

[v] It is important to note that data in this table is what was published by the BBC and that the difference in time played when a club is winning or losing is not present in the original data.

What causes added time?

According to FIFA, popular opinion, and academic research,[15] the following are justified events that should cause officials to consider the length of added time:

- the number of yellow cards shown
- the number of red cards shown
- the number of game incidents
- the number of substitutions

This means that if there are a large number of incidents, such as goals, injuries, and substitutions, a referee would be expected to play more added time than normal. And that is what we see; injury time played is, indeed, influenced by such events.[16]

To followers of football, there are no great surprises there.

However, the most significant cause of the amount of injury time played is *not* the events listed above but the score-line in the 87th, 88th and 89th minutes.[17] Bearing in mind that it is during this time period that injury time will be declared, this means that referees are more influenced by the score than game incidents.

To followers of football, *this* may come as a surprise.

It is important to note, however, that by score-line it is not *who* is winning that counts but by *how much*. To clarify, take a look at the graph shown in figure 1.2. The graph reveals that if the home side is losing by a one-goal margin, the referee is likely to play more injury time than if they are losing (or winning) by more than one goal.[18]

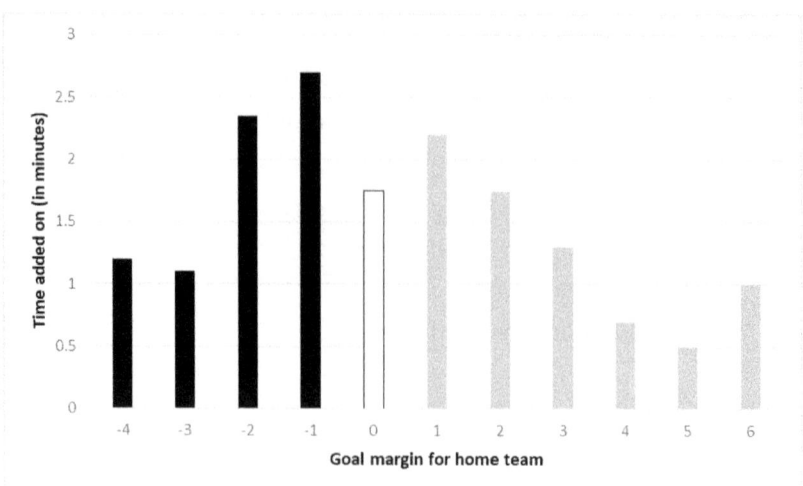

Figure 1.2: Average injury time per goal difference after 90 minutes (from Sutter & Kocher, 2004).

An important consideration here is that if the reasons stated by FIFA were adhered to by referees then, assuming other incidents such as cards shown and injuries were identical, injury time for 0-3 and 1-2 games should be the same. After all, three goals have been scored in both. This is not the case, and the research is endorsed by real examples.

For instance, in the aftermath of the 2018 League Cup Final between Manchester City and Arsenal (which Arsenal lost 3-0; the third goal coming in the 65th minute), Arsenal manager Arsene Wenger complained that the officials did not play an adequate amount of injury time, stating, "It's not down to you [the officials] to judge how long is the time, if you want it or not, give a normal [amount of] added time."[19]

Although it *is* the responsibility of the officials to decide on the length of added time, Wenger's comments ignore the point that, with a three-goal difference between the sides, research suggests that the officials were unlikely to add any more time due to the number of goals scored. In fact, they were more likely to play a minimal amount.[vi] As FIFA guidelines state that 'game incidents'

[vi] Three minutes of injury time were played which would be considered a standard amount of time to most football fans.

should be considered (such as goals), it stands to reason that more time should be played if the score-line is 3-0 than 1-0. Therefore, although Wenger was wrong when he said it is not the official's role to determine the amount of injury time, perhaps he had a point in that more should have been played?

Referees are more likely to play an increased amount of added time if the home team are losing by one goal in the 89th minute than by any other margin.

This finding is reliable even when other factors (such as the number of cards or substitutions) are considered.

Referees are not helped by FIFA not specifying how much time should be added on for game incidents.

Influence on Discipline

In February 2018, Real Madrid hosted Paris Saint-Germain (PSG) in the first leg of the knock-out stages of the UEFA Champions League. After the game, PSG manager Unai Emery stated that, "His [the referee] tendency was to whistle more in favour of Real Madrid. We saw that in the cards, the fouls and the penalty."[20]

Managers regularly comment on refereeing and discipline when games don't go their way. Players 'should' have been booked; players 'should' have won fouls.

So do referees favour the home side with regards to discipline? Again, the answer is yes. In the words of one researcher, there is "a significant home advantage in cards and penalties."[21]

What does the data show?

Figure 1.3 shows that in *no season* in the English Premier League (from 1992 to 2005) has the away team averaged fewer yellow cards than the home team. With red cards, apart from the 2000/2001 season, away teams collected more than the home teams. Think about that for a second. In only one season have the home teams accumulated more disciplinary cards than the away team. To clarify, the average for yellow cards per game is

1.171 for home teams, and 1.621 for away teams. That's nearly 50% more! For red cards, the average stands at 0.056 for home teams, and 0.094 for away teams, also just shy of 50% more likely.

Season	Home Cautions (yellows)	Away Cautions (yellows)	Home Reds	Away Reds
1992	0.595	1.035	0.022	0.048
1993	0.530	0.810	0.017	0.043
1994	1.190	1.578	0.041	0.104
1995	1.232	1.721	0.061	0.089
1996	1.292	1.782	0.026	0.082
1997	1.287	1.984	0.058	0.121
1998	1.547	2.084	0.071	0.113
1999	1.368	1.816	0.055	0.113
2000	1.313	1.763	0.084	0.079
2001	1.211	1.742	0.084	0.092
2002	1.266	1.584	0.068	0.118
2003	1.211	1.503	0.053	0.097
2004	1.089	1.611	0.071	0.084
2005	1.261	1.684	0.068	0.126
MEAN	1.171	1.621	0.056	0.094

Figure 1.3: Comparison of yellow cards, red cards, and penalties converted between home and away sides (Boyko et al., 2007).

A referee is approximately 50% more likely to show a yellow or red card to away team players than home team players.

This effect on discipline could be decisive regarding the outcome of the game.

Having established that referees favour the home side in terms of opportunity and discipline, the natural question to ask is 'why'? After all, a referee does not deliberately exercise a bias towards the home team. In the next chapter, we will investigate what influences a referee's decisions regarding home and away players.

2: Big Club, Big Influence: Are Referees Influenced by the Crowd?

Referees do not show a home bias. This term implies that they favour the home team deliberately, but they are *influenced* by elements of home advantage. Why?

One possible reason is the noise of the crowd. If you stand in front of 20 people shouting for a decision, there is presumably less pressure than when you stand in front of 20,000. While the pressure to get a decision right remains the same, the threat of others evaluating your performance negatively is multiplied.

Although one former Premier League referee has stated that large crowds become like 'working with the radio on',[22] suggesting that any noise is simply ambient, there is evidence to suggest that referees are influenced by crowd noise, and it is a major factor in home team bias.

Crowd noise is related to the number of people present; generally speaking, the more fans present, the greater the noise. And most British stadiums, at the higher levels of the game, have a lot of people generating a lot of noise. The average attendance in the Premier League during the 2016/17 season, for example, was 35,822, with a highest average attendance of 75,290 (Manchester United) and a lowest average of 11,182 (Bournemouth).[23]

When looking at crowd noise, the first thing to examine is its impact on decision-making (this subject was touched upon in the introduction). Sports are judged on either subjective or objective criteria. Athletics, for example, is based on objective measurement (e.g., the time an athlete finishes a race or the measurement of their jump) whereas gymnastics is subjectively measured (e.g., the judges award scores based on their perception of the gymnast's execution). In many sports that are judged subjectively, there are a number of external influences on the officials. For example, British figure skater Nick Buckland stated his belief that the music he and his partner dance to has a major effect on the judges' scores.[24]

Football referees are subjective decision makers on many occasions during a match. In the documentary, *Ref: Stories from the Weekend,* [25] it is stated that the section on the laws of the game that covers 'interpretation of the laws' is bigger than the section that covers the actual laws. This provides referees with both flexibility and confusion, which is frequently evident.

For example, in a match between Liverpool and Tottenham Hotspur on the 4th of February 2018, Tottenham Hotspur were awarded two penalty kicks which were debated long after the final whistle. Former Premiership referee Mark Clattenburg stated (in his column in *The Times* on the 5th of February 2018) that neither penalty should have been awarded, whereas another former Premiership referee, Dermot Gallagher[26] said that the referee was right to award both. This debate, involving two highly experienced referees, illustrates perfectly the subjective nature of officiating in football.[vii]

This is important as the impact of home advantage for sports that are judged subjectively is greater than those that are objectively measured. In fact, home teams/athletes win 74% of the time in subjectively judged sports (e.g., scoring in boxing or figure skating), whereas home sides/athletes in objectively judged sports (e.g., weightlifting and speed skating) win just 57% of the time.[27]

We shouldn't be too hard on referees here. This phenomenon even affected judging at the Olympic Winter Games throughout the 20th century![28] Whilst the crowds at the Olympic Games are typically seen as less partisan and more restrained than football crowds, it is a surprise that anyone believes football referees are not influenced! Therefore, what is it specifically about crowds that influence the referee? Additionally, and importantly, *why* does this happen?

[vii] Empirical research also supports the subjective nature of officiating in football. Fuller, Junge & Dvorak (2004) An assessment of football referees' decisions in incidents leading to player injuries. *The American Journal of Sports Medicine, 32,* 17-22, concluded that agreement rates between match referees and expert panels to be 70%.

The Influences

Figure 2.1 highlights the features of a home crowd that have been shown to affect refereeing decisions. Each of these will be explained in turn.

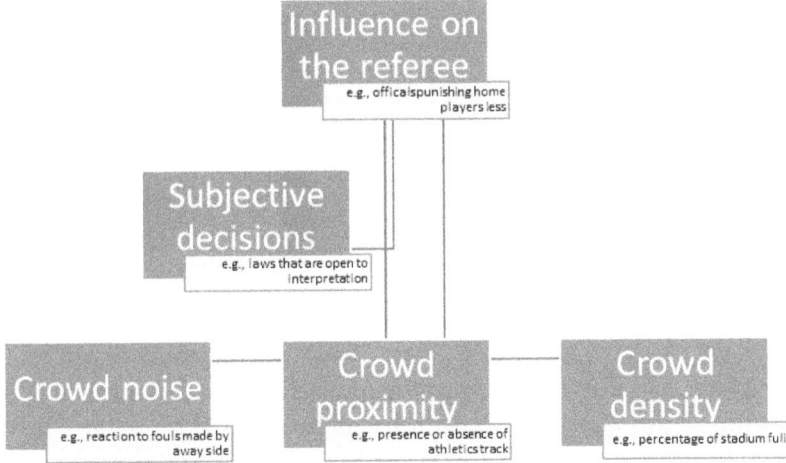

Figure 2.1: Diagram showing the features of a home crowd that impact referees.

Crowd noise

Imagine that you wanted to investigate the effect of crowd noise on whether to give a foul (or not). You would have to test it with a number of referees to make sure the influence was universal and not just applicable to one or two individuals.

Some referees would be shown scenes from a game with the sound of the crowd switched off, whilst others would watch the same clips but with the sound on, as per normal. In fact, this exact approach was used for a game between Liverpool and Leicester City at Anfield, and the results can be seen in figure 2.2.

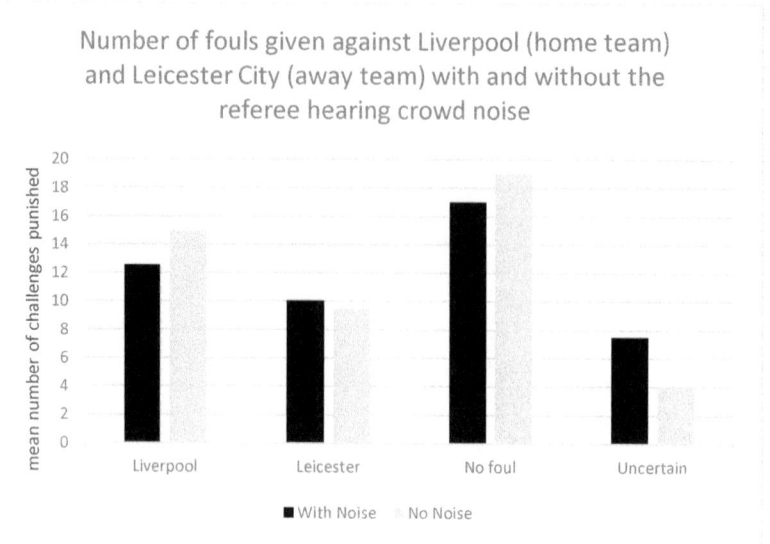

Number of fouls given against Liverpool (home team) and Leicester City (away team) with and without the referee hearing crowd noise

Figure 2.2: The mean number of challenges awarded to the home team (Liverpool) and the away team (Leicester City) when officials watched with and without crowd noise (Nevill, Balmer & Williams, 2002)

The results (and the graph above) show that referees gave 15.5% fewer fouls against the home team when they could hear the noise of the crowd. In other words, the home team was less likely to be penalised if the crowd was noisy; whereas the noise had little effect on the decisions for the away team.

Referees are less likely to call a foul against the home team because of crowd noise.

Does the volume of the crowd noise make a difference?

"Just like a library" is a chant that fans often use to mock a quiet crowd at a football match. But, bravado aside, does the atmosphere at a game (basically how loud a crowd is) influence the referee?

Undoubtedly, yes. In fact, referees are 10% more likely to award a yellow card if the crowd reaction is loud.[29] Additionally, referees often find it hard to recall whether crowds were loud or quiet after a match, which not only suggests that Jeff Winter was correct when he stated that referees do not pay attention to crowd noise on a *conscious* level, but suggests that the influence is certainly subconscious.

Although the effect is small, referees are less likely to punish a team playing in front of a noisy home crowd.

Crowd proximity

Amongst fans, the closeness of the crowd to the players is considered beneficial to the home team's performance. For example, fans and players of West Ham United have discussed, at length, the positive experience of playing at Upton Park and the negative experience of playing at the London Stadium; the common consensus is that the closer the fans are to the pitch the better the influence on player performance.[30]

What is rarely discussed, however, is the influence on the referee.

Indeed, straightforward home team bias (e.g., teams winning more at home) appears stronger in stadiums where the crowd are close to the pitch (e.g., there is no running track present).

Is it simply that home players perform better if they are close to the crowd, or that away players are intimidated? Both are a possibility. However, what is known from research is that the referee is 10% less likely to make a correct decision regarding awarding a home goal when the game takes place in a stadium without a running track.[31] (In other words, goals are awarded more than they should be.) Although goal-line technology is changing the dynamics of awarding goals, the evidence that crowd proximity influences decision making is still valid; the closer the crowd, the greater the likelihood of an incorrect decision in favour of the home team.

In addition, officials are less likely to show a yellow card to a home player if the game is played in a stadium without a running track.[32]

So any owners of football clubs reading this book may wish to minimise the distance from the pitch to the crowd, when building that new stadium!

The closer the crowd, the more likely a referee is to give decisions that benefit the home side.

Crowd density

Another concern for club owners and fans, however, should be the density of the crowd which also has an influence on the referee.[33] Crowd density relates to the percentage of the stadium that is full, and it obviously affects some referees more than others. For example, at the top end of club football, the Champions League attracted larger attendances and greater densities than the Europa League (85.4% versus 64.9% respectively) for the 2016/17 season.[viii] By comparison, some referees in the lower leagues can officiate in front of very empty stadiums!

So what is the influence of crowd density? First, the greater the percentage of the stadium that is full, the more likely the away team will receive more yellow cards.[34] In other words, the effect of crowd density appears to be not that the home team are punished less, but that the away team are punished more.[35]

Of course, this impact could be attributed to greater crowd noise (after all, a stadium that is 98% full will produce a more deafening sound than a stadium that is only 50% full). But the take home point to all this is that crowds really can affect referees!

The density of the crowd (the percentage of the stadium that is sold out) has an influence on officials.

This influence is that away team players are punished more severely than home team players.

---

viii The average attendance for a Champions League match in the 16/17 season was 43,430. The average attendance for a Europa League match in the same season was 21,218. (www.transfermarkt.com/uefa-champions-league/besucherzahlen/pokalwettbewerb/CL/plus/0/galerie/0?saison_id=2016. Cited on 28/11/18 from the World Wide Web).

But why?

It seems a strange phenomenon.

Why would a referee that has, as we will see in part two, trained and acquired a great deal of experience, allow a crowd to influence them in such a way? There are many explanations that all have their roots in psychology. One possible explanation is a phenomenon that has been termed 'charity bias'. This is where referees seek to avoid close victories as they do not wish to be accused by the losing team of helping cause the defeat. After all, the perception of impartiality is of the utmost importance to a referee. One such example of charity bias may be the likelihood of the referee to allow 'one more attack' for a losing side before blowing for full-time.

But, as stated, referees are well-trained professionals who do their best to judge events as fairly as possible. Is there another explanation for the influence of the crowd on a referee? The next chapter will look at a theory that seems well-placed to explain *why* the crowd affects a referee...

3: Feeding the Crocodile: Do Referees Try to Appease the Crowd?

Commenting on Neville Chamberlain's policy of appeasement in relation to the actions of Hitler in the late 1930's, Sir Winston Churchill said, "An appeaser is one who feeds the crocodile, hoping it will eat him last." Do referees want to appease the home crowd for fear of getting eaten? In the previous chapters, we've established that referees are influenced by a home crowd, but we've only just scratched the surface as to why.

The notion of the 'charity bias' is understandable, but not cast-iron. After all, wouldn't the referee feel just as charitable (or perhaps even more) towards the away side? It stands to reason, then, that there is something specific about the presence of the home crowd that impacts a referee's performance. The presence of others leads us to the field of social psychology. By investigating this area, we will establish whether or not the referee feels the need to appease the crowd. But first, we must establish the importance of decision-making on a referee's performance in order to understand the significance of any influence on it.

Decision-Making

The FA[36] states that the primary role of the referee is to enforce the Laws of the Game. Although there are other duties – such as timekeeping – which has been discussed in the previous chapter, the main task of the referee is to make decisions to the best of his or her ability. Fans of football, despite rarely displaying sympathy for the referee, understand that the decision-making process is not easy for a number of reasons.

First, there is the sheer number of decisions to make (see introduction). Second, the game is getting more difficult to judge as player speeds increase. For example, in 2012 it was revealed that top flight football in England is 20% faster than it was in 2007.[37] Third, the media and managers of football clubs scrutinise every decision made, as a potential 'game-changing' moment.[ix] For instance, in the 2011/12 season, Sunderland beat Manchester City with the winning goal coming from Ji Dong-won. The goal was shown, via computer analysis, to be offside and the assistant referee was calculated as being 0.3 metres (30cm) behind play because he had paused in case there was foul to be seen.[38] Fourthly and finally, the official must often make what is known as a 'discreet' decision (e.g., foul or no foul, with no other option) based on 'open' information (e.g., movement/s of the player/s, intention, and player control) within a small timeframe. This is different to the decision-making processes of the coaches whose decisions are both made and revealed over a longer period of time; a referee, by comparison, makes a decision and changes the situation instantly.[39]

This, of course, is not new information. However, popular discussion rarely examines the psychology behind decision-making, particularly for a sport like football, which is culturally significant and regularly discussed in the media. This chapter will examine if the presence of others (especially if those others are biased) influences the decision-making abilities of a referee.

Social Psychology

Social psychologists like to explain behaviour by analysing the environment around us, including the other people within that environment. This perspective, therefore, attempts to explain the decision-making process by looking at the referee's environment and consider its impact. One such hypothesis that has been made is that referees look to avoid making bad calls in order to avoid being unpopular.[40] Indeed, this line of thought could be extended to home bias; the referee, either consciously or subconsciously, wants to be popular with the majority of the fans present and therefore favours the home team. At first glance, this may seem outrageous. It does, after all, seem unlikely that an individual chooses to be a football referee with the end goal of becoming popular! However, there is both anecdotal and academic evidence to support this claim.

[ix] The influence of managers will be explored further in chapter five.

Conformity

Conformity was the explanation given by former referee Mark Halsey when discussing why match official Anthony Taylor appeared to change his mind and show Manchester City's Fabian Delph a red card after initially taking out his yellow card during an FA Cup match with Wigan Athletic in 2018.[41] As the match was played at Wigan's DW Stadium, Halsey claims that Taylor was influenced by the Wigan players and coaches and therefore changed his mind to conform to popular opinion. So is conforming to the views of the majority a motivating factor behind our decisions and actions?

Conformity is an area of psychology that has been researched for decades. Perhaps the best-known researcher, here, is Solomon Asch (1907-1996) who, in one significant experiment, showed a room of seven men a picture of three vertical lines. One of the men was a real participant; the other six were stooges. The seven men were then asked to state which of the three lines was identical in length to a fourth line. The answer was fairly obvious. However, the stooges were coached beforehand to choose the wrong line. Across the many different trials, the various participants were pretty accurate when left to make the choice for themselves (incorrect less than 1% of the time), but when subjected to group pressure, the percentage of wrong answers jumped to almost 37%. This has important implications for match officials; group pressure significantly increases the likelihood of conformity.

A further important consideration is that all the participants in the study agreed, once the experimental aim was revealed, that "independence was preferable to conformity",[42] a view that has contemporary support.[43] This offers a possible explanation as to why referees such as Jeff Winter claim they *were not* influenced by the crowd; it validates their belief that they are independent and immune to external social pressure.

Additionally, the significant increase in incorrect answers came despite people in the Asch experiment having time to respond to a fairly easy task; football referees, on the other hand, have little time to make decisions and are often presented with information that is difficult to decipher.

Do we still think that social forces and the concept of conformity would have little or no impact on a football referee? Two important factors regarding whether a person conforms are the size of the majority, and their unanimity. This is especially relevant to referees, as home crowds are both particularly large (especially in the Premier League as has been shown) and partisan to the point that fans will appeal for decisions in favour of their team regardless of legitimacy. In other words, fans will try to persuade the referee to make a decision even if they do not believe it to be the correct one.

A couple of counterpoints should be raised here. The first is that referees have two assistants and a fourth official to assist them. While they are subject to the same social influences as the referee themselves, Asch found that when the subject had a 'truth-telling' partner, conformity dropped by 75%; we can, therefore, query whether conformity really is the cause behind home bias (this will be dealt with in the following chapters).

Secondly, if home bias is attributable to a human desire to conform to a majority, then there is confusion surrounding why referees were affected by crowd noise when watching clips on TV.[44] Why would a home bias be present when the referee is not in the actual physical presence of a partisan majority? The explanation that the referee is simply 'putting themselves in the game' is too much of a stretch. Therefore, as we continue our journey, perhaps the answer lies not in social psychology, but in cognitive psychology.

Decision-making is the most important skill for a referee.

Social psychologists try to explain what affects this skill by looking at the effects of others, such as a crowd.

There is evidence that individuals are more likely to conform if they are alone in the presence of a large, unanimous majority.

Although a referee is technically not alone, it will be shown that this does not necessarily eliminate the effects of conformity.

4: "Bloody Hell, Ref!" Do Appeals Influence the Referee?

Most football fans, in the cold light of day, will state that they not only appreciate the difficult nature of the referee's job but that they also feel the referee's decisions should be respected.

In reality, fans appeal decisions all the time. They try to exert pressure on the referee to favour their side. Players do this too. But does it work? And can it explain the influence of the crowd on a referee? To answer this, we must move away from social psychology and towards cognitive psychology.

Cognitive Psychology

Cognitive psychology attempts to explain behaviour by likening the brain to a computer; we receive information like a computer receives data, we run a check and then produce a result (such as a decision or behaviour) based on our interpretation of that information. Therefore, referees may not be required to 'put themselves in the game' to replicate conformity, it may simply be a case of referees reacting to specific data. One such type of data a referee may receive is what we would commonly know as an 'appeal', but what psychologists would call a 'cue'.

What is a Cue?

A cue is something that helps guide our actions. For example, a cricketer who is batting tries to predict the path of the ball from the cues given by the bowler, such as their run-up and/or hand position. These would be classified as visual cues. Then, if our cricketer succeeds in hitting the ball, they may wait for a call from their partner to inform them whether to run and, if so, how many runs to attempt. These are verbal cues.

Individuals in all sporting contexts are required to focus attention on the most appropriate cues in their environments if they want to perform effectively.[45]

There are two key aspects to consider. First, cues influence performance in 'all sports contexts', of which officiating is surely one. Indeed, referees testify to using cues to aid decision-making.

For example, if an official cannot see (or decide) if a corner or goal kick should be awarded, they will often wait to see how the players react once the ball has gone out of play.[x]

Second, only appropriate cues must be considered, emphasising the importance of *perceptual-cognitive expertise*. This is the ability to identify and use information that – when used alongside existing knowledge – allows someone to choose and execute the correct response. For example, a goalkeeper might interpret how a striker approaches the ball and accurately predict the direction of the kick based on the information acquired.

The development of perceptual-cognitive skill, therefore, contributes greatly to the skills of decision-making; the most desirable characteristic of a match day official.[46] In turn, attention is linked to cues (after all, our cricketer cannot read the bowler's intent if they are not paying attention) and it is the ability to react to the correct cues that characterises a referee's performance.

Chapter two showed how verbal cues (e.g., crowd noise) appear to impact the decision-making process, and has been flagged up as evidence for the home advantage in football[47] but the *explanation* is often overlooked. After all, why were the referees' decisions in the game between Liverpool and Leicester City so different when watching with and without sound?

Verbal Cues and Attentional Control

Verbal cues are "concise phrases, often just one or two words that either direct a [participant's] attention to a relevant task stimuli or prompt key movement pattern elements of a motor skill."[48] Essentially, they are something we say to show someone something we want them to see, and to prompt them to act in an appropriate way. For instance, on hearing the cry of 'Offside!' a referee would look at their assistant.

While most research has observed the effect of verbal cues on teaching someone a physical skill (such as kicking a football),[49]

---

[x] Another personal favourite is that if a tackle has been made and players rush to confront the offender, it suggests the tackle is worthy of a yellow card; whereas if the players rush to the aid of their teammate, the tackle is probably a red card offence (both of these examples were given by a former Level 3 referee interviewed for this book).

34

this book is interested in the role of verbal cues on directing attention to specific information. It is imperative that we understand more about this concept because of its significance to sports performance.

As one prominent researcher in the field of skill acquisition and cue learning has made clear, it would be difficult to identify a factor that is "more important to learning and performing sport skills than paying attention to the task."[50]

It would be a mistake, however, to assume that attention is solely the ability to concentrate on something. Additionally, it would be foolish to think that it is a process that can be turned 'on' and 'off'. In fact, attention has four characteristics that relate to task concentration and performance (see figure 4.1).[51] These are:

Attentional focus, which is made up of how many things we need to pay attention to (so-called *width*), and whether something has happened previously or is happening now (so-called *direction*). For example, it is sometimes necessary to focus on many things happening at any given moment, such as direction of player travel, speed of travel, height of an attempted tackle, whether there was contact with the ball, etc. Alternatively, sometimes it is necessary to focus on a single, historical fact, such as whether a player has already received a yellow card in that game or not.

Changes in performance situations require different attention skills (e.g., a referee must observe many things going on in open play, but when cautioning a player, they must focus solely on this procedure).

Skills vary by individual (e.g., some referees are better than others at paying attention to what's going on in open play, than others).

A person's ability to attend to something can be modified. This means that everyone is different, each circumstance is different, and referees can be trained to improve their attentional skills.

What is clear, then, is that whilst attention is clearly vital to a referee across a match, attention must change, based on the issue at hand.

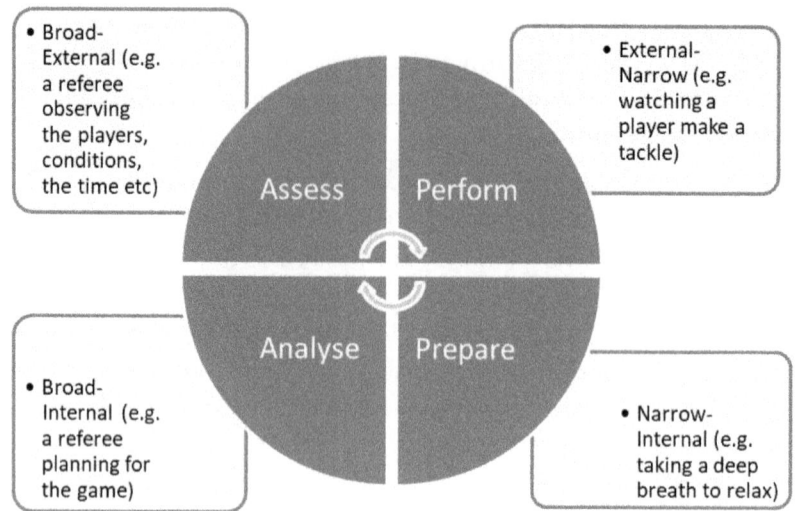

Figure 4.1: The four dimensions of attentional focus (adapted from Nideffer, 1976).

The most important part of figure 4.1 is the *practical application* of each dimension. It is clear that a match official must execute all four of these dimensions (prepare, assess, analyse and act) in any given match and, therefore, an integral skill of any referee is not only being competent in all four dimensions of attentional focus but also having the ability to *switch* their focus accordingly. This ability has a direct impact on information processing, a procedure that a referee must repeat many times per match, and under time constraints.

People in sport use cues to help guide their decisions and actions, including referees.

Cues help people direct, or switch, their attention to specific cues.

What we pay attention to, helps us make a decision.

What is Information Processing & What Impact Does It Have on Performance?

Consider the following example.

Player A is running towards the opposition goal and is chasing, but not in possession of, the ball. There are two defenders who are the same distance away from the ball also trying to reach it first. The goalkeeper from the defending team rushes out to try to win the ball but Player A gets to the ball first, touching it away from the goalkeeper who, consequently, collides with Player A.

According to the Laws of the Game, the official must perceptually process many factors in order to make the correct decision. These factors are:

- Where was the point of contact? (perception of location)

- Was the contact significant or trifling? (perception of force)

- If inside the penalty box, was it a genuine attempt to win the ball or a deliberate attempt to foul the attacker and stop them making progress? (perception of intent)

- Was the attempted tackle by the goalkeeper reckless, careless, or excessive in force? (these terms are not interchangeable in accordance with the Laws of the Game, and have distinguishing features and consequences)

- Would the attacker have reached the ball if they were not fouled, or was it going out of play? (perception of speed, space, and time)

- What was the position of the defending players in the incident? (perception of environment)

- This example illustrates the sheer amount of perceptual information an official must process. The quick analysis of this information is the first step to successful sports performance.[52]

- The next step is decision processing (deciding on the action) and effector processing (acting on the decision).

Simply put, a referee must observe a wide range of information, interpret this information, and act upon it. If there were no interfering factors, a wrong decision could be attributable to a genuine mistake or incompetence. But there may be interfering factors, such as crowd noise, and therefore the question is how do verbal cues affect the decision-making process?

Verbal Cues and Performance

As established, verbal cues influence attentional control (e.g., if someone shouts 'Look!' it will change a person's attentional focus, width, and direction). Verbal cues therefore influence the decision-making process.

Verbal cues affect this process by reducing the number of options from which a performer can choose.[53] Whilst a match day official normally only has two options to decide from (for instance, offside/onside or foul/no foul), verbal cues influence the preference of one decision over another by directing attention to specific aspects of the information available. For example, if the referee hears someone say, "Bloody hell, ref!" after a tackle, the official may choose to focus on the force of contact at the expense of other, important factors.

But can verbal cues really influence our perception that much? Unbelievably so. This is demonstrated superbly in a classic experiment regarding heuristics.[54]

Heuristics are mental shortcuts that allow individuals to make decisions and draw conclusions quickly. In the experiment, the researchers showed footage of a car accident to participants who were then asked: "How fast were the cars going when they _____ each other". The verb 'smashed', 'collided', 'hit', 'bumped' or 'contacted' was used to complete the sentence before being given to different groups. The participants then gave their estimate regarding the speed of the cars in the accident. The results can be seen in figure 4.2.

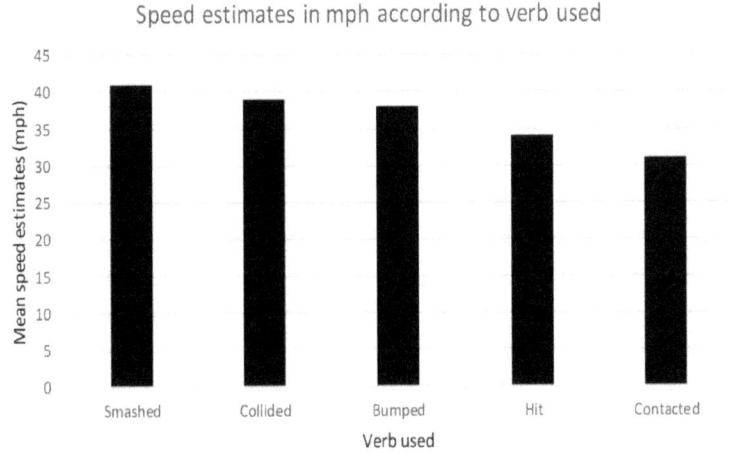

Speed estimates in mph according to verb used

Figure 4.2: Results of the speed estimates given according to which verb was used regarding a car accident (Loftus & Palmer, 1974).

The findings of the experiment demonstrated that those given more 'extreme language' (e.g., 'smashed' over 'contacted') gave higher estimates regarding speed. This can be carried over into football, and how a referee perceives a situation. For example, a tremendous crowd noise, or player appeal after a perceived foul, is similar to the verb 'smashed'; whereas a weak appeal is similar to the verb 'bumped'.

Not only can verbal cues influence perception, but they can also interfere with our memory or events.

In the same experiment, the participants were split into three groups and shown footage of the accident. One group was asked the same question as above with the verb 'smashed' used to describe the impact. The second group was asked the question with the verb 'hit'. The third group acted as the control group and was not asked a question. All the groups were asked to return a week later and given a number of questions regarding the accident on a questionnaire. One of the questions was 'Did you see any broken glass?' despite there not being any broken glass in the footage. The results can be seen in table 4.3.

"Did you see any broken glass?"	'Smashed' group	'Hit' group	Control group
YES	16	7	6
NO	34	43	44

Table 4.3: Results from the second experiment asking "did you see any broken glass" using three groups (Loftus & Palmer, 1974).

These results show that the use of verbal cues (in this case, the verb used) can not only influence our judgment but also misguide our perception and memory. The fact that 32% of the group with the most extreme verbal cue thought they saw broken glass, when there was none, suggests that the more extreme the inference, the greater the likelihood that an individual is influenced.

Don't be fooled into thinking that this phenomenon is only relevant in extreme situations, such as a car crash. Although a player's verbal appeal does not influence whether or not a foul is given in the first place, it *does* influence whether or not the referee awards just a free kick or shows a yellow or red card to the offender.[55]

Does this, therefore, explain why referees discipline the away team more severely than the home team? Possibly, but the use of heuristics is not without criticism. The most relevant of which is that heuristics are normally used when people are not motivated or held accountable for their decisions,[56] and this (clearly) does not apply to officiating in football. In turn, heuristics might not be objectively correct.

For example, in the programme *The Referees: Onside with Carragher and Neville* [57] the presenters are advised by Mike Mullarkey[xi] that unless the attacker looks at least one metre offside, he/she is probably onside. This guidance contributes to the use of cues (in

---

[xi] Senior Coach for Select Group assistant referees at the time of writing.

this case visual) to make a 'short-cut' to a decision, but this may not be the only information that a referee considers when making a quick decision.

Verbal cues direct attention towards certain factors.

With the help of heuristics, these factors can alter a person's perception of events and even their recall of them later.

Cues can interfere with a referee's performance.

The other types of information that may influence a referee will be the focus of the next few chapters. Specifically, do referees use 'short-cuts' to help them come to a decision, and do these short cuts help or hinder performance? One such short-cut may be the reputation of a team, manager or player.

5: Not Them Again: Are Referees Influenced by Reputation?

Are referees influenced by reputation? Fans think so. A quick glance at comments made by spectators on internet forums or social media demonstrates this nicely. For example, after a Premier League fixture between Sunderland and Bolton Wanderers in 2010, a Sunderland supporter stated on an online fan's forum:

> *"The unfortunate thing is that every foul Cattermole does at present is deemed a booking. The booking yesterday and his yellow against West Ham were patheticly [sic] bad decisions. It seems that refs want to get him in the book early to try to stop him tackling, which is an incredibly poor attitude to take."* [58]

During Tottenham Hotspur's 2-4 defeat to Barcelona in the Champions League in 2018, one supporter tweeted:

> *Referee clearly just as overawed as most of the Spurs players.*
>
> @_the_spaniard

Do these quotes reflect reality? If so, what elements of someone's 'reputation' impact on a refereeing performance? For example, does a prestigious manager influence the referee more than a less well-known one? Do high profile players hold more sway when arguing with the referee than newcomers to the league? Does the perceived ability of a team make a difference?

In this chapter, we will use the example of an aggressive reputation to establish that, yes, how the referee perceives a team or person influences their performance. Importantly, we'll also look at why this happens and why it affects performance. Before we do this, however, the quotes above have something in common: both fans are angry or frustrated at the referee for being, in their opinion, influenced. What is it about this belief that brings out such emotion in spectators?

Procedural Justice

The anger shown by fans when they perceive a referee not to be impartial is a result of a phenomenon called 'procedural justice': that it is not the decision that is objected to, but the perceived fairness of the process.[59] For instance, let's take a look at this quote from former Scotland international and current assistant head coach James McFadden:

> *"As a player, I wasn't the easiest to referee, but I hated injustice. I felt, if a decision is made, the referee should explain it."* [60]

Essentially, we accept an unfavourable decision more readily if we believe the decision was made fairly and without external influence. Consequently, when managers or players question a referee's neutrality, the outcome may be unsavoury. The Swedish referee Anders Frisk, for example, was forced to retire after accusations of corruption from Jose Mourinho and Didier Drogba following Chelsea's 2005 loss to Barcelona in the Champions League; he also received death threats from Chelsea supporters.

If a referee is accused of being influenced by the reputation of a team, manager, or player – it is their impartiality that is being questioned.

This angers fans because of a concept called 'procedural justice'.

Basically, if we believe it's fair, we accept it. If we believe it's not, we don't.

It's Not Just the 'What', It's the 'Who'.

It's clear to see that accusations of cheating or unfairness are harmful but, additionally, it is not just the nature of the criticism that is damaging; it's also the source. Following a disappointing draw at home to Sunderland, the Manchester United manager Sir Alex Ferguson stated in a press conference that the referee, 49-year-old Alan Wiley, was "not fit enough for a game of that standard and that is an indictment of our game."

The criticism was flawed, however. Wiley had actually covered 11,039m throughout the game.[61] This is 206m more than the average distance covered by the players. In turn, the referee had an average distance from the ball of 17.7m (the FA has a recommended limit of 20m).[62]

The validity of the criticism is irrelevant, however, when it comes from a source held in such high regard. A fundamental principle of social psychology is that behaviour and information is held in higher esteem when it comes from someone significant. It is clear that former managers such as Sir Alex Ferguson and Arsene Wenger, as well as current managers such as Jose Mourinho and Pep Guardiola, are significant and respected individuals in the world of football. Frankly, what they say, and do, matters.

In 2012, when questioned whether Sir Alex Ferguson influenced the Premier League through his 'relationships with and behaviour towards match officials', ex-Premiership referee Graham Poll answered: "Undoubtedly, yes." Despite Poll's back-tracking in the same article (he claims that he was never influenced by Ferguson), it is clear that decision-making *is* influenced by a number of external sources. But, as this chapter establishes, the outcome is not necessarily what we think it might be. Let's start by looking at the influence of aggression on referees.

Aggression Towards The Referee

Referees, at all levels, report varying degrees of verbal or physical aggression. In 2016, *The Telegraph* published online a number of emails they had received regarding aggressive behaviour towards referees. Some of the correspondence made for quite upsetting reading.

> "Only last Sunday I was assaulted and verbally abused by a coach of an under-15 team. As a 17-year-old, I was truly shaken and deeply saddened that this could happen in a sport I dearly love. The incident occurred after a fight broke out between two players. One of the coaches came running on swearing at me, then pushed me. He was claiming I should have stepped in to stop the fight but I had been trained not to get involved. I had to be escorted by the home team to my car."

*

> "Last Saturday, I was refereeing an under-10s game near Harrogate. I was subjected to constant dissent and questioning of my decisions by the visiting coaches. They play two 30-minute games at that age. After the first, I asked the coaches to refrain from their behaviour as it was a bad example to the children. During the second game, I received more insults and was accused of being a 'cheat'. Attacking the integrity of a referee, in my book, is beyond the pale. I have reported the club and their parents. The situation has left me so deflated."

*

> "Earlier this season I officiated an under-16s game. Throughout, I was subjected to escalating levels of abuse and accused of cheating. I was speaking to a team manager to try and calm things down when one of the players approached me with a torrent of abuse. I showed the player the red card. The player spat in my face and tried to punch me. I was surrounded by members of his team who proceeded to kick me and jostle me. The player's father ran the width of the pitch to shout abuse at me and threaten to 'do me'. This all happened months ago and yet the case still has not been heard by the county FA. Managers and players seemingly 'play' the system by claiming to be unavailable for hearing after hearing. I can tell you from my experience as a referees' officer that those officials who apply the law and report every incident are quickly seen as 'high maintenance' by the county FA."

These incidents illustrate the level of aggression that referees are subjected to, ranging from verbal aggression (e.g., being called a 'cheat') to physical aggression (e.g., being spat at, physically threatened or kicked). Not only may this behaviour lead to referees quitting (as in the case of Anders Frisk) it is also possible that such intimidation affects performance. For example, when recalling an incident involving Roy Keane, former Premier League referee Mark Clattenburg stated:

> *"He screamed at us for a corner and I'm sure it was a goal kick but because he screamed at us so loudly, I gave a corner. I was that petrified of him."* [63]

First, it is important to establish the extent of intimidation that occurs. Although numerous accounts have been highlighted, many may believe them to be extreme examples which do not reflect reality. Unfortunately, this is not the case. The level and frequency of abuse has led to approximately two-thirds of qualified officials contemplating quitting or quitting altogether.[64] While this avoidance tactic is both understandable and regrettable, the focus of this chapter will be the effect that intimidation has on performance.

Before this is examined, however, it is important to understand *why* spectators, players, and coaches abuse referees. Is it simply convention to abuse the referee (which will be discussed in chapter six) or is there something more to it? A possible explanation can be found in a concept known as Attribution Theory.[65]

"The Referee Cost us the Game": Attribution Theory

Attribution Theory explains what people attribute success and failure to. This attribution has an impact on not only their emotions, but how they approach similar situations in the future.

Four areas can be identified for attributing success or failure, and can be seen in figure 5.1.

Figure 5.1: Attribution Theory matrix (Weiner, 1976).

Let's break them down.

1. Ability (e.g., "We played better than them" or "They played better than us")
2. Effort (e.g., "We worked hard today" or "They were first to every ball")
3. Task Difficulty (e.g., "We put out a strong side today" or "They have fantastic players")
4. Luck (e.g., "We were a bit fortunate with the second goal" or "Everything went their way today")

There are two important considerations regarding these areas. First, some are stable over time (whilst others are not). For example, ability is relatively stable. Ballon d'Or winner Luka Modric may have a bad game but he wouldn't become a bad footballer overnight. Luck, on the other hand, is relatively unstable. It can change. Modric may miskick the ball because of a poor playing surface in the 10th minute before scoring via a fortunate deflection in the 12th, for example.

The second consideration is that some causes are within our control and some are not. For example, task difficulty is out of a team's hands; they must play who they are told to play. Effort, on the other hand, is controllable. It is up to the team how much effort they put in.

But this is the important bit: when an individual succeeds they tend to attribute it to things they can control (such as "I played very well" or "I tried really hard"). When they fail they tend to attribute it to things that can change and/or outside their control (such as "they played better on the day" or "I was unlucky").

This is human nature and makes sense. After all, if we have just taken part in a competitive situation and we believe that we are not good enough to succeed, or at least improve, then why bother continuing? Additionally, what we attribute 'results' to also has an *emotional outcome* (see figure 5.2). Simply put, if a manager thinks they won a game because of a bad refereeing decision they express that emotion in gratitude (e.g., "we were a bit fortunate"). If they believe they lost the game because of a bad decision, they express it in anger (e.g., "that ref was a joke").

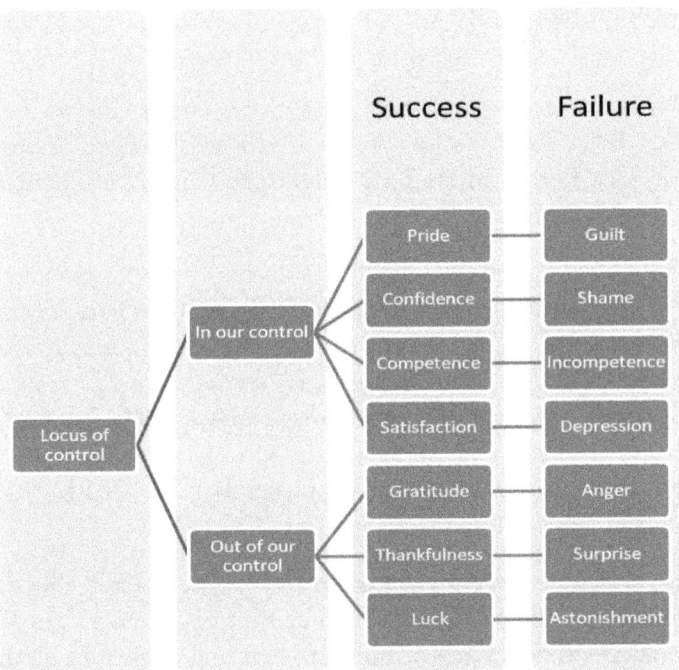

Figure 5.2: Emotional Outcomes of Attributions (taken from the New Zealand Institute of Health & Fitness, 2018). [66]

Do Managers and Players Actually Do This?

Attribution Theory is a nice theory, but those involved in football don't actually do this, do they? Without a doubt, they do! Let's look at some post-match interviews and relate it to the emotional outcomes shown in figure 5.2.

"They [his players] tell me it was a penalty. We are not having any luck with referees, who are human, they can be wrong, but we lack fortune in that respect. We played an outstanding game, we did everything we had prepared, but their individual quality is tremendous." Alaves manager Abelardo Fernandez after a 2-1 loss to Barcelona at the Camp Nou on January 28th, 2018.

*

"You want a fair referee - or a strong referee, anyway - and we didn't get that. When I saw who the referee was I did fear it. I feared the worst." Sir Alex Ferguson after a 2-1 defeat to Chelsea at Stamford Bridge on March 1st, 2011.

*

"In other countries…it [a refereeing error] would be a front-page scandal because it is a scandal. It is not a small penalty, it is a penalty like Big Ben… we will just say that it was a big mistake with a big influence on the result. I will go to the referee and wish him a good year and tell him he will be ashamed." Jose Mourinho after Chelsea drew 1-1 with Southampton at St. Mary's on December 28th, 2014.

These statements are revealing for two reasons. First, they were extremely common.[xii] Secondly, they support Weiner's theory that failures tend to be attributed to external causes. In all the examples given, the referee (an external factor) is blamed. Of course, managers do not always blame the officials for a loss. These examples were picked because that is our focus. But external factors nearly always are. Indeed, in the first example

---

[xii] Typing 'coach blames referee' into a search engine provides more examples than are needed for this book.

from the coach of Alaves in the Spanish league, the defeat is attributed to both external causes – task difficulty ("their [Barcelona's] individual quality is tremendous") and luck ("we are not having any luck with referees"). This example highlights how a coach can bemoan a refereeing decision without attacking the official in question.

The two following quotes, however, indicate how coaches often attribute defeats to the referee in a more aggressive manner. Figure 5.2 explains why coaches can react like this: because the emotion that results from attributing failures to external causes is often anger.

Anger is a human emotion and research has established that emotions may be regulated in order to meet goals or objectives. In other words, people will try to manipulate their mood if they think it will help them.[xiii] For example, anger may be used as a method of intimidating someone to give in to your demands or appeals.[67] Linking this with the emotional consequences of failure, it is clear why coaches might react in an angry manner to perceived, or genuine, refereeing mistakes.

Coaches and players attribute victories and losses to one of four things: ability, effort, task difficulty, or luck.

Losses tend to be attributed to external factors (such as the referee).

Attributions have emotional outcomes that explain why coaches and players may show anger towards officials.

Now we understand why the referee may be blamed for a loss, we must establish the influence on performance. Would referees have been intimidated by Fergie's 'hairdryer'? Let's find out.

---

xiii We will investigate how and why officials do this in chapter thirteen.

Team Reputation – Does It Influence The Referee?

Football fans may wonder whether teams that have a reputation for being aggressive or abusive are treated differently by match day officials. After all, as discussed earlier, many have asked Graham Poll if he was intimidated by Sir Alex Ferguson. While referees may be reluctant to say if this is the case, or not, one former Level 3 referee and current FA official's coach interviewed for this book stated that the reputation of a team or individual will undoubtedly influence a referee because they are only human.

Although a valid one, it is still only an opinion. To confirm this, we need more evidence. Fortunately, we have some. We know that when referees are told which team is the 'aggressive' one before making decisions in a game, the 'aggressive' team is more likely to receive a yellow or red card for a foul than the opposition.[68]

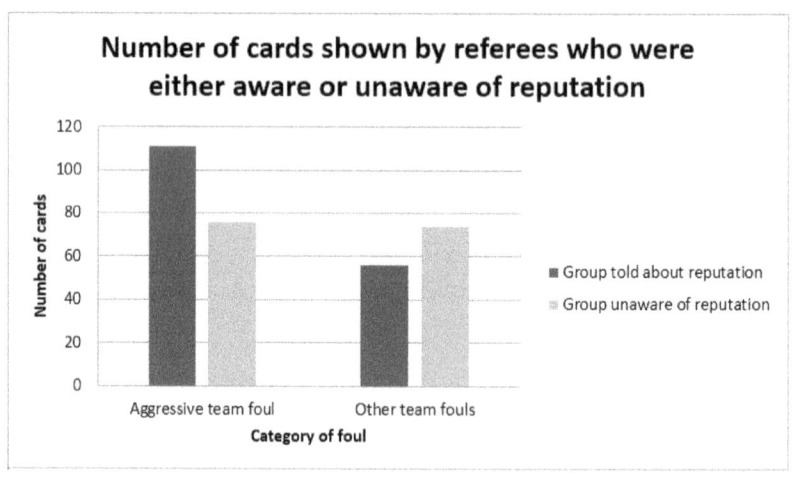

Figure 5.3: The number of red and yellow cards given to each team after 'certain foul' incidents (from Jones, Paull & Erskine, 2002).

When referees are aware of a team's aggressive reputation, they will punish them more severely when a foul has been given.

Figure 5.3 shows that when referees are aware that a team has a reputation for being aggressive, they are more likely to show a card for the foul. The referees that were unaware of any reputation were more likely to be 'consistent'; showing an almost identical number of cards to both teams. Simply put, reputation counts.

There are two important considerations that arise from this research. First, referees did not give more fouls against the aggressive team based on reputation (they award more cards). So, credit needs to be given here to referees who do an excellent job of trying to remain impervious to irrelevant factors such as reputation.

However, another point (and this is key) is that referees took longer to make a decision about whether or not to show a card after a foul when they knew the offender had a reputation as being aggressive. Could this provide us with the answer as to why officials are swayed by external factors despite their best intentions not to be?

Why Does This Happen? Explicit v Implicit Decision-Making

Taking longer to make a decision may seem innocuous, but it reveals that not only are referees influenced by team reputation but also *how* they are influenced. The bottom line is that it alters the implicit, 'natural' nature of decision making into a more explicit and unnatural process. To understand this impact, let's dig into how we learn a skill in the first place.

Skills – both physical and cognitive – are acquired. We are not born with them. In turn, it has always been thought that novices must pay more attention to learning and performing a skill than experts.[69] Skills are then developed from the cognitive (having to think about doing something) stage to an autonomous stage.[70]

Essentially, this means that when we are learning a skill we have to pay such attention to it that our focus is very conscious. However, as we progress, we obtain a level of expertise that allows us to execute a skill without having to pay our full attention. Think about when you were learning to drive. At first, you thought about every movement and action, such as pressing the clutch to change gear or reminding yourself to check the mirror before signalling. But after years of practice, you change gear or manoeuvre while singing along to the radio or thinking about what to have for dinner. The skill becomes what psychologists call autonomous but is more commonly labelled as 'natural'.

But what is of particular importance is that expert performers are admired because their skills are not readily acquired. Indeed, they must dedicate a significant amount of time to obtaining them, making them unique. This is why so many fans, for example, admire the free-kicks of David Beckham. After all, not everyone can 'bend it like Beckham'. Importantly, as anybody who saw 'that' game against Greece at Old Trafford will testify to, these performers are capable of executing their skills under intense pressure. This includes match officials.

At first, it seems logical that paying conscious attention to decisions would be advantageous to referees. However, our working memory is limited and therefore we can only dedicate so much attention to a certain number of factors at any given time.[71] For a match official then – who has many responsibilities and a lot of information to consider – this is detrimental to performance and is why cognitive theories of skill acquisition and execution have been criticised due to their "context conditioned variability".[72] Simply put, learning a skill in the traditional way means we struggle to reproduce our best performance when we are taken 'out of context'. For example, although you may be able to drive competently, you may not perform to your best if you were chauffeuring the Queen.

It would therefore be beneficial to referees to train and to act implicitly.[xiv] There are powerful arguments to suggest that

---

[xiv] The implications of training implicitly (and what this means) will be discussed in chapters seventeen and eighteen.

implicit processes are better than explicit ones regarding skill retention in conditions of fatigue, multi-tasking, and over time.[73] In other words, when we're tired and have to make a decision quickly, the skills we've learned implicitly are performed better. As fatigue, multi-tasking, and time constraints are conditions that affect a referee, it strengthens the case that implicit decision making is best for performance.

So this is why reputation may impact a referee's performance; it halts their implicit decision-making, prompting them to think too much about irrelevant factors. Are the aggressive team deliberately trying to injure the other team? If they are not punished with a yellow or red card, will control of the game be lost? Will I be criticised if I don't send him off? Much like a footballer who is asked how they scored a particularly good goal is likely to say that they 'just hit it' (rather than giving a detailed analysis of their strike), a referee would perform better if they didn't need to think about it, but 'just did it'.

The traditional way of learning a skill is to pay attention to what we are doing until it becomes automatic.

However, when something interferes with this process (such as new information), we think about it, meaning our 'natural' performance is disrupted.

This may be why reputation influences refereeing performances.

So, would it be better if referees made an instinctive decision, preventing them from 'over-thinking' and allowing irrelevant details, such as reputation, to influence their decisions?[xv] Referees already do this. In fact, we all do. We create short-cuts

---

xv It could also help combat the influence of crowd noise. Remember the study that used the Liverpool v Leicester game (figure 2.2)? Have another look and you'll notice that crowd noise nearly doubled the number of 'uncertain' decisions. It's entirely possible that crowd noise is interfering with the referee's 'instinct', and harming performance.

to help us with decision-making. Let's see if this has a positive impact on performance.

6: Get In The Box: Do Referees Categorise Teams and Players?

The examples given previously about Roy Keane intimidating Mark Clattenburg, and fans of Sunderland believing that Lee Cattermole's reputation led to him being booked more often than other players, suggests that how a referee sees a player can influence their decision-making. This is particularly important as professional referees are highly likely to work with the same players on many occasions. For example, in 2009, former referee David Elleray stated:

> *"All refs would say there are some players they get on with and some they don't. Most of them are nice guys. The longer you referee and the more you know them, the better they are. I've refereed [Manchester United] 36 times in my career, so you do get to know them."* [74]

As we'll soon learn, the referee's opinion of a person can greatly impact their decisions and performance.

Schema Theory – Why a Referee's Opinion Influences their Decision-Making

In addition to the quote above, former referee David Elleray also stated that Paul Gascoigne, Ian Wright, and Darren Anderton were the players he disliked officiating the most, stating that Anderton was "one of the biggest moaners in the game." Although this claim may frustrate fans of the teams these players represented, it is a perfectly human admission.

The issue, however, is how these opinions affected decision-making. In his book entitled *How the Mind Works* [75], the author, Steven Pinker, stated that humans tend to 'put people in boxes and treat them all the same.' In this case, Anderton has been labelled 'a moaner'. This is what psychologists refer to as 'schemata'.

Schemata is an area of psychology that has been used to explain how humans use a sense of prediction and control to reach decisions, as opposed to the more time-consuming approach of receiving then interpreting information in order to reach a decision.[76]

Essentially, this means that when people enter an environment of social interaction (e.g., going to a place of work or officiating a football match), they try to categorise others into a schema. A schema is a classification that allows an individual to generalise. For example, someone may put all the different breeds of dogs into one schema called 'canines', inadvertently attributing the same characteristics to all those types of dogs. Although, in reality, not all dogs share the same characteristics, this grouping enables the individual to generalise a group quickly, encouraging faster understanding and decision making (e.g., 'There is a dog. Dogs bite. Do not go near the dog'). The downside of this process, however, is that inferences and decision-making might not be correct. After all, not all dogs bite. Figure 6.1 illustrates how an official may develop a schema for different types of football players.

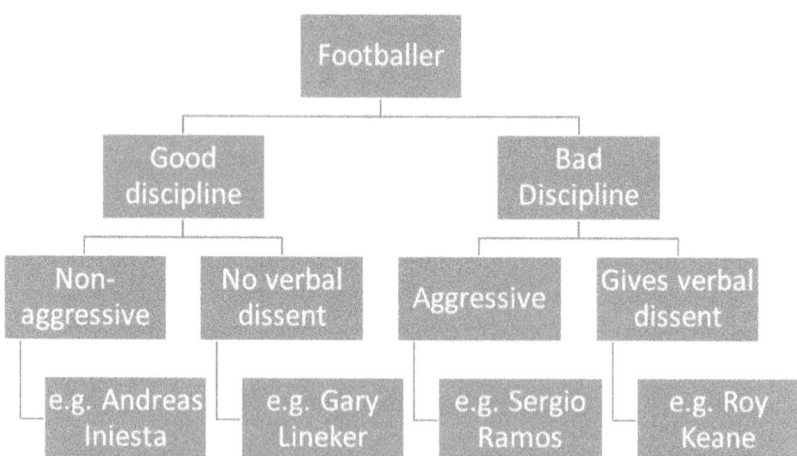

Figure 6.1: Diagram to demonstrate a simple schema of types of footballer. NOTE: This is an incredibly simplistic representation as there are, of course, more than two types of footballer (here only 'good' and 'bad' players with regard to discipline are shown). A more complex model – although it may

be a more accurate representation – would not serve to help explain schema theory.[xvi]

> A referee will come across the same players frequently.
>
> This means they build up a schema of these players – a simplified image of them – which impacts how they interact with them.

Once a Diver, Always a Diver? Referees and Schema-Theory

There is empirical research to support the suggestion that sports officials use schemata to make decisions, especially in fast-paced events when decisions must be made in short periods of time.[77] Given the time constraints that match day officials are faced with in professional football, it is logical to apply this finding.

Additionally, it has been proposed that when an individual is experiencing heightened levels of arousal, schema-driven processing is encouraged.[78] While some might argue that professional referees are experienced and therefore, at that level, unlikely to experience nerves or high arousal levels, former referee Howard Webb recognised that he experienced nerves. Indeed, he said, "The more nerves I felt, the better I felt I performed."[79]

However, it is important to exercise caution before accepting the shortcuts to decision-making that schemata provide. Use of schemata may enable quicker decisions but not necessarily more accurate ones. The already mentioned Loftus and Palmer study (involving the car accident) indicated how information recall might be flawed if an individual frames the problem incorrectly.

[xvi] In an attempt to be as unbiased as possible and not be influenced by my own schema, I have used examples that are couched in evidence. For example, Sergio Ramos is La Liga's record holder for the most red cards (20 at the time of writing) and Roy Keane is often cited as a player who was 'verbally intimidating' (see Sky Sports, 2017c). Whereas Iniesta and Lineker are cited in UEFA's records as players with the best disciplinary records in Europe (UEFA, 2017).

This is especially true when considering schema theory as an official may frame information (e.g., aggression/speed/height of a tackle) in the context of a schema (e.g., 'aggressive' player v 'non-aggressive player'). It is, therefore, possible that schema theory may aid the official in coming to a quick decision (e.g., show a yellow or red card to a player categorised as 'aggressive') but the decision may be incorrect.

This incorrectness may well be because schema-driven processes contribute to confirmation bias, which we shall cover next.

Schemas help a referee make a decision when under time-pressure.

This does not necessarily mean it will be the correct one.

Confirmation Bias

Confirmation bias occurs when we have pre-formed ideas about a subject, and they lead us to accept information that supports these prejudiced ideas (and reject conflicting information) regardless of any validity. For example, say we believe that all rugby fans like to drink beer or that all Americans like baseball. We accept it as confirmation that we were right when we come across someone who meets our expectation. Although these are trivial examples, there is evidence that confirmation bias can be more dangerous.

For example, black athletes have been subjected to the stereotypes of 'lacking work ethic' and 'arrogance'.[80] This stems from the stereotype that black people are naturally-gifted athletes and therefore do not have to try. This bias is perpetuated by the media. For example, announcers on US television emphasise athleticism when discussing African-American players but emphasise abilities such as intelligence or speed of thought when discussing white players.[81]

This not only affects the perception of those individuals but it also has practical, and sometimes worrying, consequences. For example, in 1991 former Crystal Palace chairman Ron Noades stated:

"The problem with black players is they've great pace, great athletes, love to play with the ball in front of them...When it's behind them, it's chaos. I don't think too many of them can read the game. When you're getting into the mid-winter you need a few of the hard white men to carry the athletic black players through." [82]

The consequence of this attitude ranges from issues such as filtering and stacking[xvii] in sports, to the prevention of participation. Although the Noades quote is from 1991, a study from Moskowitz and Carter in 2018 shows that racial stereotypes are still prevalent and influence people's thinking. This attitude permeates popular media. An article in January, 2019, for instance, highlighted that TV pundit and tabloid columnist Jamie Redknapp lauded Paul Pogba's "pace" and "power", ignoring his obvious passing ability.[83] Those that stereotype may even be complimentary, such as 'Brazilians are good at dribbling' or 'Germans are disciplined', yet the impact is the same: it distorts what we actually see into what we think we see.

But what does this have to do with referees?

Confirmation bias is relevant to decision-making as it can influence how we process information without paying attention to *relevant* cues.[xviii] After all, if someone can attribute a personality characteristic such as arrogance (or their ability to play a game, or specific position, based on nothing more than skin colour), then it is entirely possible that a referee can attribute an action or intention to irrelevant cues.

Implicit biases influence our responses in many ways.[84] For example, the previously discussed interview with David Elleray[85] provides us with this insight into confirmation bias in football (and officials):

Q: Did you pick up on European refereeing techniques?

Elleray: Yes, especially when we had that huge influx of foreign players. Those of us who were refereeing in Europe found it

---

[xvii] Filtering is the name given to the process of pushing players from ethnic minorities into certain sports. Stacking is then pushing those individuals into certain positions.

[xviii] See chapter four.

much easier to deal with international players. *We knew they were inclined to fall over more easily* [italics mine].

Q: So they brought bad habits with them?

Elleray: They brought a mixture, but it's fair to say that most of them were already here. I remember watching Francis Lee of Manchester City when I was a kid. He always had a reputation for going to ground easily. That was way before it was seen to be continental.

It is easy to see an implicit or confirmation bias in Elleray's statements. He endorses the view that foreign players are more likely to dive than British players. Interestingly, when asked about this, he contradicts himself, saying that most of the 'bad habits' were 'already here'. This is a good example of how, when an individual is asked to *think* about their statement, they can categorise information differently from their instinctive viewpoint. In the first question, Elleray appears to put all continental players in the 'diver' box whereas, when probed, he re-frames this perception. Unfortunately, when an individual is under time pressure, schema theory is used to come to quick conclusions,[86] and mistakes can be made.

A contemporary example came on the 29th of April 2018, during the live match feed of the Premier League game between West Ham United and Manchester City, provided by *The Guardian* online, which included this update:

57 min: *Sterling goes down under Cresswell's challenge and that's the clearest penalty ever ... but it's not given, and in fact Neil Swarbrick [the referee] points the other way! Cresswell's trailing leg absolutely took Sterling out there.*[87]

There are a number of possible explanations for the referee not awarding the penalty. One is that he simply did not see it (although if it was indeed the 'clearest penalty ever', that seems difficult to comprehend). Another is that the referee was influenced by an implicit bias resulting from a schema that Raheem Sterling is a 'diver' and therefore framed the information incorrectly. This is the view put forward by *The Times* journalist Alyson Rudd[88] in her match report the next day.

It is, of course, impossible to know whether the match day official holds this view of Sterling (either consciously or subconsciously) but evidence has been provided to show how the beliefs an official may have – regarding individual players – influences their decision-making.

Confirmation bias is when we ignore evidence that challenges our beliefs about something.

This is why schemas are hard to change and why reputation counts in football.

This chapter has revealed why establishing short-cuts to eliminate the influence of reputation may not help a referee's performance. In the next chapter, we will see that this influence does not stop at schema theory and confirmation bias. In fact, the more a referee knows about a player or team, the worse they may perform.

7: The More You Read, The Less You Know. Do Expectations Influence a Referee?

Keith Hackett was a FIFA referee from 1981 to 1991 and former boss of the PGMOL. Nowadays, you may be familiar with his *"You Are the Ref"* books. He kindly agreed to be interviewed for this book.

Keith's career saw him travel around the world, refereeing players from a variety of countries and backgrounds. Consequently, Keith says that managing players of different nationalities was a particular challenge. For example, "Italians would attempt to surround you on big decisions", whereas "Eastern bloc countries reacted positively to officialdom. If I asked for ten yards, they would go back further."

These comments illustrate that we are conditioned to attribute characteristics to people (see schema theory in the previous chapter) based on a number of criteria, such as nationality.

"I Know How to Deal with Players Like Them" – Expectancy Effects

How we expect someone to behave may influence our response to them. For example, if a referee perceives a player to be aggressive, then they may feel the need to punish them more readily in order to control them. This makes sense and is suggested by fans (and academics[89]) as to why certain individuals are often booked or sent off when others escape such punishment.

Is this a reality or simply fans exercising their own confirmation bias (or paranoia)? Actually, the fans have a point. Research from 2012 concluded that: "Officials' judgments have been shown, in some situations, to be influenced by information gained or formed prior to the event."[90] In other words, officials may base decisions on previous knowledge or assumptions as opposed to the facts presented in front of them. This is not the fault of a referee but a human function, so let's understand this better.

What We Saw... or What We Think We Saw

There are situations in sport where the difficulty in judging an action is obvious. For example, many spectators would find it impossible to know with certainty how many rotations a figure skater completed throughout their jump, which gives credibility to the expertise of subjective judges.

Football referees are also subjective judges, so perhaps we should not be so quick to query their decisions. Regardless, there is evidence to suggest that, occasionally, officials and judges use information that is *not* relevant to the action being judged in order to be more objective. For example, judges in gymnastics give more favourable scores to gymnasts competing towards the end of their team routine based on the accepted practice that the better gymnasts perform later in the scheduled order.[91] This effect has also been shown in figure skating, where figure skaters were scored higher by judges who were made aware of their positive reputations, compared to judges who did not know them.[92]

These are examples of expectancy effects.

Interestingly, though, "expectancies that mirror true differences can... improve accuracy in complex judgment tasks."[93] Simply put, what we *expect* to see can, on occasion, improve our decision-making abilities.

For example, imagine a referee observing the actions of players during a set piece. Prior knowledge of a player's illegal intentions may benefit the official. Mark Clattenburg stated in an interview that this is exactly what occurred during the 2015 Champions League semi-final between Bayern Munich and Barcelona.[94] Clattenburg was informed by Pierluigi Collina[xix] that the Bayern Munich player, Thiago Alcântara, would move into a deliberately offside position and then position himself to block the run of the Barcelona player, Gerard Piqué. Clattenburg said that in the 13th

---

[xix] Collina was a former FIFA referee who was appointed UEFA's first ever Chief Refereeing Officer in 2010. He won FIFA's 'World's Best Referee' award six consecutive times from 1998-2003.

minute of the second leg this incident occurred, as predicted, and Clattenburg awarded a free kick against Alcântara.

Therefore, it would appear that prior information and expectation was beneficial to Clattenburg's performance. However, it is also possible that having this expectation meant he ignored other incidents going on at the same time. After all, if he is looking at one player deliberately, can he observe the actions of the 21 others? This is not to suggest that Clattenburg was wrong or that he did miss any other incidents, but to highlight that expectations of behaviour can just as easily hinder the performance of an official as help them.[xx]

A Referee and Their Beliefs About a Team

So, if a referee holds a belief about a player or team, does this mean that their behaviour towards them is affected? Absolutely, but perhaps not in the way we may think.

Before we discuss officials, it must be acknowledged that people behave towards others in a way that is consistent with their beliefs and judgements about them.[95] Our perception of others affects decision-making[96] and, alarmingly, it takes a lot for us to change our mind about someone. For instance, parents who believed boys were stronger than girls at maths and sport perceived their sons to be better than their daughters in these fields, regardless of any information to the contrary.[97] This is due to socialisation: the notion that we are raised to believe certain things about people (and that we believe them). It's hard to escape and we all do it. For example, you may assume that a Brazilian would be better than an Australian at samba dancing because, well, Brazilians are good at samba right?

So how does this affect a football referee? Referees are more likely to punish aggressive females with a card than males, even if more aggressive actions occurred during the male game.[98] Referees also resist using cards against nations with

---

xx In chapter thirteen, we will also discuss how individual referees may try to adopt strategies for dealing with aggressive people in advance, which may influence performance.

temperamental reputations. For example, Head of Referee Education, Paul Rejer, wrote the following in support of the referee of England's 2018 World Cup match with Columbia after the official was criticised for not being firm enough with Columbian dissent after awarding England a penalty:

*"Geiger [the referee] has experience in CONCACAF where he has refereed Central American teams in the Gold Cup and World Cup qualifiers, whilst also refereeing South American nations in the Copa America, and, by the way, he has refereed Colombia twice before including at the World Cup in 2014. So he's highly experienced dealing with these types of teams in previous games, and he'll be the first to know that you don't start issuing cautions repeatedly, **that would not work with their temperament, and would only serve to anger them further.**"* [my emphasis] [99]

So, why didn't Geiger punish the Columbian players despite their reputation? Or why were the females punished more severely than the males?

Simply put, because of expectancy effects. If an individual believes that males are more aggressive than females, or that Columbians are likely to lose their temper if disciplined, they are more likely to allow aggressive behaviour because this is what they believe *should* be happening. At the very least, it is more acceptable.

On the face of it, this appears to go against our previous conclusion that teams and players with an aggressive reputation will be punished more severely. However, there is an important distinction. Reputation is not socialised (e.g., it is a widespread opinion of something or someone that is couched in what an individual believes to be evidence). Essentially, it is *earned*, not *learned*. Of course, a reputation may not be true, Gareth Bale and Raheem Sterling don't always dive for example.[xxi] However, the referee has built that image through personal or vicarious experience. Expectancy effects are implicit biases that we have

---

xxi See the next chapter for further discussion on this.

because of the environments we have been brought up in. Let's look at an example to explain this.

> Reputation is different to expectancy effects.
>
> Reputation is not socialised; expectancy effects are.
>
> If a player has an aggressive reputation, a referee will be more likely to punish them with a card.
>
> If a player is expected to be aggressive, because of a cultural expectation, they are less likely to be punished severely.

"He Doesn't Look Like a Footballer" – Social Expectations

One such bias that is often discussed is the colour of a team's shirt. This discussion isn't entirely without foundation. Judges in Taekwondo award 13% more points to competitors wearing red protective equipment as opposed to blue.[100] While it could easily be argued that this phenomenon does not apply to football (for every team in red that is successful, such as Manchester United or Bayern Munich, there is an equally successful counterpart playing in another colour, such as Real Madrid or Juventus), this would be to miss the point.

The reason behind favouring the red competitor in Taekwondo is due to the judges' association of red with aggression; a characteristic that is rewarded in combat sports. Although aggression may not be rewarded in football (it may even be punished), one valid link is the association between personality and player size and body shape.

Sports socialise[xxii] masculinity both physically and psychologically.[101] In other words, they tell us what a good player should look like. Journalist Will Jackson, for example, stated that

---

xxii Socialisation is the process in which we accept the norms and ideologies of societies. Remember the samba example before? There is no evidence that people born to Brazilian parents are genetically stronger at doing the samba than Britons, Canadians or Australians. But we would expect a Brazilian to come out on top of this particular contest!

Leicester City defender Harry Maguire "doesn't look like a footballer."[102] While this seems like a harmless comment, it reflects the biases that we all hold. One such bias is that we attribute personality characteristics to body shapes (which are known as somatotypes).

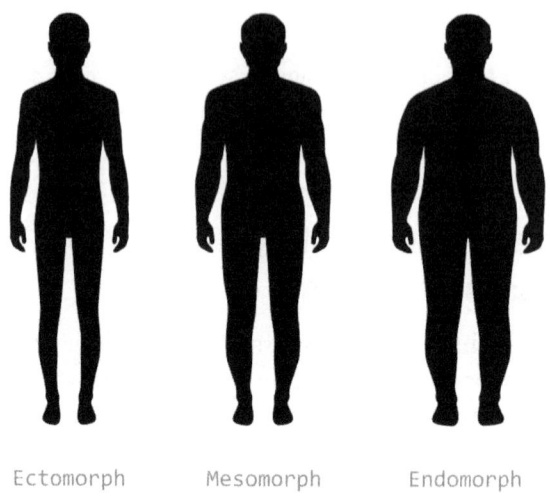

Ectomorph   Mesomorph   Endomorph

Figure 7.1: Somatotypes to categorise human physique (Sheldon, 1954).[103]

A thin body shape (an ectomorph) is associated with attractiveness,[xxiii] success, control and social obedience, whereas a large body shape (an endomorph) is associated with unattractiveness, laziness and social aggression.[104] Body shape is also linked with our ideas of dominance, power, and success.[105]

As established, referees utilise cues to aid decision-making, and referees use associations with body shape as cues in the decision-making process. For example, the taller the player, the more likely they are in having a foul awarded *against* them when they are involved in what the referee perceives to be an ambiguous situation.[106] As can be seen in figure 7.2, the average height of

---

[xxiii] It is interesting here to see the many ways that human psychology intertwines. For example, does somatotype contribute to the halo effect? See the next chapter for a discussion on this influence.

the perpetrator was greater than the average height of the victim across three different competitions throughout all seasons, demonstrating that height (without doubt!) is a variable that influences decision making in referees.

Data Set	Player Height (cm)		Difference (cm)
	Perpetrators	Victims	
German Bundesliga			
2000/01	182.55	181.74	.81
2001/02	182.59	181.80	.79
2002/03	182.64	181.76	.88
2003/04	182.92	181.96	.96
2004/05	182.89	181.90	.99
2005/06	183.38	182.46	.92
2006/07	182.81	182	.81
UEFA Champions League			
2000/01	181.02	180.12	.90
2001/02	181.21	180.46	.75
2002/03	181.30	180.50	.80
2003/04	181.25	180.59	.66
2004/05	181.55	180.79	.76
2005/06	181.78	181.05	.73
2006/07	181.44	180.82	.62
FIFA World Cup			
1998	180.84	179.84	1
2002	180.94	180.17	.77
2006	180.96	180.45	.51

Table 7.2: Average height of perpetrators and victims in three different competitions (adapted from van Quaquebeke & Giessner, 2010).

The average height difference between perpetrator and victim is .86cm which would be indistinguishable to the referee, especially at a distance. But if we look at things more broadly (e.g., a much taller player versus a short player) the greater the difference in height between two players, the greater the probability in a foul being called against the taller player. For instance, when the height difference between the players is 1cm to 5cm, the average chance of the foul being called against the taller player is 51.4%, and therefore any bias is minimal. However, if the height difference is greater than 10cm, the likelihood of the foul being called against the taller player jumps to 58.4%!

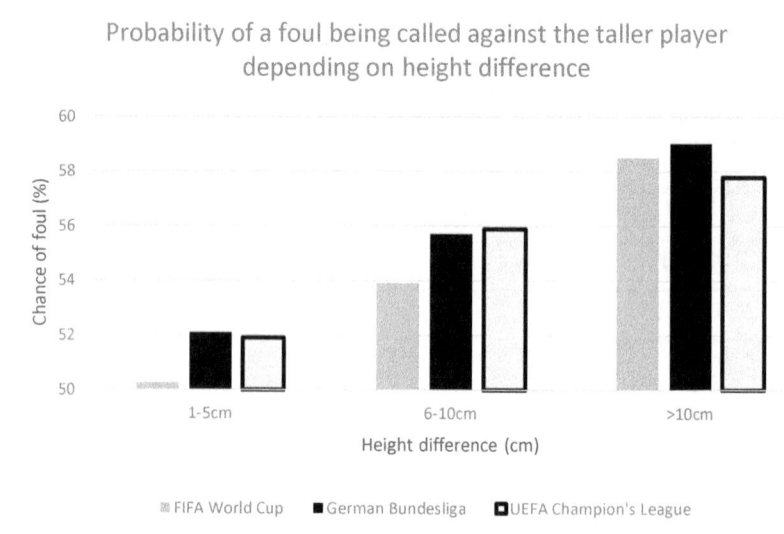

Figure 7.3: Mean probability of fouls being called against the taller player depending on absolute height categories (from van Quaquebeke & Giessner, 2010).

Interestingly, when a taller player goes down after a tackle, it is often attributed to a dive or an accident.[107] If we associate height with power and dominance then Goliath can't be brought down by David, can he?

We associate characteristics to people based on their appearance. For example, tall and muscular people are associated with power and dominance.

Referees are more likely to punish taller players for fouling shorter players than the other way around. The bigger the height difference, the more likely the foul will be given.

This is because of the associations a referee makes with certain body shapes.

This chapter has built upon the influence of a team or player's reputation and shown how a referee's beliefs (about who they are in charge of) will impact their performance. However, is it possible that the effect could go the other way. Might referees hold some people in such high regard that they are not punished when they should be?

Certainly, fans think that some coaches and players get special treatment. For instance, in one pre-match press conference, Jose Mourinho once accused Stoke City of being an aggressive team.[108] However, as Mourinho did not explicitly mention the referee, he was not charged with misconduct for his comments, despite the inference that the referee should be aware of Stoke's approach. Could it be that Mourinho, a high-profile manager with an international reputation, is given special treatment? Therefore, the next section will focus on whether officials are influenced by an individual's reputation because of our need to categorise people. Could it be that a referee's opinion of an individual guides their judgment, or are officials immune to allowing personal feelings to dictate behaviour? For example, former Premier League referee Mark Clattenburg was accused of telling former Southampton player Adam Lallana, "You are very different now, since you've played for England – you never used to be like this."[xxiv][109] Is it possible that personal opinions influence a referee? We shall establish this next.

[xxiv] This complaint was dismissed by the PGMOL.

8: All Men Are Equal... But Some Are More Equal Than Others. Do Referees Show Favouritism?

In 2011, former Premiership referee Mark Halsey showed a player a yellow card because the player asked him to. The player, who is unnamed, wished to be suspended for the next game instead of risking being suspended for a derby game. Halsey instructed the player to "leather the ball 50 yards" after he conceded a free-kick, which is a mandatory booking for dissent. The PGMOL said they had no knowledge of the incident and would have looked into it had they known.[110]

After the game, the player approached Halsey and said, "Thanks for that, Mark."

As established in chapter six – remember the David Elleray interview? – referees get to know players. At the highest level, they are on first name terms, demonstrating a mutual respect that is considered vital for effective officiating.[111]

But does this familiarity ever cross the line into favouritism? After all, we've seen that referees disliked working with some players, so it stands to reason that there were others that they liked. While this in itself is not a problem, it becomes significant if their personal opinion influences performance.

"A putative offence should be judged according to its severity, not the identity of the person who commits it."[112] This quote from journalist and author Matthew Syed summarises an ideal: that participants are judged purely on their actions. However, human beings are subject to a phenomenon that has been evidenced so much, it has its own name: the 'Halo Effect'.

The Halo Effect

The Halo Effect is a positive bias toward someone who possesses, in the eye of the perceiver, something we admire, respect or value.[113] This bias is so strong that we can even attribute positive personality traits based on nothing more than whether or not we find them attractive.[114]

The effect has a powerful impact on judges in subjective sports. Reigning champions, for example, are judged more favourably because of the qualities they must have in order to have achieved so much.[115] Many sports have taken measures to minimise the Halo Effect's impact, such as the highest and lowest scores being discarded in figure skating.

The Halo Effect and Football

The Halo Effect was examined, recently, in an article that compared the treatment of Pep Guardiola (who had a physical altercation with Wigan manager Paul Cook in 2018 during a shock 1-0 win for Cook's side and a red card for Manchester City's Fabian Delph), to that of Jose Mourinho, who kicked a water bottle in frustration when Manchester United midfielder Paul Pogba was booked during a 1-1 draw with West Ham United at Old Trafford.[116]

Guardiola escaped punishment whereas Mourinho received a one-game touchline ban. This discrepancy was attributed to the Halo Effect, with many fans voicing similar opinions. Here are some tweets from fans on the subject:[117]

If Mourinho acted like that in the tunnel he'd get a 5 match touchline ban. Let's see if Guardiola gets anything…@FA

@tanvir10_

Guardiola to get a ban? Oh no, he's not Mourinho.

@MikeMaloney1992

If Pep Guardiola doesn't get a ban by the FA then it's a shambles because whose [sic] the real victim here, the poor water bottle?

@JadeStamate

Guardiola could shoot a referee with a semi-automatic on live TV and the @TheFA wouldn't charge him and Mourinho could wink at a ref and get a lifetime ban. Shocking how the media treat it too. Insane bias towards Pep and City.

@HtotheQ

Are the fans right? Are people treated differently? Although it's difficult to comment on individual cases generally, yes, they are. And it is because of the Halo Effect, which states that we expect better performances (and behaviour) from individuals who we believe have positive characteristics. In turn, and importantly, when they fail or let themselves down, we are also *more likely to forgive them*. This has tremendous consequences regarding refereeing. It explains why professional referees are more likely to be deceived by certain players but not others. For instance, former referee Mark Clattenburg stated:

> *"I've been conned many times, but the most memorable was Cristiano Ronaldo for Manchester United against Spurs at White Hart Lane... I knew at half-time that I had made a mistake because I got dog's abuse when I came out for the second half. The fans had reviewed it, and they were screaming. I was furious when I watched it back. He was that good at it. He went into the penalty area and dropped."* [118]

We'll look into this statement in more detail later, but the most important aspect is that, following this statement, Clattenburg states Gareth Bale was denied many free kicks because he was labelled a 'diver'. Why, then, could Ronaldo 'con' an experienced official but Bale was not awarded genuine free-kicks? Because Bale was a victim of the negative aspect of the Halo Effect.

The Halo Effect is so powerful it even trumps expectancy effects. While female football players are punished more severely than males for aggression because it is not expected,[119] a negative Halo Effect means a referee will take stronger action should they personally dislike a player. Consider this piece of anecdotal evidence from an amateur referee, for example:

> *"I've had a run in with him in the past where I gave a penalty to the other side because he fouled someone... since then I've cautioned him on numerous occasions shall we say, simply because of the way he speaks to me... he's an idiot and he gets me angry... During the game, he did his first foul, so I cautioned him, I honestly think it was a genuine attempt for the ball but he mistimed it... it was literally the first five minutes of the game, normally I would have spoken to them... but on that occasion I knew who it was, and I thought, 'great', I remember thinking, 'I've got him really early, I'll give him a yellow early, he can't do anything else, no grief, no chat, I've got him in the first five minutes."* [120]

This testimony supports earlier evidence that teams with an aggressive reputation will be punished more severely when transgressions are perceived.[121] Additionally, the Halo Effect may be resilient to experience and training – as a more experienced, Level 5 referee stated:

> *"I've refereed [team name] three times and sent him off three times... When I saw him again, I thought to myself 'when will I be sending him off?' because I knew he'd give me a hard time... it literally went through my mind... I went out with the idea I'm going to send him off and I started the game, looked at him, gave him a smirk and thought you're going to be walking... pretty much every tackle he did I gave a foul."* [122]

This effect is therefore powerful, robust, and highly damaging to a referee's decision-making ability.

Referees get to know players well through frequent meetings.

Our opinions about people can be based on minimal information, and we attribute characteristics to irrelevant factors.

These characteristics can cause us to like or dislike someone.

People we like are less likely to be considered in the wrong, and are more likely to be forgiven.

How Does the Halo Effect Work?

The Halo Effect is another example of an implicit bias, which is comprised of eight effects: [123]

1. How we categorise information
2. Where attention is allocated
3. The expectations and standards we set
4. The type of judgments and inferences we form
5. What we consider valid
6. Our approach and avoidance tendencies
7. How we generally act
8. How we feel

When applying these effects to both refereeing, and the Halo Effect, it is obvious how performance can be influenced. For example, let's go back to the Clattenburg anecdote about Ronaldo and apply the Halo Effect. For clarity, the effects of an inherent bias will be added in italics.

- To begin, Clattenburg may have attributed positive characteristics to Ronaldo. He is an incredible talent, playing for a successful club, and is generally considered attractive. This would lead the referee to *categorise* him as a 'very good footballer with lots of positive characteristics'.

- When Ronaldo travels with the ball into the penalty area the referee's *attention* is going to be solely focussed on him as his implicit bias would demand it. Of course, experienced referees will be watching closely whenever anyone dribbles into the penalty area but, as indicated in chapter 3, there are different levels of attention and focus.

- Clattenburg may be *expecting* Ronaldo to succeed in his attack or at least perform a good action, such is the regard he holds him in. However, the dribble is not successful as he falls to the floor. Psychologically, there is now a discrepancy in expectation and outcome which may have led Clattenburg to form an *inference* from the information that Ronaldo was illegally tackled. He considers this a *valid* outcome.

- Consequently, Clattenburg does not *avoid* action but *approaches* it and his *act* is to award a penalty.[xxv]

- Finally, it is revealing to see how Clattenburg *feels* after realising he has been fooled ("I was furious"). Only those we hold up to such high standards can make us feel so angry when they have let us down.

The Halo Effect often sees us ignore the transgressions of people we admire. On the occasions we cannot ignore them, we forgive them more easily.

This effect creates inconsistency in judgements.

It is, of course, impossible to say whether or not this is the reason why Clattenburg was fooled. Even asking the referee would be unhelpful because he may not be aware himself. However, the Halo Effect is clearly a powerful phenomenon that, as has been shown, can explain many behaviours. That said, there is another view that may explain why some individuals are treated more favourably than others...

Idiosyncrasy Credit

During the 1998 FIFA World Cup match between England and Argentina, many England fans blamed the defeat on the theatrics of Diego Simeone after he fell to the ground following a kick

---

[xxv] Avoidance is an area that will be investigated in more depth in chapter eleven.

from David Beckham, resulting in a red card for the Englishman. However, there was not much blame or attention given to how Michael Owen won a penalty in the same game, despite the player himself stating that he went down too easily.[124][xxvi] This begs the question, are some 'questionable' acts forgiven more easily depending on the person?

First, we know that fans forgive the transgressions of their own team more readily than the nefarious acts of the opposition, because humans defend their 'in-group' (basically the group they identify with).[125] It's why Simeone is a villain in England for 'making a meal of it', whereas Owen is a hero.

But this doesn't apply to refereeing, right? After all, officials are not part of a club and cannot referee their own country. The truth may not be as 'cut-and-dry' as it seems.

The concept of *Idiosyncrasy Credit* stems from the leniency shown to those who do things differently, and are excused for it. In fact, it may even make them more appealing. This is the appeal of the 'maverick player', such as Cantona, Di Canio, Cassano, and Balotelli, and they are often given special treatment by those in authority positions. For example, upon being appointed the manager of Paris Saint-Germain, Thomas Tuchel stated that Neymar was an 'artist' and that "artists are special players, they need special treatment; it's common sense."[126]

It is possible that the appeal of the 'maverick' extends itself to the referee; if spectators and coaches can forgive those that bypass the norm, then why not the referee? Suppose that Lionel Messi commits a foul that the laws of the game state is a red card offence, is it possible that the referee would choose not to send him off because he is such a magnificent player? A former Premier League referee, in the documentary *'The Truth About Referees,'*[127] said that if he sent off 'big name' players such as Wayne Rooney, Thierry Henry and Frank Lampard for arguing or swearing at him then the FA would be 'having a word' with him. Although some may argue that this is because of the

---

xxvi Owen repeated the act in the 2002 World Cup finals group stage game against the same opposition.

economic impact of having 'marquee players' suspended,[xxvii] it is more logical to assume that it is because these players have such appeal they are excused more readily when they deviate from accepted behaviour.

A good example of this arose in 2008 when Liverpool's Javier Mascherano was shown a red card for dissent during a game with Manchester United. Although it is easy to justify the dismissal, the poignant fact is that during this particular season the FA were publicising their 'Respect' campaign and stressing their desire to minimise dissent. However, the previous week Chelsea defender Ashley Cole was only booked for dissent that many, including Liverpool rival Sir Alex Ferguson (who mentioned the incident in his interview after the Liverpool fixture), felt was much worse than Mascherano's offence. Is it possible that Ashley Cole, as an England player, was awarded more leniency? Was Mascherano a big enough name that he could be made an example of, but not big enough that he had any Idiosyncrasy Credit?

A key aspect of Idiosyncrasy Credit is that belonging to a 'group' (like fans would perceive themselves to be) is irrelevant.[128] Whereas, with the Halo Effect, we tend to attribute positive characteristics to those we associate with – remember that England fans disliked Simeone's theatrics in 1998 but admired or ignored Owen's – Idiosyncracy Credit can be awarded to anyone, whether we associate with them or not. You don't need to be a Barcelona fan or Argentinian to not want Messi to be shown a red card. Therefore, Idiosyncrasy Credit can also explain why referees favour certain individuals over others.

---

xxvii This argument is flawed because tickets and TV subscriptions are mostly paid in advance.

Idiosyncrasy credit is when we forgive those who do something wrong because we believe they are special in some way (such as being an exceptional player).

This is a big influence on referees because it does not require the judge to be part of an 'in-group' (such as being the same nationality as the offender).

In this part of the book, we have examined a number of influences on the referee and shown their impact using practical, real examples. All these influences, however, are external: they have nothing to do with the referee themselves as an individual. Could it be that the most important factor regarding these influences on a referee is the referee themselves? The evidence seems to suggest so.

So far, we've discussed a variety of influences that can be described as implicit bias. Although I would disagree with the use of the word 'bias' due to its negative connotations (namely that it implies cheating), the 'unconscious roots' of our decision-making has been demonstrated.[129] However, how immune are these 'unconscious roots' to individual factors, particularly self-presentation? In other words, do internal influences – such as a referee's motivation, personality, and ability to control their emotions – determine how influenced they are by these pressures?

That is what we shall discover in part two.

PART TWO

INDIVIDUAL DIFFERENCES AND
THEIR IMPACT ON PERFORMANCE

9: Motivation Matters: Does It Matter Why a Referee is a Referee?

The influences discussed in part one exist. But it is fair to assume that individuals may read about the impact of things like player reputation or player size, and think that they would not be affected. They may believe that they would be strong enough to defy the influence of the crowd, team reputation and player appeals. In fact, they have a point. Individual differences (e.g., time spent training) minimises the impact of crowd noise.[130]

In this part of the book we will explore individual differences, and why they are important. These differences are what separate the 'best from the rest' with regard to football referees.

It is important to remember that referees at the top level are scrutinised by their governing bodies after every performance,[xxviii] with mistakes being punished depending on their "severity and frequency."[131] Therefore, a referee needs to ensure that their errors are rare and of little consequence. This is where the individual behind the whistle reveals their significance.

First, let's look at why someone becomes a referee and whether or not this is important for performance.

There are nine levels of football officiating in the UK.

Level	Description
1	National List (English Football League and English Premier League)
2a	Panel Select (National League Premier)

---

xxviii Referees at lower levels are still observed and receive constructive criticism but less frequently.

Level	Description
2b	Panel (National League North and South)
3	Contributory (contributory Leagues)
4	Supply (Supply Leagues)
5	Senior County (County Leagues)
6	County (County Leagues)
7	Junior (Amateur Leagues)
8	Youth (Junior Referee below the age of 16)
9	Trainee

Table 9.1: The referee development pathway.

Starting at the bottom, levels 9 and 8 are for trainees or under 16's who have completed the FA Referees course. Level 7 is for over 16's who have completed it. Referees can then apply for promotion through levels 7, 6, 5 and 4. Promotion involves training, examinations based on the laws of the game, and marks received from observers. There is no specific timescale in relation to this process, but typically a referee can expect to spend approximately a year at each level.

At level 4, promotion is dependent on a merit table. This table is derived from marks given by clubs that the referee has officiated at (called 'club marks'), and by independent observers. The psychological impact of 'club marks' on referees is discussed in chapter 4. Promotion from Level 2a includes an interview. Once a referee reaches Level 1, a possible final promotion is available to the 'International List'.

This pathway indicates two things: first, that a referee must have their skills continually tested in order to progress. Second, anyone wishing to become a Level 1 referee must be motivated to do so.

It is a long and arduous process. This second point prompts two questions: why would someone want to do it, and does their reason matter?

In this chapter, we shall look at the importance of motivation for football referees and how it affects both participation and performance.

Motivation – Why Would Anyone Want To Be a Referee?

The pathway (above) from grassroots refereeing to the Premier League and Football League is not easy and requires time, dedication, learning, and practice. In other words, an individual must be motivated. In a 2017 interview, former referee Mark Clattenburg stated that he became a referee due to being a 'failed footballer'.[132] A level 6 referee interviewed for this book, meanwhile, stated the following when asked why he decided to become a referee:

> *"I originally wanted to be a coach… but first I wanted to understand the game more. I'd played at amateur level… but I was so bad. So I decided I needed to understand everything. Because I have season tickets, for 11 years now, I've watched a lot [of football] and find myself pretty educated [on all things related to football] but refereeing was an aspect I didn't understand. So I started refereeing. I took my coaching badges but realised while I enjoyed coaching I was actually a really good referee. I'd had really good feedback off a lot of people, and this was without any training from being in a CORE[xxix] group or FA development group… so I decided that [refereeing] would be my pathway."*

While some may focus on the suggestion that referees are 'failed players', this is neither here nor there. The poignant fact is that

---

xxix Centre of Refereeing Excellence.

referees are individuals who wish to be involved because of their enthusiasm for the game. This was perfectly summarised in a newspaper feature, 'Why would anyone be a Sunday league referee'?[133] where one referee put it best, "You have to enjoy the game to be a referee." Enjoyment is a recurring theme in the article and can be summed up by one phrase: 'The love of the game'.

But why do some referees wish to make a career out of officiating while some are happy to participate at a recreational level? Why do some continue to participate in a role despite the incredibly difficult demands, and the potential for abuse? A matchday official may be motivated by any number of factors but eight main motivators have been established and ranked.[134] Here they are:

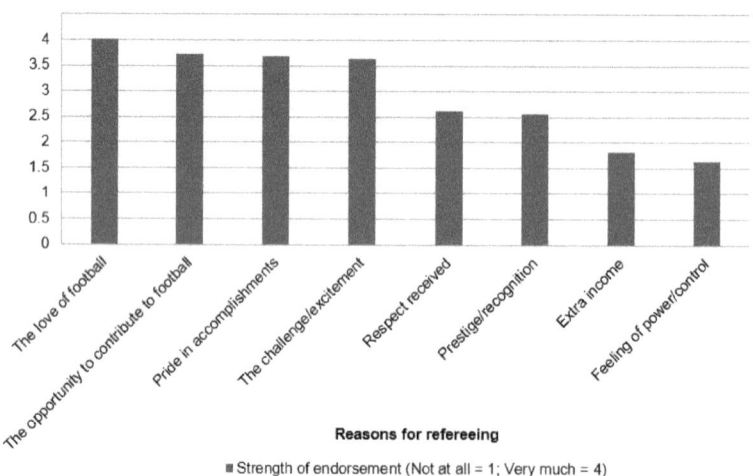

Strength of endorsment for reasons given for refereeing

Reasons for refereeing

■ Strength of endorsement (Not at all = 1; Very much = 4)

Figure 9.2: Reasons given for refereeing (adapted from Wolfson & Neave, 2017).

The top two reasons support the anecdotal evidence that referees are intrinsically motivated and want to participate in football for 'the love of the game'. Intrinsic motivation is all about 'participating in an activity for its inherent satisfactions',[135] meaning that the individual does not receive anything other than personal pleasure for doing the activity. This is important, and has a powerful consequence on performance, as it essentially dictates whether or not we choose to perform in the first place. Would you take up something that gave you no pleasure at all? I wouldn't!

Intrinsic motivation also contributes to whether or not we *continue* the activity, and is especially important in situations where we will be judged (such as a sporting context). Imagine you are about to compete in a game of football, for example. You may love playing, but you also feel nervous. Not only might your team lose the game, you will also be evaluated (e.g., did you play well or not?) Participation in situations such as this is dependent on intrinsic motivation. Essentially, if we enjoy the activity more than the anxiety it may cause us, we will continue to participate.[136]

The impact this has a on a referee cannot be underestimated. Theirs is a situation that is ripe for evaluation and criticism, often in an unpleasant form. Without continued participation, a referee cannot improve performance, and so we must acknowledge that referees really do love the game.

For example, take this testimony of a level 6 referee, who stated:

> *"By the time my second season rolled about, I was given U14 and U15s and being 17 at the time I was nervous. I worried about how the players would receive me as a referee and if they would respect me."*

As this referee is now in their fifth year of officiating, it shows how their intrinsic motivation outweighed the nerves experienced, and he kept doing the job.

Intrinsic motivation is how we measure the level of personal satisfaction we get from doing something.

If an activity causes us anxiety or worry, our intrinsic motivation better be high or we won't do it.

If we don't do it, we can't be good at it!

What Influence Does Motivation Have on Performance?

Having established the importance of motivation on participation, it is also imperative to understand the impact a motivator can have on performance. The FA have identified 17 'key personal motivators' for officials. These are:

Respect – to gain respect and admiration from others in your life

Challenge – to experience the excitement of difficult, risky tasks/situations

Achievement – to see, and feel satisfied, by excellent results in your work

Progression – to be recognised and promoted to higher levels within your organisation/company based on your results and achievement

Health – to remain as fit and healthy as you can

Status – to have the best job title, grade or position for your personal fulfilment

Career/Job Security – to belong to a strong organisation/company and have job security

Power/Control – to be in a position to mainly influence and control others

Harmony – to be accepted by others and have harmonious/strong relationships

Financial Stability – to acquire plenty of material reward (e.g., money and possessions)

Society – to serve both a good cause and your society (local or in general)

Learning – to gain new skills and knowledge; to mature to be as good as you can be in what you do

Work Satisfaction – to be able to do what you actually enjoy doing, and actually enjoy the process of working

Acknowledgment from Above – to gain acknowledgment for being good at what you do from your hierarchy

Life Balance – to have enough fruitful time for your family and friends

Self-Drive/Motivation – to be able to work towards your own goals in work/life, needing only support and guidance rather than full direction

Placid Enjoyment – to simply enjoy life wherever it may take you

Understanding someone's motivation is important as it has an important influence on performance. We assume that if we have passion for an activity then that can only benefit our ability regarding that activity. This assumption, however, is incorrect.

Harmonious and Obsessive Passion

In 2015, a Norwegian study into football referees applied a new perspective to motivation. Two types of passion were identified: harmonious passion and obsessive passion.[137]

What is passion?

It's something we really care about. It's something where we feel good when things go our way and bad when things don't. The behavioural consequence of our passion is that someone will invest a large amount of time, effort, and resources into achieving goals when they mean something to them.

As we have seen, earlier in the book, most referees report a 'passion for the game'.

The first type of passion is harmonious passion, and it is characterised by the following:

- Feeling good after doing the activity

- Not defining success or failure in 'absolutes', such as thinking "I must perform well or I am a failure"

- The activity does not define them as a person

- If things go wrong, negative emotions (e.g., depression or anxiety) don't last long and aren't very strong

- People feel in control of the activity (e.g., they *want* to do it, they don't *have* to do it)

In other words, the activity that the person is passionate about does not define them; failure is rationalised and any resulting negative emotion is minimised. Additionally, the individual will feel positive emotions following the activity and a sense of control. A good example comes from Rory McIlroy who stated "There are other things in my life that are more important than golf."[138]

On the other hand obsessive passion has the following characteristics:

- Individuals don't feel in control of the activity (e.g., they *have* to do the activity, they don't just *want* to do it)

- They only feel socially accepted (and only accept themselves) if they are good at the activity

- The activity conflicts with other aspects of their lives

- If they cannot do the activity, they experience negative emotions (e.g., anger or depression)

When a person has high levels of obsessive passion, however, the individual cannot focus on the task at hand because they cannot control their emotional experience, or prevent themselves from thinking about the task too much.[139]

Why is this important? First, controlling emotions is of the upmost importance when officiating in football.[140] It is easy to see why. If an official is angry at a particular player then their judgment may be influenced. Secondly, referees interviewed for this book highlighted the importance of moving on from 'one decision to the next'. In other words, a good official cannot let a previous decision influence the next, and this quality is compromised by those experiencing obsessive passion.

So, what do refs have? Obsessive or harmonious passion?

Elite referees, at the top level of officiating, have more harmonious passion than obsessive passion, compared to their non-elite peers.[141] Seeing as it seems safe to assume that elite referees perform better than non-elite counterparts, we can conclude that the type of passion a referee has for their role is important.

Harmonious passion is when a person feels in control of the activity, experiences pleasure when doing it, and doesn't let success or failure define them as a person.

Obsessive passion is when a person is controlled by the activity, they experience negative emotions if they cannot do the activity well or are denied the opportunity to participate altogether, and their self-worth is directly associated with success or failure.

Elite referees are more likely to experience harmonious passion about officiating than non-elite referees.

Having established that the type of passion someone has for an activity can influence performance, it must also be said that how a person defines success also has an impact. To show this, we need to look at what psychologists call goal orientation.

Goal Orientation

Goal orientation is what motivates us to try to excel at a particular task and can be divided into two parts.[142]

Task-orientation: this is where the individual sees skill improvement as the end goal. The development, or mastery, of a skill, is the ultimate aim. A good example would be a footballer staying behind after training to practice free-kicks.

Ego-orientation: this is where the individual defines success as performing *better than others*. An example of this approach would be a footballer who does not do their best in training, believing that their ability will be 'enough' to perform well on the day. Additionally, they would justify this approach by comparing their performance to others who performed worse (those who performed better were probably just lucky).

Figure 9.3 compares task and ego-orientation characteristics.

Task-orientation characteristics	Ego-orientation characteristics
Mastery of skill is success	Being better than others is success

Task-orientation characteristics	Ego-orientation characteristics
Self-referenced	Externally-referenced
Practice and hard work is important for development	Perceived ability more important than effort
More likely to persist if they fail	Less likely to persist if they fail
More likely to invest time in new strategies	Less likely to invest time in new strategies
Less likely to drop-out	More likely to drop-out

Figure 9.3: Characteristics of task-orientated and ego-orientated individuals (see Cox, 1998[143]).

At first glance, it is easy to assume that task-orientation is the better approach if you want to become an elite referee. But, in reality, people have a mix of both task- *and* ego-orientation, and this mix is best for peak performance in sporting situations.[144]

The benefits of task-orientation are obvious: people practise, persist, and try to adopt new strategies for success.

But what is the benefit of ego-orientation? Simply put, those who perceive their ability to be *high* will demonstrate the positive approaches normally found in task-orientated athletes. Only those who perceive their ability to be *low* will adopt negative approaches, such as quitting.[145]

Task-orientation is when we see success as improvement or mastery of a skill.

Ego-orientation is when we see success as performing better than others.

For optimum performance, it is beneficial to be both task- and ego-orientated.

Motivation is integral to optimum performance. Specifically, it brings out potential, improves welfare, and reveals how people respond to challenges.[146] If someone with high ego-orientation perceives their ability to be low, they will quit or avoid challenges.

So, if a mix of both task- and ego-orientation is important for optimum performance, elite referees not only compare themselves to others but perceive their ability to be high. In the next chapter, we will not only establish this but reveal why the perception of referees as 'arrogant' is not always a bad thing.

10: Narcissistic Control Freaks: Are Referees Arrogant?

People respond to challenges in different ways. Judgements are then passed on how they coped with such challenges. Indeed, footballers are often assessed like this: "He's too casual", "She needs to be more aggressive", "They need to believe in themselves more".

The way referees approach their challenges often see them labelled as 'arrogant'. In 2017, former Republic of Ireland player Stephen Hunt said that Premier League referee Mike Dean is "probably the most arrogant man I've ever met on a football pitch", whilst former Notts County manager Ricardo Moniz bemoaned how the officials were "arrogant" following a League Cup defeat in 2015.[147]

Are these labels fair and, more importantly, do they matter with regard to performance?

Self-Efficacy

When faced with a challenge, we attempt to meet it or avoid it based on whether we *think* we can achieve our goals.

That's what self-efficacy is. It is the self-belief that an individual is competent at a particular skill or task and can succeed when challenged to do it.

> Self-efficacy = the self-belief that I can achieve a particular task.

Importantly, self-efficacy often dictates whether a person will actually tackle a given situation (versus avoiding it altogether).

For example, a person with low self-efficacy in terms of footballing ability is not likely to sign up for a football club trial. This is because a football club trial is an evaluated environment (e.g., you are judged and evaluated whenever you play).

As referees are judged and critiqued, post-performance, it is clear a referee must believe in their ability to get the job done, or they would avoid the situation altogether.

What Causes Self-Efficacy?

There are four factors that impact self-efficacy.

Figure 10.1: Bandura's model of self-efficacy (1977).

Let's take a look at each arm of the model.

Successful previous performance(s) relates to past success and is considered the most important factor. If a referee feels they have experienced success in the past, they are more likely to referee similar situations again. This can be seen in the quote presented earlier in chapter 9, "I was actually a really good referee".

Vicarious experience (learning from others). This is seen as particularly important when training referees. An FA tutor and former Level 3 referee interviewed for this book stated that one of the most important things a referee can do to improve their understanding is to *watch* others at their level.

Verbal persuasion relates to the messages that others give an individual regarding their performance. Referees might receive positive persuasion regarding their competence from observers and colleagues; however, verbal persuasion may also be negative as officials are often singled out for abuse by fans, players, coaches, and the media. This may contribute to low self-efficacy (e.g., "I can't do it") and may lead to referees quitting.

Emotional arousal refers to how a referee feels (calm, anxious, focussed, etc.). For example, one referee interviewed for this book explained that, before the game, they listen to music and 'get themselves into a zone'. People often do things – such as listening to music – to get themselves into a desired emotional state that boosts self-efficacy.[148]

So, do professional referees believe in themselves? The answer is a resounding yes. Indeed, a lot of the time, referees think they are better than their colleagues.[149]

As can be seen in the following table, accredited referees genuinely perceive their role-specific abilities to be better than those of their peers!

Quality as an official	% better than others	% worse than others
Visual perception	55	2
Commitment	69	0
Honesty	67	0
Willingness to accept a mistake	67	0
Accurate judgments	50	2
Fitness	50	10
Decisiveness	64	0
Dealing with heated situations	59	2
Confidence	76	2
Knowing the intentions of players	64	5
Reading the game	67	2

Quality as an official	% better than others	% worse than others
Interacting with fellow officials	57	5
Spotting a player 'cheats' (i.e. 'simulation')	41	0
Making offside decisions	64	0
Knowledge of the rules	62	0
TOTAL MEAN AVERAGE	60.8	2

Figure 10.2: Perceptions of superiority amongst professional referees (adapted from Wolfson & Neave, 2007).

For example, 67% of referees believed they were better than others (fellow referees) at accepting mistakes, and 62% believed they had better knowledge of the rules than others. On average, almost 61% of referees felt their qualities were better than those of their colleagues.

So, Are Referees Arrogant?

This depends on your definition of arrogant.

It could be that a referee's 'demeanour' is mistaken for arrogance by fans, even though this quality – normally shown with a confident body posture and good eye contact with players – is encouraged by ex-referees.[150]

Additionally, when the importance of self-efficacy is appreciated, unshakable self-belief can be more readily accepted and understood. Indeed, when a football player displays qualities that are labelled as arrogant, some may argue that this is a pre-requisite for excellence. Would a player such as Thierry Henry, who is labelled as arrogant in his native France,[151] have been as good without his swagger? As one Level 3 referee claims, "Referees live on confidence."[152]

Success in a role is not achieved overnight; it's the reward for persistence, hard work, and dedication as seen in the referee pathway. High self-efficacy will encourage a referee to keep going, despite the inevitable challenges that lie in wait.

Professional referees have a high perception of their own abilities.

Sometimes seen as arrogance, this is actually important for performance.

11: Welcome to the Pressure Cooker: How Does Stress Influence a Referee?

Imagine it is the 90th minute of the World Cup Final and the red team are winning 1-0. A player from the blue team has gone down in the penalty box after a challenge from a member of the red team. You awarded the red team a penalty earlier in the game for a similar challenge but you are not sure that this one is a foul. The crowd appeals with a roar. It's deafening. The blue team instantly shout their protests at you. You have approximately one second to respond. What do you do?

This would be considered by many to be a stressful situation for a referee. Indeed, a referee will face many. But is this – what is termed in refereeing as a 'key match decision' – something that provokes feelings of stress in officials? Surprisingly not. Referees (as seen in the previous chapter) are confident in their abilities. Making a call that could change the game is not seen as a stressful situation. However, in games that are of great importance, such as a final or local derby, players commit more fouls.[153] In other words, the greater the stakes, the greater the likelihood of mistakes, regardless of confidence. And Referees feel stress. Former Premier League official Bobby Madley says:

> *"Scrutiny from the media has increased a hell of a lot...They [the public] don't just want highlights of goals any more...You can feel it [pressure], no doubt about it, especially on the biggest stages."*[154]

This chapter will examine three things: first, what exactly is stress? Second, what causes a football referee to feel stress? And finally, how does stress influence the performance of a referee?

What is Stress?

Before considering the relationship between stress and performance let's clarify some terms. Psychology literature views behaviour on only two dimensions:

1. Intensity (meaning the strength of an action)
2. Direction (whether the behaviour is helpful or not)

Some other terms are worth listing before we move on.

Arousal (or activation) relates to the intensity of behaviour.

Anxiety or eustress (the perception that stress is beneficial)[155] relates to the direction (e.g., a positive or negative sensation).

The most important consideration here is that stress is non-specific; what causes stress and how we react to it is entirely down to an *individual's* perception and beliefs. Everybody's different.

However, are there certain things that cause a football referee stress? To establish this, let's see what referees across all levels (and both genders) have to say on the subject.

One level 5 five referee interviewed was asked to recall a stressful incident when officiating. It is easy to believe that the answer would involve a mistake or a physical confrontation. Let's take a look at their answer:

> "One time I was given a game on the Thursday for the upcoming Sunday. Match confirmation didn't come through at all. I had to go through one of the players… I also wasn't told who my assistants were until Friday and when I asked for their contact details… they didn't reply. Eventually I got emails… so I had to email them Saturday for the game. Last minute, very stressful. I didn't get any reply, so I wasn't sure if they were coming. I get to the game feeling stressed. I'm waiting around for a long time… It gets to 2:15PM, kick off at 3PM and they still aren't there… One of my ARs [assistant referees] arrived at 2:30PM but refuses to join me on my warm up. It gets to 2:50PM and my second AR arrives.

> "That whole experience was so stressful, not knowing if they were going to turn up. I had to do a speed session of my pre-match to get out on the pitch on time.

> "They didn't turn up on time. They didn't turn up smartly dressed like required. And that alone annoys me because it's part of first impressions… It worries me that people may think it was down to my poor leadership."

This example shows that a particular stressor for referees is reputation and the image they project. This is echoed in another example, given by a former Level 3 referee, who stated that, after awarding a penalty for a handball on the goal-line, he knew he had to show the culprit a red card. The difficulty was, however, that he hadn't seen who had actually done it because of the vast number of players in a congested penalty box![xxx]

Why did these incidents provide stress? The answer is in the groundwork laid by two prominent researchers on the subject, Richard Lazarus and Susan Folkman.

Lazarus and Folkman helped establish that what causes us stress can be classified into three distinctive groups:[156]

1. 'Harm' – the psychological damage that has already been done (e.g., not turning up on time which results in a negative opinion of you)
2. 'Threat' – the anticipation of harm (e.g., someone may attack me physically or evaluate me negatively)
3. 'Challenge' – the demands made on us that we feel we can overcome (e.g., a referee that is concerned there will be a difficult game to officiate).

Threat can be broken down further.

1. Threat to a person's ego (e.g., a referee who believes they are excellent but then makes a big error)
2. Threat of physical harm (e.g., amateur referees are concerned about the threat of physical violence more than professional referees[157])
3. Ambiguity (e.g., events being unclear, such as the previous example where the referee was unsure who to send off)
4. Disruption to routine (e.g., the previous example of a referee's pre-match routine and organisation not going to plan)

[xxx] His solution was ingenious. He spoke to the assistant to give the illusion that they had seen who had done it and then, with an authoritative tone, called out, "yes, please" while giving an inviting gesture with his hand towards the group of players. The culprit stepped forward. The referee then asked, "Why did you do that?" to check he had the right man, which prompted a full confession.

5. Threat of negative social evaluation (e.g., fans or players thinking you're not a very good referee).[158]

Although these fears are not exclusive to referees, speaking to match officials – such as in the examples given already – shows that that some are stronger than others. Dr Tom Webb, an expert on match day officials and author of *Elite Soccer Referees: Officiating in the Premier League, La Liga and Serie A*,[159] has identified time and travel issues and commitments as particularly stressful for officials.[160]

Therefore referees tend to feel stressed about the same things, but the causes of their stress is not what we probably thought. This brings us onto our second point.

Although referees may feel stressed about the same things, that is not to say that they are affected in the same way. For instance, one referee stated that they experienced stress when dealing with their first "mass confrontation" on the football pitch, while others stated that this didn't bother them because they had seen it all before! Simply put, people respond differently to similar situations.

If we take the issue of aggression and intimidation, for instance, individual differences and their effect on performance can be seen in these quotes from two referees:[161]

> "*You do feel that that the pressure is put on you so much that you get to the point where you are so angry that you say, 'sod it, I'm going to give everything against you'... You think, 'sod it, I don't care if I'm wrong... I don't care, for a 50/50, I'm going against you', even though you then think 'I actually got that wrong'... I think it's done just to shut them up, 'you're not going to get anything so shut up'.*"

*

> "*It was a tough game to referee, but it goes back to getting the decisions right, if there was a decision to go to [the team that had been aggressive towards him] I'd give it to them, if there was one to go against them, it would go against them. There's no point getting decisions deliberately wrong because you're cheating yourself, you're cheating the players and you'll be found out... I definitely thought about this before making the decision.*"

These separate pieces of referee testimony illustrate the potential for individual differences. After all, one referee seems to be less influenced by aggression than the other. Interestingly, not only is each referee different, but the same referee may be different *one game to the next*!

> Stress can differ in intensity and direction (basically, it could be perceived as good or bad).
>
> Anecdotal evidence suggests that not knowing what to do in a situation (ambiguity) and disruption to routine are the most common stressors to officials; not making big decisions and worrying about mistakes are less stressful.
>
> Referees are individuals and so may react to the same event differently.
>
> Not only that, but the same referee may react differently to similar circumstances at different times.

Why Are Some Influenced More Than Others?

The variation in the attitudes and behaviours of officials often encourages spectators, journalists, coaches, and others to assess them.

For instance, one journalist claimed that the referee of the fight between Anthony Joshua and Joseph Parker – Giuseppe Quarterone – was the type of referee who is intoxicated by power, likening him to "a bouncer at a dodgy nightclub who wants to be the centre of attention."[162]

Football referees, as a result of officiating a sport that dominates the media, are often subject to personality analyses. For example, Mark Clattenburg claimed that spectators believe him to be an 'egotist',[163] former Leicester City manager Nigel Pearson said that referee Mike Dean is "one of the most arrogant men I have ever met"[164] and Jose Mourinho labelled Slovenian official Damir Skomina as "weak and naïve."[165] Although such comments are most likely borne from frustration (would Mourinho label an official 'weak' if they agreed with his view every time?) they imply that personality impacts upon performance.

Individual differences in sports performance are well established. They influence any number of things, such as how athletes react to different leadership styles, group cohesion, and how motivational a training environment is.[166] Individual differences also influence the performance of the referee.

In chapter four, the concept of *attentional focus* was discussed and it was stated that attentional skills vary across individuals.[167] Here are three areas where individual differences come to the fore:[168]

1. Individuals have different levels for developing attention. These levels influence how many things they can pay attention to, and also *how* they interpret the information (e.g., a referee considering the rules of the competition, the location, the conditions and specific tactics for the game). Therefore some individuals are better suited to roles where taking in large amounts of information is important than others.

2. Some individuals are more sensitive to information that they cannot control (e.g., the environment, the players, the current action area, and visual or verbal cues) than others. This means that they can read and react to information from these sources more effectively. They also deal with large amounts of this type of information without getting overloaded or confused, performing better in critical situations.

3. Some individuals are better at focussing *narrowly* (e.g., watching a specific action or taking a deep breath to compose themselves) and not become distracted. This especially true of those involved in world class sport.[xxxi]

[xxxi] This is called 'gazing performance' and is used by many high performing groups such as the New Zealand All Blacks. Essentially, it is about using triggers (e.g., looking at the grass or taking a breath) to in order to focus on relevant information and block out unwanted stimuli. See http://trainingground.guru/articles/red2blue-how-to-think-like-an-all-black-or-gurkha for an excellent review.

In the next two chapters, we will focus on how we attend to our own emotions[xxxii] and how they impact on performance. First, however, let's look at the ability of an individual to deal with large amounts of information.

Personality is seen as an important factor regarding performance as it dictates how we perceive stressful situations. This is what makes us unique.

Some people are better at certain types of attention under stress than others. Some types of attention are better in certain situations (such as refereeing a football match). For example, at some points during a game, a referee must be aware of many things, such as the conditions, the contact between two players, whether a player has had previous warnings, the location of the incident, input from their assistant, et cetera). At other times, the referee may need to focus their attention on themselves. For example, after a big decision, taking a moment to calm down and re-focus.

Dealing with External Information and Preventing Confusion

Confusion is a symptom of psychological stress, and often appears in sport. Why is this? Because sporting competition is seen as culturally and personally significant, with the end goal of winning perceived as extremely desirable. This 'high stakes' environment is what can cause stress on participants and officials.

An example of this stress could be seen in the actions of British tennis player Johanna Konta who, on Sunday 17th June, 2018, said to the umpire, "This is an absolute joke. We are out here busting our chops. You are making decisions that affect all our lives."[169]

---

xxxii Labelled 'narrow-internal' attention

Like players, officials want to do a good job. They do not want to make mistakes and want to avoid the stressors discussed earlier. This, however, is sometimes unavoidable which can lead to a decrease in performance. Ultimately, stress is considered to be "a major factor in the failure of athletes to fully and effectively utilise their skills in diverse types of performance."[170]

When levels of activation or arousal are high, an individual's focus may become so narrow that they miss relevant stimuli. Loris Karius' mistakes in the Champions League final against Real Madrid was an example where this happens to a player.[171]

In essence, the less psychologically aroused someone is, the more events they can process.

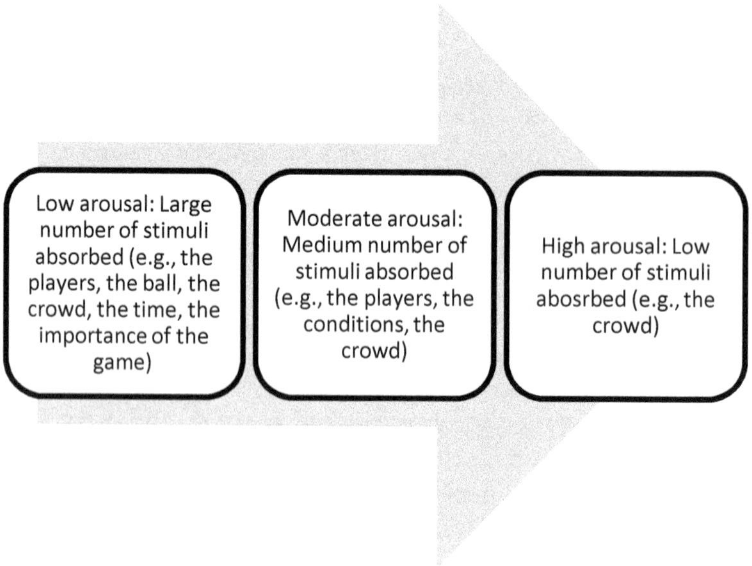

Low arousal: Large number of stimuli absorbed (e.g., the players, the ball, the crowd, the time, the importance of the game)

Moderate arousal: Medium number of stimuli absorbed (e.g., the players, the conditions, the crowd)

High arousal: Low number of stimuli abosrbed (e.g., the crowd)

Figure 11.1: Cue utilisation theory (Easterbrook, 1959).[172] NOTE: the arrow indicates an increase in arousal.

The premise of cue utilisation theory is that as our levels of anxiety increase, we narrow our field of attention, resulting in a focus on only one or two stimuli.

For some activities, this may not be an issue. For example, a power lifter does not have many relevant things to focus upon that may affect their performance (e.g., weather conditions or an opponent trying to stop them succeeding) and therefore such narrowing of attention may not be harmful to their success (indeed, it may help it). However, a football referee has an abundance of factors to consider that are relevant to performance. Consequently, an increase in anxiety may be detrimental to performance.

This is supported by our second example. Let's recall the situation:

It's a tense game and, at one stage, the players occupy a crowded penalty box. There is a lot of noise and shouting and appeals from players and fans alike. You are constantly positioning yourself to provide the best view while, at the same time, trying not to interfere with play. The ball is hit at high speed towards goal. An arm flashes up and stops the ball crossing the line. You award the penalty for deliberate handball but, with so much information to be aware of (and the fact the incident is over so quickly), you are not sure who the guilty party is. A failure to show a red card would indicate a lack of control and weakness. You would be open to criticism. Showing the card to the wrong player would be worse; it would show you are guessing at best, or just plain wrong at worst.

Cue utilisation theory suggests that, in such a 'busy' situation, our arousal increases and our attention narrows to such an extent that we concentrate on only one or two factors. And as our attention narrows, we get anxious that we might get things wrong.

Enter: the inverted 'U' theory.

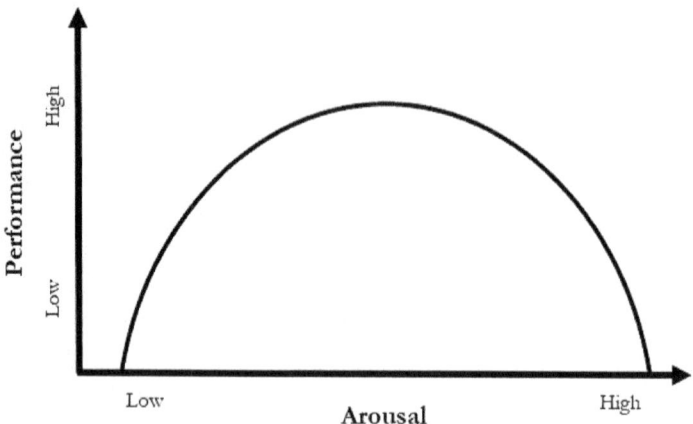

Figure 11.2: The inverted 'U' theory.

The inverted 'U' theory helps explain what happens when people are affected by stress and anxiety. As can be seen from the illustration, under-arousal and over-arousal will result in poor performance,[xxxiii] with maximum performance coming when individuals are moderately aroused.

Although there are clear strengths are to this model of human behaviour – namely that its generic nature means it can be applied to all individuals in all sporting contexts – this is also its main weakness: it is *too* generic. As the pathway shown in chapter ten reveals (figure 10.1), referees acquire a great deal of experience and training on their way to becoming an elite referee and therefore it may be possible that they not only deal with arousal more efficiently than others, but they actually *seek out* challenge – bigger and bigger stages. For example, referees frequently cite progression to larger stadiums or events as motivating.[173] Additionally, we know that some athletes (and referees) perform *better* in high pressure situations. This is what separates good performers from outstanding performers. A large part of this is because what we may consider a stressful situation

---

xxxiii A good example of apparent over-arousal and poor performance in football is Joe Hart's 'energetic' display in the tunnel before England's Euro 2016 game with Iceland.

(such as having 22 professional athletes and 60,000 spectators trying to influence our every decision) is *not* perceived that way by others. Why is this?

A female referee was asked if she ever worried about making mistakes. Her answer was "no". When pushed, and asked if there was a time during a game that she became stressed or anxious, she said the only time she could recall stress was during her "first mass confrontation". The most significant part of the quote is the word 'first'. Another level 3 referee stated that he doesn't find situations like this stressful because he has experienced them all before. Therefore, experience is a key factor in influencing the impact of stress and anxiety on performance.[xxxiv]

So before we think that an increase in arousal always leads to poor performance, let's consider another perspective: drive theory.

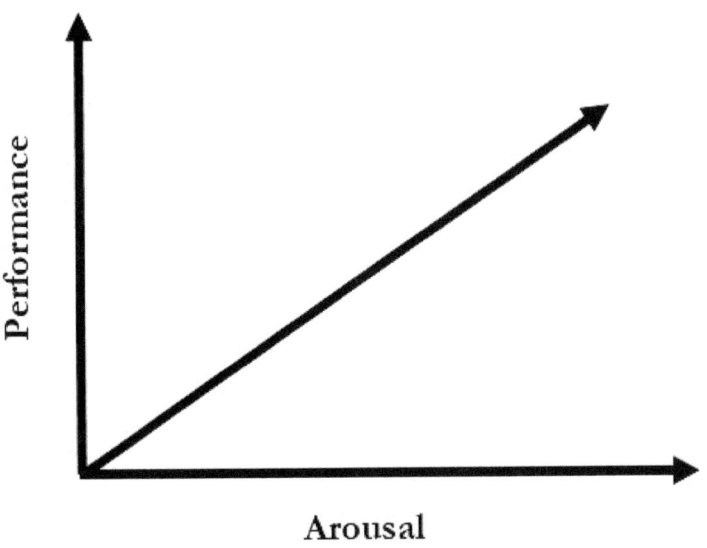

Figure 11.3: Drive Theory (Hull, 1943[174]; modified by Spence & Spence, 1966[175]).

---

xxxiv The importance of experience and how it helps will be discussed in greater detail in part three.

115

Drive theory posits that the higher the arousal of an individual, the greater the performance. Okay, there is an important proviso; namely, that the *dominant response* (the most likely reaction) of the individual is the correct one. In other words, as arousal (and stress) increases, performance also increases (providing the referee is not making mistakes). As Howard Webb elaborated, "The more nerves I felt the better I felt I performed."[176]

However, take this conclusion with caution. Experience alone does not protect us from the effects of nerves! For example, players with current high status regarding ability – such as those who placed in the top three for the FIFA World Player of the Year award, who are all highly experienced – are more likely to perform worse in a competitive penalty shootout than those who do not share such acclaim.[177]

This can also relate to referees. In the 2006 World Cup, Graham Poll, who had 26 years of experience, showed three yellow cards to the Croatian player Josip Simunic, during Croatia's 2-2 draw with Australia. FIFA referees chief Angel Maria Villar Llona stated that Poll's experience would help him overcome the situation,[178] (presumably other referees would not be able to recover from such a mistake) although this does not address the fact that an experienced official made such an error in the first place.

These three theories demonstrate the difficulty in understanding whether nerves 'bring out the best' in those involved in sports. Essentially, it is unknown, too complex, or both!

It is also difficult to establish the difference between over-arousal and passion[179] which has a powerful impact on performance (see chapter ten). This confusion is because *individual differences* dictate the outcome of arousal and stress on the referee's performance. How to deal effectively with the vast number of factors outside a referee's control is a result of how a referee deals with the factors *they can control*. Essentially, how a referee responds to external influences boils down to the emotions they experience as a result of that influence. A good example of this is what fans call 'evening things up' but what psychologists call 'sequential effects'.

The jury is out on whether arousal (e.g., the strength of stress or eustress) is good or bad for sporting performance.

This is because how we respond is down to individual differences.

An important difference between referees is the emotions they experience while officiating. These emotions are influenced by experience.

Sequential Effects

Social psychology may explain some of the decisions made by match officials, particularly by looking at the emotions an audience can cause an individual to experience.

For example, research has shown that, in certain social circumstances, actions can have contrast or assimilation effects.[180] This means that a specific judgement of an event will be more or less likely depending on *what has occurred before*. Football fans often speculate, for instance, that a referee wishes to 'even things up' if they have made a decision that is likely to influence the outcome of a game.

During the Premier League fixture between Bournemouth and Everton in 2018, for instance, Sky Sports stated on their online updates feature that the decision to send off Bournemouth's Adam Smith in the second half was influenced by the referee's decision to send off Richarlison of Everton in the first.[181] Coaches may buy into this concept too. Following Liverpool's 1-1 draw with West Ham United on February 4th, 2019, which saw Liverpool score a goal that was shown to be offside, manager Jürgen Klopp said:

> *"I heard our goal was offside, I'm pretty sure the ref knew that…In 50-50 situations it was always a free kick for the other team…As a human being, if I know I made a big mistake in the first half, I don't want to open the gap any more."* [182]

Referees are aware of this. One former Premier League official says that forgetting about a decision or possible error is important as one bad decision can "quickly become two or three."[183] An interesting experiment illustrated this effect where 115 people were shown 20 scenes from a match between Rayo Vallecano and Real Madrid from 1999.[184] This match contained three successive ambiguous foul scenes; two in the penalty area of one team (Team A) and one in the penalty area of the other (Team B). The participants were asked to state what they believed to be the correct decision in each scene.

The results revealed four important outcomes:

1. None of the participants who awarded a penalty kick in the first incident (in Team A's penalty area) awarded the second penalty kick.
2. 33.9% of those who did not award the first penalty to Team A awarded them the second.
3. If a penalty kick was awarded to team A (either the first or the second), then participants were almost *twice as likely* to award a penalty to team B.
4. Finally, this impact of sequential events did not apply to free kicks, only to penalty kicks.

In other words, if a referee gives a team a penalty they are less likely to award them another, and more likely to award one to the opposition.

'Charity bias', discussed in chapter one, is a possible explanation for a second penalty being awarded, but penalty kicks are more valuable than free-kicks, so another explanation stems from an unlikely source in French philosophy.

Pascal's Wager

Blaise Pascal (1623-62) was a French mathematician and theologian (amongst other things) who put forward an argument regarding the existence of God which is now known as 'Pascal's wager'.

Essentially, Pascal argued that it makes more sense to believe in God than not. His reasoning was that a human being has two options: believe or do not believe. If he/she believes in God and

He does exist, they will go to heaven. If He does not, they simply wasted a few hours every Sunday.

On the other hand, if they do not believe in God and He does not exist, they get a lie-in on a Sunday, but if He does exist then they go to hell (he was a Catholic theologian).

Therefore it is prudent to believe in God, as the worst case scenario of not believing (an eternity in hell) is worse than the worst case alternative for believing (wasting time). Additionally, the best case scenario for believing in God (going to heaven) is better than the best case scenario of not believing (some extra hours in bed). Hence it is logical to seek out actions that have the least disastrous outcome.

Relating this to refereeing, it explains why the participants in the previously discussed study were statistically unlikely to deny team B a penalty if they had previously awarded one to team A (and why they were unlikely to award two to the same team). As humans, we like to avoid negative social evaluation and seek to minimise the worst case scenario.

A key researcher in how we deal with stress, Norman Endler (who identified the five main stressors we discussed earlier), concluded that the initial reaction to many situations that could result in stress and anxiety (such as negative social evaluation) is to avoid the situation altogether.[185][xxxv] Therefore by 'levelling up' the penalty decisions (or seeking to avoid awarding them altogether), match day officials avoid the worst case scenario of being labelled biased.

[xxxv] The topic of stress avoidance will be further discussed in chapters twelve and thirteen.

Referees are less likely to award a penalty if they have already given that team one.

Similarly, a referee is more likely to award a penalty if they have already given one to the other side. These are known as sequential effects.

This is because humans tend to avoid the worst case scenario in order to avoid negative emotions (such as stress, guilt or anger).

To be labelled as biased is considered a great insult to a referee.[xxxvi] It explains the resultant furore after Giorgio Chiellini insinuated that match day official Michael Oliver was bribed after awarding a penalty to Real Madrid in injury time during their Champions League quarter-final match with Juventus on the 11th of April 2018.[xxxvii]

Oliver's decision was hailed as 'brave' by ex-referee Graham Poll,[186] which is an interesting choice of word as it perhaps suggests that it would have been safer not to apply the laws of the game and prevent negative attention.

Away from the referee, research has also shown that, *if in doubt*, assistant referees are more likely to raise their flag for offside than to keep it down.[187] This is because it is considered worse to allow an illegal goal than to prevent a legal one; officials want to avoid the negative emotions that come with perceptions of bias or incompetence. In the next chapter, we will look at emotions and their impact on performance in more depth.

---

xxxvi One referee interviewed for this book stated that 'cheat' is the real 'c' word for referees.

xxxvii The irony here is that Juventus were stripped of their 2005 Serie A title, demoted to last place (surrendering their title to Inter Milan), and relegated to Serie B for the 2006-2007 season for their role in *Calciopoli*, a scandal involving Juventus officials influencing the selection of certain referees for specific matches.

12: I Feel, Therefore I Am: Do Emotions Affect Performance?

In January, 2018, Nantes hosted Paris Saint-Germain in France's Ligue 1. In added time, Diego Carlos of Nantes and referee Tony Chapron accidentally collided causing both to fall to the ground. As Carlos got to his feet, the referee kicked him. Carlos was then shown a second yellow card for dissent.[xxxviii]

Why did the referee do this? Why perform such an unprecedented action that resulted in his suspension?

Director of the Referees' Technical Directorate in France, Pascal Garibian, said:

> *"His action was unacceptable... It was a bad reaction. He lost control of his emotions in the context of the fall."* [188]

You are probably aware of how you behave or perform when you are emotional, and it would be normal to assume that everyone responds in a similar way, but it turns out that our emotions and subsequent reactions are quite a personal thing. The Individualised Zones of Optimal Functioning (IZOF)[189] model suggests that everyone has their own, personal level of arousal that results in optimum performance. If we transfer this to the football pitch, for example, we might see that player A performs well when feeling high levels of activation whereas player B performs well when calm.

Furthermore, it turns out that performances are hugely influenced by our previous emotional experiences. Did I react well last time I felt nervous? Did this feeling help me? If the answers to these questions are positive then performance will benefit. If not, then I will probably be making some bad decisions soon! Our irate referee, Chapron, for example, said that his kick was an instinctive reaction after the collision caused

---

[xxxviii] We can only imagine what he said but the dismissal was overturned.

pain brought on by a recent injury. Assuming the injury was a negative emotional experience, it may be that the recurrence of pain created frustration that caused Chapron to lash out. More broadly, therefore, a referee's emotions can partially dictate their performance.

So, what causes our emotions? And what outcomes do emotions promote? To answer this, we can turn to the Cognitive-Motivational-Relational (CMR) Theory of Emotions.[190]

Emotions can have a huge impact on performance.

The emotions we experience are personal to us and our experiences.

Cognitive-Motivational-Relational (CMR) Theory of Emotions

There are three principles to this theory that help us understand the effect of emotions on performance. These are:

1. People can react to the same situation in different ways. This is obvious. But despite these differences, these reactions share a 'common relational meaning'. Simply, this is what the situation means to us (such as 'gain' or 'loss'). Let's look at figure 12.1 to help clarify. A referee is appointed a high-profile, derby game (such as Roma v Lazio or Rangers v Celtic). They may foresee this fixture as a challenge (e.g., it will be a good test of their abilities) or a threat (e.g., it will be so difficult, they believe their abilities will be criticised). Consequently, it is how they *approach* the role that will dictate both the immediate outcome (e.g., personal gain, such as development or satisfaction, or personal loss, such as a decrease in confidence or reputation) and the long-term impact (e.g., personal benefit or harm).

Outcomes	Anticipated	Occurred
Gain	Challenge	Benefit
Loss	Threat	Harm

Figure 12.1: A two-factor schematisation of relational meaning and time (from Lazarus, 2000).

2. The resulting emotion we feel is an appraisal of how important this meaning is to our emotional well-being. We are continually appraising events, and experience an emotion to promote a helpful behaviour. For example, when we experience something that makes us angry, that anger has come from our desire to not experience that again and we hope our anger will help us achieve that goal. Therefore, emotions are motivation-led. However, our appraisal may be unrealistic, leading to a maladaptive or unhelpful emotion. For example, if we feel that we *must* be treated with respect all the time then being a football referee will result in a lot of anger. Getting angry about dissent will do nothing to better the situation.

3. Therefore, it is an individual's 'relational meaning' of an event that is important in determining emotional experience. This emphasises the importance of individual difference in refereeing performance; how one official appraises an action may be very different to how another would. How an individual may appraise situations using themes - (figure 12.2).[191]

Emotion	Theme
Anger	A demeaning offense against me and mine.
Anxiety	Facing uncertain, existential threat.
Fright	An immediate, concrete, and overwhelming physical danger.
Guilt	Having transgressed a moral imperative.
Shame	Failing to live up to an ego-ideal.
Sadness	Having experienced an irrevocable loss.
Envy	Wanting what someone else has and feeling deprived of it but justified in having it.
Jealousy	Resenting a third party for loss or threat to another's affection or favour.
Happiness	Making reasonable progress toward the realisation of a goal.
Pride	Enhancement of one's ego-identity by taking credit for a valued object or achievement, either one's own or that of someone or group with whom one identifies.
Relief	A distressing goal-incongruent condition that has changed for the better or gone away.
Hope	Fearing the worst but yearning for better, and believing the improvement is possible.
Love	Desiring or participating in affection, usually but not necessarily reciprocated.
Gratitude	Appreciation for an altruistic gift that provides personal benefit.
Compassion	Moved by another's suffering and wanting to help.

Figure 12.2: The core relational theme for each emotion (from Lazarus, 2000).

The table shows how emotions are appraised across situations. For example, a referee that feels they must get every decision right will feel shame as they cannot expect to live up to that ideal.

The importance of CMR cannot be emphasised enough. How a referee interprets a situation is the very foundation of their performance! This can be seen using real referee testimony.[xxxix] Here, we can see how referees really react – emotionally – to certain triggers. For verbal abuse from the crowd, two referees reveal two very different emotional reactions.

Referee one, a female amateur referee reflecting on being told 'these ******* women should be at home doing the cooking', stated:[xl]

> "*I was fuming* (emotion)...*when the spectator said it. I was livid* (emotion)... *It made me make decisions that the team he supported wouldn't like because I thought that they were willing for him to speak like that* (type of ego involvement/harm appraisal). *Looking back, a few of the decisions did go one way, when they should have gone the other way* (decision making). *At the time, I didn't think about it, but after I thought, 'I gave it that way!' It was horrendous. I hate that I did it but I did.*" [192]

Referee two, a Level 1 referee, reflected on what happened when a member of the crowd called him a 'paedophile':

> "*I felt sick... getting called something like that for not giving this person's team an offside is hurtful* (type of ego involvement/harm appraisal), *and in this case it hurt and angered me* (emotion)...*however, you hear comments from the crowd every game, but it's all part and parcel of the game, I've never thought, 'oh he's shouted at me so I'm not going to give that decision'... I can't honestly say I've been like that, you just shut it off as if being along the lines of pantomime, you get it every game, so it's the same old story and I use the*

---

xxxix Particularly the testimony published in the wonderful study from Rich Neil and colleagues in 2013.

xl For clarity, the stage of the stress-emotion process is in parenthesis in the following quotes and are taken from the findings of Neil et al, 2013.

expression 'water off a duck's back'. That's what it becomes as you know, before the game, that you're going to get it so you're expecting it to come. It's just part and parcel of the day, you've got to switch it off (emotion-focussed coping)*... so it didn't affect my decision making.* " [193]

In these examples, both individuals have had the same experience (personal abuse from a crowd member). Additionally, they have both appraised the event in the same way (harm appraisal). However one referee has not, to the best of their knowledge, allowed it to affect their performance, whereas the other did. Not only that, they felt *guilt* afterwards ("I hate that I did it but I did.") This will not promote good performance the next time they feel that particular emotion.

So what can help people appraise and manage situations in a helpful way?

Experience is one way. For example age helps referees deal with aggression more effectively, leading to better performance.[194] Is this because the older the person the better they are at disarming aggression in others? No, it is more the case that they have learned how to control *their* emotions.

Training is another approach. It is worth remembering that the second quote is from a Level 1 referee and the importance of training – in focussing on helpful cues – is reflected in these two quotes:[195]

> *"A [player] came in and fouled another player... I'd normally get away with not booking him, but the fans who saw the challenge went ballistic, and with this reaction I felt I had to caution him, because they put me under pressure to think 'what happens if I don't punish this one?... I got anxious and booked the player."*

> *

> *"It's interesting, people have this concept that the referee will go with what the crowd says... when you get decisions wrong you get more dissatisfaction in yourself and more abuse from players, just because the crowd thinks they should get decisions their way...So, big crowds never bother me as I think of it as a pantomime, which is to my benefit as it*

doesn't affect my performance… I get excited to play in front of these crowds."

The first of these quotes came from a Level 5 referee whereas the second from a Level 1 referee, supporting the notion that individual differences – notably how emotions create different responses – is influenced by training and experience.

However, to attribute referee performance solely to experience and training is to underplay the relevance of personality differences. For example, sequential effects (e.g., awarding a penalty to team B because one was given to team A earlier) is an influence that is likely to affect everyone, even if they are not a referee.[196] Simply, training and experience do not completely eliminate the impact of stress and social pressure. There must be something else that helps define a referee's performance.

> How we appraise a situation (e.g., do we see it as threatening or wrong?) dictates our emotional response (e.g., anger or guilt).
>
> Different emotions affect a referee's performance (e.g., not giving a particular decision because their captain annoyed you).

So, What Separates Good Performances From Bad?

The answer to this question is the aim of the book. If we know how to protect referees from the factors that can influence their performance, then we can improve the standard of officiating. Who knows, referees may even get more respect!

The answer is not to stop referees experiencing such influences or stress. This wouldn't work, because it is unrealistic; a crowd will always be biased and achievement situations (situations where we will be evaluated) will always promote nerves. The solution is to help referees *regulate* emotions. It is how they deal with what the game throws at them that counts.

13: Controlling the Controllable: How Do Referees Control Their Emotions?

In the documentary 'Ref: Stories from the Weekend',[197] an amateur referee claims that "you have to be a certain type of person, psychologically" to referee. They were referring to how a person deals with conflict, setbacks, and challenges in order to perform their role.

Although how we regulate our emotions is not often discussed, this chapter will explore how important it is for an official's performance. Not only is there a benefit to emotional control, but it is also something that occurs frequently.[198]

But before we discuss the 'how', let's look at the 'why'.

Why Regulate Emotion?

We regulate emotion to "modify behaviour or mental states to achieve desired outcomes."[199] In other words, we try to change how we're feeling to get something we want.

We do this all the time in everyday life. Think about the time you didn't tell someone what you were really feeling because it would get you in trouble, or perhaps a time when you changed your feelings of frustration or anger to one of patience or tolerance.

We also see this happening in sport. For example, a footballer may slow down their breathing and take their time before taking a penalty kick in order to improve their chances of scoring (which it does[200]).

There are two fundamental motives for regulating emotions: *hedonic* and *instrumental*. Let's clear this up by looking at some examples.

Consider the time you laughed at a comedian's joke, despite not finding it *that* funny, in order increase the happiness you were experiencing at that moment. Why would you do this? Well, you'd invested time and money in going to see the comedian, so that was a *hedonic* motive for emotional regulation (hedonism: feeling pleasure).

Now think back to when you returned home from work feeling tired, so you tried to energise yourself in order to go to the gym. That was an *instrumental* motive for emotional regulation (performance: 'to do').

These desired outcomes are shown in Tamir's taxonomy of motives in emotion regulation (figure 13.1).

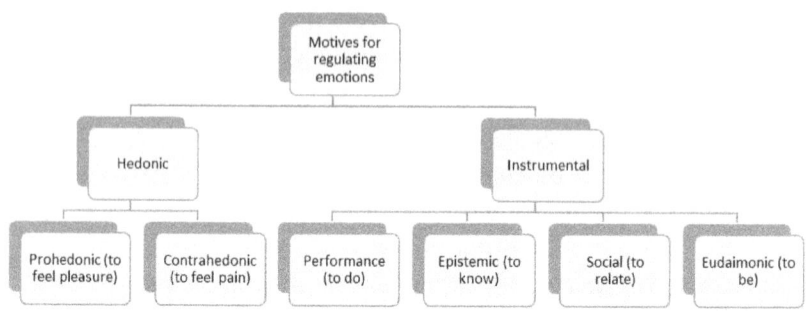

Figure 13.1: A taxonomy of motives in emotion regulation (adapted from Tamir, 2016).

When applying these two main drivers to refereeing performance, it is clear why an individual may wish to regulate their emotions. For example, Premier League referees are required to evaluate their performance every week with an assessor and therefore a referee may wish to get their emotions in check (e.g., reduce anger or hostility) in order to accept criticism.

If a referee wishes to influence a player on the pitch they may regulate their emotions by demonstrating understanding and showing tolerance (social regulation: 'to relate'). This is particularly relevant as individuals who expect their emotions to influence others (which a referee would) demonstrate a greater motivation to regulate them.[201] In other words, referees understand that their emotions can influence the behaviour of others and, therefore, are motivated to manage themselves.

Perhaps this explains why referees appear better than players at controlling their emotions. According to former referee Peter Walton, referees "take context of the [player's] reaction into account. They [the players] don't necessarily get cautioned for the initial reaction."[202] After all, it's not the player's role to influence the behaviour of the referee (even if they'd like to), but it is the official's role to keep players under control!

While these examples show instrumental motives – to learn something or to relate to someone – referees are also motivated by hedonic outcomes. For example, a referee's desire not to make a bad or controversial decision in order to avoid being unpopular.[203][xli]

A practical example to support this view comes from the 2015/2016 Premier League season. Tottenham Hotspur visited Stamford Bridge to play Chelsea, with Tottenham needing to win in order to preserve their chance of winning the league title. The game ended in a heated 2-2 draw in which many players could have been sent off. The referee, Mark Clattenburg, later explained:

> *"I allowed them [Tottenham Hotspur] to self-destruct so all the media, all the people in the world could go: 'Tottenham lost the title'. If I sent off three players from Tottenham, what are the headlines? 'Clattenburg cost Tottenham the title'. It was pure theatre that Tottenham lost the title against Chelsea and Leicester won the title. Some referees would have played by the book… but I didn't give them an excuse, because my game plan was: 'Let them lose the title.'"*[204]

Clattenburg reveals that one of his aims was to keep his name out of the 'headlines'. Therefore, presumably, he regulated his emotions (e.g., increased tolerance) to feel subsequent pleasure (prohedonic regulation) by *avoiding* displeasure (contrahedonic regulation).

Avoiding unwanted attention is something that other Level 1 referees have mentioned as a desirable outcome. For example, when reflecting on an incident involving a high-profile manager

---

[xli] This can be linked to the theory of conformity discussed in chapter three and the theory of sequential effects discussed in chapter eleven. For example, if a referee has already turned down a penalty appeal for team 'A', they may not wish to give team 'B' a 'soft one' to avoid being called biased or incompetent.

one referee stated, "Here we go, my name's going to hit the papers again."[205] This concern has been labelled 'impression management'[206] – in order to avoid controversy and experience pleasure (and/or avoid displeasure), a referee may regulate emotions in order to tolerate transgressions.

Regulating emotions helps someone achieve a desired outcome.

These outcomes are either hedonic (to promote pleasure or displeasure) or instrumental (to help us do something, know something, relate to something or be something).

Regulating emotions can harm performance but can also help it.

Emotional Regulation and Performance

For some people, emotional regulation may not always be seen as something that is beneficial to performance. For example, former Premier League official Dermot Gallagher stated that Clattenburg's performance in the match between Chelsea and Tottenham Hotspur was poor, "You saw players who took the law into their own hands because the referee didn't apply the laws firmly, fairly and consistently."[207]

However, there are occasions when emotional regulation undoubtedly improves a referee's performance. For example, a referee who is feeling particularly anxious before a match may attempt to calm themselves down in order to improve performance, particularly as calmness is seen as desirable amongst referees.[208]

Additionally, the desire to avoid negative emotions can prompt someone to focus on specific, helpful areas.[209] This is directly applicable to refereeing as a match official would want to avoid feelings of ambiguity or confusion and therefore do their best to pay attention to relevant cues. For example, a referee may ignore the protests of a grounded player, despite them being frustrating and distracting, in order to concentrate on an advantage being played.

Although no guarantee of a good display, emotional control is usually beneficial to a referee and their performance.

How Do Referees Regulate Emotion?

Now we know *why* a referee may regulate emotions, and its impact on performance, let's discuss how emotions are regulated. The model shown in figure 13.2 shows us how this is done.

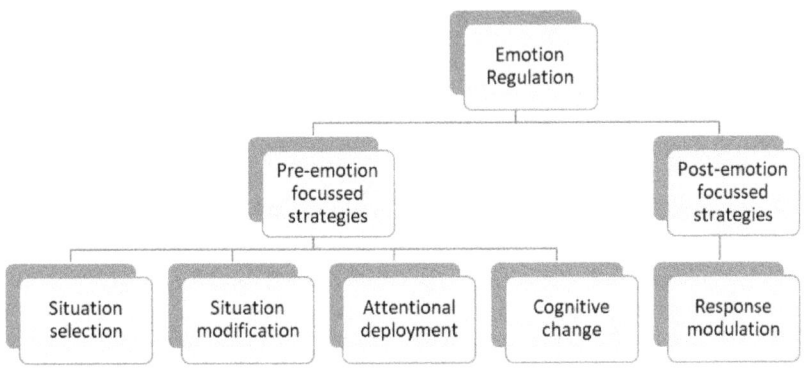

Figure 13.2: Adapted process model of emotion regulation (adapted from Gross & Thompson, 2007).[210]

This model provides us with five strategies for controlling our emotions. The first two – situation selection and situation modification – refer to how a person will manipulate their situation in order to control their emotions. For instance, someone who doesn't like flying might look into other modes of transport to attend a meeting in order to minimise the feeling of anxiety.

The third strategy – attentional deployment – informs us that an individual will direct attention to certain factors that will not cause negative emotions. The learner driver taking their practical test, for example, will attempt to concentrate on relevant information to pass the exam in order to avoid feelings of disappointment.

The fourth approach – cognitive change – reveals how someone can alter the *meaning* of an event or situation in order to avoid undesirable emotions. Think about a time when you were driving and someone pulled out in front of you, forcing you to brake. If you wanted to avoid being angry you may tell yourself that the person didn't mean to do that; it was an honest mistake, rather than thinking of it as a reckless or dangerous act.

Finally, response modulation refers to attempts to control both physical and mental aspects of already experienced emotions. This may be done directly before an event (e.g., trying to calm down beforehand) or after (e.g., suppressing a negative emotion that is experienced because of an event).

There are numerous examples of referees exercising all of these strategies. Let's explore each in turn:

Situation Selection

An easy one to start with; referees have already chosen to participate in a role that has the potential to increase negative emotions such as anxiety or distress. If they were to experience negative emotions as a result of the role then they could choose not to continue.[xlii] For example, one amateur referee interviewed for this book stated that the distress he experienced as a referee led him to temporarily withdraw from the role.

Situation Modification

Referees may wish to regulate emotions by modifying a situation.

A good example came from a fixture between Leicester City and Manchester City in 2016. Referee Michael Oliver stated in his pre-match briefing that he did not wish to have communication with his assistants if the ball was in their area of the pitch, allowing them to officiate visually, with no audio communication, in order to minimise distraction and unnecessary discussion. Additionally, Oliver also told the captains of each team, Wes Morgan and Pablo Zabaleta, that he was happy to discuss decisions but asked the players to decide which were important 'in the grand scheme of the game'[211] (in other words, he asks players to only discuss major decisions, not

---

xlii See chapter nine.

a 50/50 throw-in decision on the half-way line, for example). Here, Oliver was trying to modify situations in which he may become challenged; he is likely recognising that consistent appeals or 'debates' with players could lead to negative emotions (such as frustration) which could impact his performance.

Modification can also occur *after* an event. Again, Oliver provides us with an example. During the 2018 FA Cup Final, Chelsea player Eden Hazard was fouled in the penalty box by Manchester United's Phil Jones. Oliver awarded a penalty and then three things happened:

1. Chelsea players begin demanding that Jones was sent off for denying a goal scoring opportunity. Oliver stated: "Listen, listen, listen, it's in the area, it's a genuine attempt to play the ball." The protests didn't cease so Oliver said: "I'll talk to you, I'll talk to you. Listen, listen. Let's talk to Gary [Cahill, Chelsea captain].

2. After explaining the decision to Cahill, Manchester United's players decided to protest the decision. Ashley Young, for example, said that there was no foul in the first place. According to the newspaper report of this incident, Oliver "*calmly* explained the decision."[212] [emphasis mine]

3. After the penalty was awarded, Oliver (in an *authoritative* tone) said "Paul [Pogba, Manchester United player], stay out [of the box]."

These events reveal excellent situation modification. In the first instance, Oliver demonstrates patience when explaining his decision in order to defuse any possible anger from Chelsea players for not sending Jones off. In the second part of the event, Oliver calmly explains to Young why he has awarded the penalty. Finally, the referee firmly tells Paul Pogba to stay out of the box.

The motive for all of these actions is to avoid an undesirable emotional outcome. For example, if Paul Pogba does encroach into the penalty area before the penalty kick is taken (and is missed), Oliver will be in a position where any decision he makes – either insisting the penalty is retaken or allowing play to continue – will anger half of the players (and the crowd).

Additionally, if he had not stayed calm when dealing with Young then the situation would probably have deteriorated. It is hard to argue that – in this case – situation modification did not enhance performance.

However, this strategy may not always have such a positive outcome. There is evidence to suggest that when faced with a situation in which the potential for making an error is high – such as refereeing – an individual is more likely to pick the choice with the least detrimental consequences and not necessarily the 'correct course of action.'[xliii] This is labelled 'Error Management Theory'.[213]

A practical example of this came in an FA Cup game between Norwich City and Chelsea in 2018 when referee Graham Scott gave a corner to Chelsea despite the correct decision appearing to be a goal kick to Norwich. His body language after this decision suggested that he thought a mistake had been made and – as soon as the corner was taken – he awarded Norwich a free kick in their penalty box. We can't read Scott's mind, perhaps he did see something amiss. But the concept of error management explains his behaviour and the press coverage after the game justified the approach. For instance, both Chelsea manager Antonio Conte and BBC pundit Dion Dublin criticised the referee for not awarding Chelsea's Brazilian attacker Willian a penalty, while the free kick awarded to Norwich (for reasons unknown) was not discussed at all.[214]

Attentional Deployment

"You have to be the right sort of person, psychologically" is a statement from an amateur female referee discussing the importance of 'moving on from mistakes quickly.[215] The ability to 'move on quickly' has a major impact on refereeing performance; thinking about previous incidents may cause an official to re-frame future incidents and affect decision making (this influence has already been highlighted during the discussion on sequential effects).

Sequential effects cross over with emotional regulation; a referee does not want to be negatively evaluated as biased and so will

---

xliii In the terraces, this could be termed 'bottling it'.

pay closer attention to fouls committed by one team over another if he or she has already awarded a penalty. This explanation is speculative, however, since there is other evidence that attentional deployment both influences performance and is *driven by* emotions.

During the FIFA World Cup group stage fixture between England and Panama in June 2018, several England players are seen trying to direct the referee's (Ghead Grisha) attention to the behaviour of the Panama defenders who were grappling with England players Harry Kane and John Stones at corner kicks. Towards the end of the first half, Grisha awarded England a penalty for a foul on both of those players after making it clear that he would be watching for any infringements.

This is a good example of attentional deployment but now it is clear *why* his attention may have become so focussed: to *avoid* negative and unhelpful emotions that would result from missing such obvious violations. After all, if he had failed to award a penalty kick, Grisha would have been criticised, since infringements were brought to his attention so explicitly. In fact, his actions possibly led to positive emotions as he was widely praised for his performance as this tweet from former Premiership ref Mark Halsey indicates:

Excellent performance from the Egyptian referee GRISHA, two penalties awarded to England rightly so, pleasing to see him give a penalty for a holding offence, stamping his authority on the game when needed.

@RefereeHalsey (via @therefonline)
June 24th, 2018

Cognitive Change

Cognitive change is related to appraisal. However, this time it is not appraisal of the self (e.g., of personal resources) but the appraisal of a *situation*. Essentially, the referee may change the meaning of an event when faced with a decision that may promote negative emotions. This is something that occurs frequently in everyday life. For example, after we miss out on a job opportunity, we may change the way we think about that job (e.g., "I didn't really want it anyway" or "I might have got bored in that role after a while"). This has been labelled 'emotion-focussed coping.'[216]

But why would a referee do this? Surely all they need to do is witness an event, interpret it as accurately as possible, and then administer the appropriate action? Why reappraise what happened at all? Indeed, this is a source of frustration for many fans, who believe that this may lead to inconsistency. Take these tweets from supporters for example:

...the ridiculous part of the rule is that some refs give yellow cards for offences that other refs do not. There is no consistency.
@Lucioronio, June 28th, 2018

And how in the world is that not a penalty? It's a card if it happens anywhere else on the pitch.
@Kagawa_Red,
December 31st, 2016

WTF why didn't the guy get a yellow card?? That's not fair the ref is biased!!!
@frantasticwOrld, June 27th, 2018

Criticism from the media and the public can result in negative emotions,[217] but a referee may interpret actions differently to others because of what has been described as "the art rather than the science of refereeing".[218] In refereeing circles, it is labelled 'game management'.

Game management is the use of two things. First, the use of effective communication skills in order to positively influence the game. These communication skills have been identified as gaze, posture, movement, and verbal explanation.[219] The ability to do these things efficiently is not only important in minimising negative emotions (as a failure to explain a decision in an appropriate manner may increase player aggression and then, in turn, referee frustration or anxiety) but also *instrumental in career progression.*[220]

This leads us to the second aspect of game management: knowing *when* to strictly enforce laws and when not to. In essence, to exercise common sense. Those that know when to be a law-enforcer, and when to be a game-manager, are more likely to progress as a referee. Indeed, referees in Germany's *Bundesliga* see their role as weighted more towards game manager than law-enforcer.[221]

To clarify the concept of game management, former referee Howard Webb explained, in 2016, that when faced with a disciplinary issue, officials are encouraged to use a 'stepped approach': a private warning, a public warning, a yellow card, a red card. This is to give the official 'somewhere to go' in managing player behaviour. Without this, a referee who has cautioned a player early in the game for a foul may be required to send that player off if they commit another foul or break another regulation of the game. Webb stated:

> *"There are so many situations that fall into the margins where the referee has to make an interpretation. So if a tackle goes in after 30 seconds and you think to yourself 'manage this situation,' will a warning work if I speak to this player, and everyone else sees me doing it? That might absolutely do the job."*[222]

This is a good example of cognitive change in order to regulate emotions: the referee has interpreted the incident as one that can be eliminated by a verbal warning as opposed to a card. If a referee sends a player off for two yellow card offences when one may have been avoided, he or she may experience negative emotions – such as anxiety or frustration – as their decision may be challenged.

In the same Howard Webb interview, former footballer Robbie Savage challenges game management by claiming this is giving people a 'free whack' early in the game, and that it creates inconsistency. However, this is to miss the point. Referees must interpret events and their meanings to enable best performance. Hence, a referee may see a situation differently when thinking about *their* impact on the game and future performance.

Additionally, a referee may also be interpreting the situation for hedonistic reasons; specifically to avoid displeasure as they are often criticised for sending players off for two 'soft' yellows. For example, after the World Cup Final in 2010, the manager of the Netherlands, Bert van Marwijk, criticised Howard Webb for failing to control the match. Webb produced 14 yellow cards in the game and this is a good example of cautions sometimes not being the most effective tool in controlling players. This is a view shared by journalist Dominic Fifield who wrote:

> *"The 38-year-old [Webb] was helpless here, all attempts to calm down players whipped up into a frenzy by the occasion proving utterly fruitless. Nerves had set in, anxiety gripping the play. From the moment van Persie became the first name in the book on the quarter-hour mark for fouling Joan Capdevila, Webb was on a hiding to nothing. The striker was the first of five bookings in 13 minutes thereafter, the game being played to a flash of yellow where we had hoped it would be glorious* roja *or dazzling* oranje *on show."*[223]

The revealing aspect of this passage is that the first booking is highlighted as the start of Webb's problems in this game, supporting the referee's claim that a stepped approach, if possible, is best. If a referee needs to interpret a situation to allow for greater emotional coping of future events, the reader must decide for themselves whether or not they believe this helps or hinders them.

It is also worth noting that the interpretation of an event in a football match may not always be attributable to the referee. For example, before the 2010 World Cup Final, Webb was advised by FIFA officials to 'understand the players' emotions' and to 'keep the cards away for as long as possible'.[224] In the 109th minute – the game went to extra time – Webb sent off Dutch defender Johnny Heitinga; however, many claimed that Dutch midfielder Nigel de Jong should have been shown a red card earlier in the game. Perhaps Webb felt he no longer had anywhere else to go and that his only course of action was to send Heitinga off. Simply, there was no further scope for cognitive change. Or perhaps Webb interpreted Heitinga's action not as a violent or reckless act but as a way to fix the mistake of not sending off de Jong, and escaping a negative evaluation from FIFA officials?

Criticism from such high office may promote negative emotions to a much greater extent than from other areas. For example, it has been found that referees find aggressive acts from coaches and players harder to cope with than aggressive acts from spectators.[225] This is explained by the referee perceiving the abuse from coaches and players at "a more personal level, whereas that of the spectators was perceived as coming from an anonymous, ignorant mob."[226] Consequently, an individual may be more likely to change the meaning of an event if they are influenced to do so by significant others. In other words, if FIFA officials request patience and tolerance, a referee is more likely to interpret an event with these qualities than if they are not encouraged.

It is likely that some reading this chapter will still disagree with 'game management'; that the referee should simply enforce the laws of the game strictly. Whilst this is a valid opinion, those that hold it need to be aware that even when a referee adopts this approach they are not immune to criticism. Mike Dean is an obvious example here.

Dean is a referee who is often criticised for being too harsh or 'card-happy'. Even former FIFA referee and PGMOL boss Keith Hackett has criticised his style, claiming his "tolerance levels are low."[227] Statistics appear to support this; Dean, as of February 2019, had shown nine red cards in the 2018/19 Premier League season, which is four more than the next highest referees (five by both Michael Oliver and Jon Moss). He is the referee who has shown the most red cards in the history of the Premier League (100). Hackett advises that better 'game management' would benefit Dean.

However, the benefit of being such as a rigid law-enforcer (as opposed to a game-manager) is that consistency is increased at the cost of being pedantic or a stickler for the rules.[228] It's a tough situation for referee. Damned if you do, damned if you don't!

Response Modulation

So far, we have looked at how an individual may control their emotions by modifying the meaning of an event or the event itself. However, if these strategies offered *the* explanation behind every decision, then how do we explain examples where referees make 'game changing' decisions when they would be justified in not awarding them? An example might be a match-winning, last minute penalty (that is questionable) for instance?

Surely such a decision would result in undesirable emotions, such as embarrassment after a negative performance evaluation (especially since we know that humans tend to pick the safest option over the riskier one)? The answer can again be attributed to individual emotions.

How someone feels is a simple but powerful factor that determines what type of decisions they make. For example, individuals who feel sad are biased in favour of high risk/high reward options (such as awarding a penalty or showing a red card) whereas individuals who feel anxious tend to choose low risk/low reward options.[229]

There are referees, however, that disagree with this conclusion. For example, one amateur referee interviewed for this book stated that although he agreed that feelings of anxiety would result in him making more cautious decisions, he also stated that the same outcome would occur if he was feeling depressed or sad. Therefore all negative emotions would lead to the same outcome. It is possible that this is the case but it is also possible that the referee *believes* his decisions to be safe, despite the truth being to the contrary. It is also possible that those who genuinely aren't influenced by mood (which could be argued as unlikely) are those who are simply more proficient in coping with any subsequent negative emotions. Either way, the significant effect of personal difference has been established.

Therefore, the salient issue could be an individual's ability to modulate their emotional response. In other words, how do they deal with an event emotionally after it has happened and they haven't had time (or the possibility) to re-frame the meaning? It has been suggested that a person may either adopt strategies to help them cope with such negative emotions or suppress the negative emotion experienced.[230]

A significant cause of whether or not a person re-appraises their emotions (in other words, 'copes' with them) or suppresses them is their ability to regulate them.[231] Therefore, everything we have discussed in this chapter boils down to the simple fact that it is an individual's emotions that most influence their decisions.

There are five different approaches to regulating emotions, each of which are commonly used by referees in order to improve performance.

How well a referee regulates their emotions may be the ultimate influence on performance, allowing them to overcome (or succumb to) other influences.

14: More Than a Game: Do Referees Suffer From Poor Mental Health?

It goes without saying that the role of the referee comes with a number of stressors. The previous chapter established strategies that referees may use in order to avoid undesirable emotions and improve performance. However, it is possible that preventing negative emotions may not always be possible. This is because a referee must – first and foremost – make decisions that may not be popular and also because emotional regulation takes effort and endurance.[232] Simply, we all let our patience and tolerance slip from time-to-time!

As discussed, suppression of such emotions may lead to negative outcomes, so an individual may seek intervention to effectively deal with them, such as exercise, therapy, substance abuse, withdrawal (quitting), or perhaps something more severe. These strategies have varying degrees of effectiveness in terms of managing mental health.

Sports people are at particular risk of poor mental health as a result of a culture that celebrates mental toughness and discourages the disclosure of weakness.[233] Unfortunately, recent incidences support this conclusion. For example, the father of British snowboarder Ellie Souter – who took her own life on her 18th birthday – felt she "may have been struggling with the pressure of competing in high-level sport."[234]

Football is not immune to these consequences, with some believing that player welfare is potentially 'the biggest problem that modern football faces.'[235] Indeed, recent players who have publicly discussed mental health issues include former England international Michael Carrick, who stated that he suffered from depression following Manchester United's Champions League final defeat to Barcelona in 2009[236] because of a mistake he made; former Coventry, Liverpool and Wigan goalkeeper Chris Kirkland[237]; and Tottenham Hotspur and England full-back Danny Rose.[238]

While these issues should of course be explored, our focus is on referees. There is much less public awareness of officials and mental health because many assume that referees are not under the same pressures as others involved in the game, such as players and coaches. This is incorrect.

To illustrate this, let's look at the role of the football coach – which experts consider to be so stressful that they should be seen as performers themselves[239] – and highlight how a referee experiences the same pressures.

So what exactly causes coaches to experience negative emotions that could lead to unhelpful or harmful behaviours? Essentially, it is how someone appraises their capability to cope with a demand. It is these demands that promote such pressure.

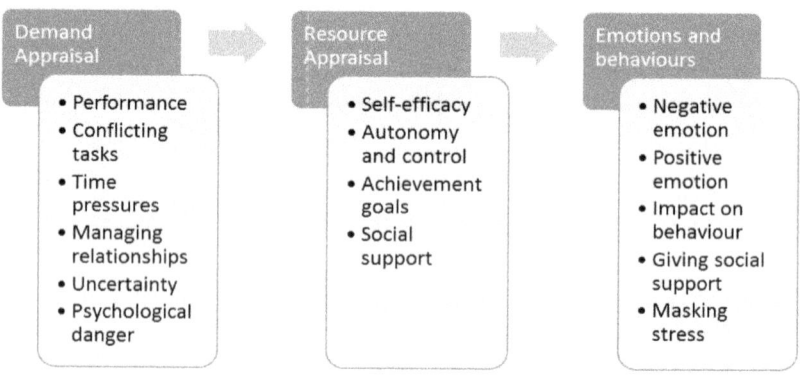

Figure 14.1: Representation of stress appraisal research with UK soccer coaches (adapted from Dixon & Turner, 2018).

The model (14.1) shows these demands that a coach experiences. They are:

- Performance (e.g., am I getting the results I want?)
- Conflicting tasks (e.g., having to spend more time doing paperwork which detracts from 'on the grass' coaching)
- Time pressures (e.g., experiencing a lack of free time due to travel, planning, or the fulfilment of other expected duties)

- Managing relationships (e.g., having to deal with others and experiencing conflict)
- Uncertainty (e.g., having to react to unexpected events)
- Psychological danger (e.g., worrying about performance).

It is clear that each of these demands can also be related to referees, supporting the notion that referees are under the same pressures as athletes and coaches. To illustrate this, let's relate each of the demand appraisals to *real* referee testimony.

Demand Appraisal	Referee example
Performance	"I was thinking, 'what are they [chief referee officer and assessors] thinking about my performance?" (cited in Neil et al, 2013:pp.36)
Conflicting tasks	"I was concentrating so much on everything else that I wasn't thinking about the one thing that's important" (cited in Neil et al, 2013:pp.30)
Time pressures	"Considerable amounts of time must also be spent on pre-match preparation, travel and post-match reports" (Wolfson & Neave, 2007:pp.233)

Managing relationships	"When they all started fighting I started to get anxious" (cited in Neil et al, 2013:pp.33)
Uncertainty	"What happens if I don't punish this one? I got anxious" (cited in Neil et al, 2013:pp.29)
Psychological danger	"I get very nervous, unusually nervous" (cited in Neil et al, 2013:pp.36)

Table 14.2: Application of demand appraisals to actual referee experience.

Referees experience the same demand appraisals as coaches; as such, the impact of their roles on their mental health should be acknowledged.

In sport, mental health issues tend to focus on players not officials.

Research shows that coaches also experience stressors but, when analysed, referees experience the same stressors.

Demand appraisals are only one part of the model shown in figure 14.1. The second aspect is that these demands cause an individual to evaluate their resources. Basically, they ask themselves if they have the ability to deal with these demands. And four areas can be identified:

- Self-efficacy (e.g., how have I coped/performed before? And do I possess the relevant skills and knowledge to succeed?)

- Autonomy and control (e.g., the extent to which an individual perceives they are in control of their situation and its demands)
- Achievement goals (e.g., appraisal of their approach goals: such as striving for competence; and appraisal of their avoidance goals: hoping to avoid incompetence)
- Social support (e.g., the feedback that an individual receives from their peers)

If an individual appraises their resources to meet or exceed the demands placed upon them then they are less likely to experience negative emotions.

A referee will also appraise their own resources, much like a coach or athlete. For example, a referee's previous training or experience will contribute towards their feeling of self-efficacy.

As Howard Webb stated in 2017, a referee will think back to their own experiences at certain grounds to help themselves prepare for the game.[240] Previous experience is a key predictor of self-efficacy (see figure 10.1); if this previous experience was positive then an official is likely to believe they *can* meet the challenge ahead.

Autonomy and control is also important. For example, a Level 2 referee stated:

"In my last season I refereed a youth game and it was one of those mass melees…I thought 'stand back, they'll split up eventually, look at it [the situation]…ok, I'll have that one [player], that one, and that one.' Nice, clear, concise, and I was in control of the situation, giving cards out to the right people."[241]

In this example, control obviously contributed to a positive emotional state and impact on behaviour/performance. Feeling a lack of control would have the opposite effect.

Achievement goals also contribute to referees' emotions. The aim of moving up the leagues and refereeing at a higher level is a particular motivating factor for officials and leads to increased job satisfaction.[242] For example, a Level 2 referee explained, "It's that drive to achieve that keeps me going."[243]

Finally, social support is a key to emotional management.[xliv] Consider this testimony from a Level 1 referee: "You need that mutual support to… bounce experiences off each other to make sure that when you… do go through a bad experience… you've got someone to talk to."[244]

It is clear that what causes positive and negative emotions in athletes and coaches is also applicable to referees. So, by extension, matchday officials are also vulnerable to mental health issues. Now we will focus on the second aim of the chapter which is to establish whether or not referees actually suffer from poor mental health as a result of their occupation.

> Referees appraise their resources in the same way that coaches do.
> Referees are as vulnerable to mental health issues as players and coaches.

Do Referees Suffer from Poor Mental Health?

This is a difficult area to investigate for a number of reasons. Perhaps the biggest is the perception that mental health issues are seen as a weakness.[245] Indeed, a number of high-profile athletes have discussed the difficulty in talking about their mental health struggles.[246]

Another difficulty is that attention is naturally drawn to extreme cases. For example, in 2018, long-serving Australian NRL referee Matt Cecchin announced he was quitting at the end of the season as a result of receiving "hundreds and hundreds" of death threats and "vile" abuse following his decision to disallow a try for Tonga against England in the World Cup semi-final in

---

[xliv] This topic will be explored in greater detail later.

2017.[xlv][247] While most members of the public would accept that the death threats sent to Cecchin and his family overstepped the mark, and would not dream of reacting in such a manner, it is possible that people do not realise that less severe abuse or pressure can equally contribute to mental health problems.

This is particularly important in light of recent reports from referees. For example, in 2013, former Premier League referee Mark Halsey claimed:

> *"It will not be long before a referee has a nervous breakdown… I also believe that if we do not do something to help referees with mental health and stress issues, then we could see a suicide."* [248]

These comments were made in reference to an incident involving Babak Rafati, a *Bundesliga* referee who had attempted suicide before undergoing treatment for depression. Halsey himself was forced to report fans to the police after suffering abuse on social media regarding his treatment for throat cancer in 2009, after officiating a 2-1 win for Manchester United over rivals Liverpool.

What exactly is mental health?

In order to ascertain whether referees are likely to suffer from poor mental health it is important to define the term. In 2014, the World Health Organisation (WHO) defined mental health as "a state of well-being in which every individual realises his or her own potential, can cope with the normal stresses of life, can work productively and fruitfully, and is able to make a contribution to his or her community." This definition highlights the importance of coping strategies, discussed in chapter sixteen, which is of particular importance to a match day official as they are often under significant mental burdens.[249] Consequently, it is important to understand what these burdens are.

[xlv] It was the correct decision.

What could harm a referee's mental health?

We've previously discussed stress and referees in chapter eleven, however, to be more specific, there are four factors that cause a football referee to experience arousal: fear of failure, fear of physical harm, time pressure, and interpersonal conflict.[250] But do these cause mental health problems, or are they simply things that a referee could do without?

In 2018 the mental health charity MIND[xlvi] highlighted the following as the main causes of anxiety and depression. I have added in italics how a referee's stressors may be linked to these causes:

- exhaustion or a build-up of stress (*fear of failure and/or interpersonal conflict*)
- long working hours
- being out of work (*interpersonal conflict may result in referees being 'demoted'*)[xlvii]
- feeling under pressure while studying or in work (*time pressure, fear of failure, fear of physical harm*)
- having money problems
- homelessness or housing problems
- losing someone close to you
- feeling lonely or isolated (*fear of failure, fear of physical harm*)
- being bullied, harassed or abused (*fear of failure, fear of physical harm, fear of interpersonal conflict*)

It is possible, then, that these stressors could cause mental health issues such as anxiety and depression. However, many individuals may experience the same causes and not experience

---

xlvi To illustrate the contemporary nature surrounding mental health in sport, the charity MIND is an official partner of the English Football League for the 2018/2019 season.

xlvii In the Premier League, for example, Mike Dean and his assistant Simon Beck were both demoted to the Championship as 'punishment' following Manchester United's 2-1 home defeat by Chelsea and criticism from Sir Alex Ferguson, who claimed it was a 'poor, poor performance' from the referee. In Europe, German referee Deniz Aytekin was demoted from Champions League football after criticism from then PSG coach, Unai Emery, following their 6-1 defeat to Barcelona.

harmful emotions such as depression. Why is that? This takes us back to the importance of resource appraisal (figure 14.1), as someone's perceived ability to cope with such demands is an important factor regarding how they react to them.[251] As shown in figure 14.1, a feeling that you are not 'up to the job' may lead to negative consequences.

One such outcome is 'impact on behaviour', such as quitting. Approximately two thirds of qualified referees say they intend to quit, citing time constraints, and criticism they had been forced to accept, as the main reasons behind their decisions.[252]

Four factors as seen as stress-inducing by referees: fear of failure, fear of physical harm, time pressure and interpersonal conflict.

All of these stressors are related to what mental health charity MIND state as causes of anxiety and/or depression. Therefore the role of the referee, by nature, may cause mental health issues.

The notion that quitting is the only way to avoid such stressors suggests that referees are at high risk of suffering from mental health issues. So why is more attention not paid to this area? One is that referees have developed coping strategies to deal with their demands which will be discussed in chapter sixteen. However, could the main reason be that we expect the referee to be able to deal with it because it is their role to be the villain?

15: "It's What They Signed Up For." Do We Just Expect Referees to Handle Abuse?

So far, this book has looked at psychological influences on referees, including their own emotions. What can often be forgotten is that people don't exist in a vacuum; we are all influenced and shaped by our society and our culture. To ignore the power of our environment is to assume that we are little more than computers; taking in information and processing that data in the same way. But we are not computers. Our environment and the beliefs of others have a significant influence on us, and they have a great impact on the football referee.

For instance, in chapter eleven, we discussed how humans tend to avoid the 'worst-case scenario'. Preeminent management thinker Geert Hofstede has identified different areas in which we can measure a culture, one of which is labelled 'uncertainty avoidance'. This means that some cultures (such as Germany) encourage uniformity and emphasise the importance of formal rules, whereas other cultures (such as China) are less interested in conformity and therefore take a less risk-adverse approach to many aspects of life.[253] Simply put, individuals are a product of their culture and how they are treated; how they respond is dependent on their society. But this is a book about referees, so the question is – are referees perceived the same around the world?

Yes and no.

While it is a bit of a stretch to suggest that there is a land where officials are always treated with respect, some are certainly much more tolerant – and some are much more cynical – than others.

Before El Clásico[xlviii] in Spain, for example, newspapers will review and analyse the chosen referee's previous performances, ramping up the pressure and attention on them. In England, commentators and pundits will often criticise a wrong decision

---

xlviii The name given to any match between rivals Barcelona and Real Madrid.

from an official but, when the right call is made, the usual comment is normally something along the lines of "the referee has just about got that one right", implying either an element of luck or a reluctance to give meaningful praise. Assistant referees, in turn, wish for more credit when they get a tight decision correct.[254]

Not only this, but Sky Sports have a feature every Monday called 'Ref Watch', where every major decision of the weekend is scrutinised. With limited time, only controversial decisions are typically covered which is hardly conducive to a helpful and supportive environment for officials! The situation in Scotland is no better, where professional referee John McKendrick says an 'abuse culture' is in place.

> *"There are concerns the climate just now is very anti-referee… Unless we make a concerted effort to remove this from our game then something more serious will happen."* [255]

Perhaps one of the most difficult cultures to referee is in Italy. Officials in Italy are subject to television shows called *'Il Processo del Lunedì'* (Monday's Trial) and *'Controcampo'* (Counter-Pitch) where referees have their decisions dissected. Fans and players alike have a deep mistrust of the officials according to leading author and expert in football officials Dr Tom Webb, due, in part, to the country's history of corrupt and oppressive leaders such as Mussolini. Author Tim Parks, in his outstanding book *A Season with Verona*, illustrated the national suspicion or cynicism of those in power:

> *"Every small town's footballing dream is dreamed despite the* bastardi, *against the* bastardi; *every victory is achieved in the teeth of the* bastardi. *Apart from the referees, we have no idea who they are."* [256]

No wonder referees get such a hard time. Cases of violence against referees are frequently reported and, in 2018, members of the Italian Referees' Association even received bullets in the post.[257] Even in the aftermath of the *calciopoli* scandal, which saw a number of high profile clubs found guilty of cherry-picking certain officials for matches, it was the referees that came out worst in the eyes of the public.

Could it be, however, that it is like this everywhere? That this is 'just the way it is'? Absolutely not. For example, in Japan players have been known to bow to the referee before a match as a sign of respect and in Holland just 2.2% of officials say they experience verbal abuse in every game, in comparison with 14.4% and 60% in France and England respectively.[258] Culture and society are therefore of great importance. Even in the (relative) refereeing haven of the Netherlands, officials are not immune to abuse, as the cartoon shown in illustration 15.1 shows. While this piece of satire is small-fry compared to contemporary criticism (such as a recent tweet from an Arsenal fan suggesting that Michael Oliver be 'shot in the head' for sending off Ashley Maitland-Niles against Leicester City in April 2019), it reveals our traditional views towards football officials.

Speler: Hé, waar is je hond?
Scheidsrechter: Wat hond?
Speler: Je bent de eerste blinde, dien ik zonder geleidehond zie.

(The Humorist)

Illustration 15.1: Dutch cartoon from 1929 (artist unknown. Source: DelpherNL).[xlix]

---

xlix With thanks to Koninklijke Bibliotheek for their help in trying to identify the artist.

Translation:

Player: Hey, where's your dog?

Referee: What dog?

Player: You're the first blind person I've seen without a guide dog.

The cultural understanding (and acceptance) that a referee is there to be disliked and abused, when possible, begs the question as to whether refereeing attracts a certain type of individual. Particularly, it may attract someone who is proficient at dealing with stress, for example. After all, abuse is a reason that many referees state they wish to quit[259] and, therefore, surely the ones that stay must be ones who have good coping skills? Indeed, one former Level 3 referee interviewed for this book stated that refereeing *helped him* in dealing with stress as it enabled him to forget everyday stressors because the role commands such attention.

Before we look at the importance of coping strategies in the next chapter, however, let's discover why there is a social acceptance to dislike the referee by investigating the historical development of the role.

The Historical Role of The Referee in The UK

Many may believe that the abuse a referee receives is 'part of the game' and therefore professional referees must be 'mentally tough'.[1] This is the view of Norwegian referee Tom Henning

---

[1] For clarity, mental toughness is defined as: 'The presence of some or the entire collection of experientially developed and inherent values, attitudes, emotions, cognitions and behaviours that influence the way in which an individual approaches, responds to and appraises both negatively and positively construed pressures, challenges and adversities to consistently achieve his or her goals', in Coulter, T. J., Mallett, C. J., & Gucciardi, D. F. (2010:p.715). Understanding mental toughness in Australian soccer: Perceptions of players, parents and coaches. *Journal of Sport Sciences, 28*, 699-716.

Ovrebo[li] who, when asked about an incident involving former Premier League referee Mark Clattenburg being accused of racism,[lii] stated:

> "*Referees at the top level are very strong. They are mentally and physically fit so they will cope with situations like this. So it's a problem for the new referees, the young referees and the promising referees. And then it will be a problem long-term because you don't get the best referees because they don't like to be… put under this kind of pressure. But for top referees, like Mark Clattenburg, they cope with things like this. They are already strong and they cope with it.*"[260]

This statement makes two key points. First, Ovrebo suggests that age is an important factor regarding the negative emotions that a referee may experience. He is right. Certain pre-match feelings, such as worry, not only effects concentration but are experienced more frequently by younger referees.[261] His second point is that abuse is not only accepted but 'part of the game' – and referees must, therefore, learn how to cope with it.

Again, Ovrebo is right. Abuse, or at least a distrust of the referee, is culturally accepted in the UK. One qualified referee sums up this attitude nicely by saying, "referees get verbal abuse on a weekly basis, I guess it is part and parcel of the job."[262] This view is nothing new, of course. Even in 1968, Goal magazine asked why there isn't more respect for referees![263]

Perhaps this is because the values of British sport traditionally dictate that teams and players regulate themselves, which is evident when British sports are compared with other cultures. This was expertly done by sports philosopher David Papineau in 2017, who compared the morality and ethics of catching in baseball compared to cricket:

[li] Best remembered for turning down four penalty appeals from Chelsea in their 2009 Champions League match against Barcelona, resulting in criticism from Jose Mourinho and Didier Drogba, as well as death threats from Chelsea fans.

[lii] The situation was a claim from Chelsea FC that referee Mark Clattenburg racially abused one of their players, Jon Obi Mikel. The claim was dismissed, Clattenburg cleared, and the FA charged Mikel for misconduct.

"When a baseball player traps a ball as it bounces – or picks it up on the half-volley, as non-Americans would say – he will generally leap up as if he has caught it cleanly, hoping to persuade the umpires that the batter is out. This is by no means considered bad behaviour in professional baseball. It's what good fielders do. You'd be letting your side down if you didn't try your hardest to take advantage of the umpires' uncertainty.

The contrast to cricket is striking. Fielders in cricket are supposed to say whether or not they have caught the ball. Traditionally the batsman and indeed the umpires have accepted the fielder's word on whether a catch was fairly made, even at the highest levels of the game." [264]

This example demonstrates beautifully that our psychology is affected by our culture and history. It does not exist in a vacuum, nor is it exclusive to the UK. For instance, Australian referee Ben Williams (the first Australian chosen to referee a FIFA World Cup game past the knock-out stage[liii]) believes a lack of respect for officials is something attributable to Australian culture, stating:

"I don't know whether it's a part of our Aussie culture that goes back to the colonial days or what, but we struggle to show respect for people in authority. It doesn't matter if we're talking about a police officer, or in my case a qualified teacher and referee. Respect just isn't there as a given." [265]

In football's primitive years, referees were only given the power of decision making if both captains agreed to it[266] as, before 1847, the game was not considered 'serious enough' for any player to deliberately transgress any rules or regulations.[267] The cultural reaction to the appointment of assistant referees in 1891 is revealed in this article published by the Referees' Association in 2012:

[liii] 2014 FIFA World Cup in Brazil

"The neutral referee was disliked from the outset. Clubs did not like his absolute authority, preferring a mutual agreement between their umpires. Spectators disputed decisions and referees were even assaulted." [268]

It became increasingly acceptable to criticise the referee from the 1920's[269] and criticism is still present today, not just from spectators but from former professionals. This is shown in a 2018 tweet from registered charity Ref Support UK, following criticism from former players aimed towards referee Craig Pawson after he showed a red card to Everton's Phil Jagielka:

We really don't understand why 'pundits' make such statements: "If you want to know why Premier League referees were not invited by FIFA to the World Cup, then evidence is provided by the decision by Craig Pawson to send off Phil Jagielka, for what was at best a bookable offence."

@refsupportuk, August 12th, 2018

So referees have always been abused, but the situation will improve as we progress from this 'old-school' mentality, right?

Wrong.

It is entirely possible that changes to the laws of the game, and an increase in the demands we make on referees, will only serve to open up more opportunities for criticism to occur, and for referees to become more vulnerable to mental health issues.

For example, FIFA provided referees with a protocol to follow should they hear any racist chanting by fans at matches during the 2018 World Cup in Russia.[liv270] So not only was the referee in

---

liv A three-step approach was advised for referees to follow: first, pause the match and request an announcement over the public address system asking for the chanting to stop. Second, if chanting persists, request another announcement and only resume the game once chanting stops. Finally, abandon the match.

charge of 22 highly competitive athletes who were doing everything to win under intense time pressure, but they were also expected to control the behaviour or the crowd!

Additionally, from the 2018/19 season, managers will be allowed to watch replays of key moments and decisions during games following a relaxing of the rules regarding technology in the dugout.[271] I'm not sure that managers and coaches will be forgiving when they have evidence of a mistake by the referee at hand.

So is anything done about it?

There have been attempts made to change disrespectful and negative attitudes towards referees, most notably the FA's 'Respect' campaign. However such action has not been well received with many officials seeing it as mere lip-service.

First launched in 2008, most referees do not feel the 'Respect' campaign has made a noticeable difference. For example, one Manchester-based amateur referee reckoned it was "dead in the water".[272] While some believe the 'Respect' campaign has helped at the elite level, many think it ignores the concerns of those at the grassroots. One amateur referee made clear, "The attitude of players has not benefitted from the Respect initiatives."[273]

Our society and culture deeply influences our attitude towards officials.

Britain traditionally has a negative view of the football referee, leading to an acceptance of abuse.

Campaigns to change this view are largely unsuccessful so, while this view must still be challenged, it is important to understand how we can help referees cope with their demands.

16: Dealing With It: How Do Referees Cope With The Demands Of The Job?

In part two of this book we have established three things. First, all referees are different and are influenced to varying degrees. Second, referees are subject to a number of stressors that – at best – make their job difficult and – at worst – could contribute to a decrease in mental health. Finally, referees have always been objects of abuse and, in most cultures, are just expected to deal with it.

So how on Earth do referees cope with the pressures of the role? The answer lies within the individual. As established, individual differences influence the impact of psychological influences such as player appeals or crowd noise. Could it be that how individuals *perceive* stressors – such as being judged negatively by a crowd or a player swearing at them – can help them to cope and perhaps even improve as a referee? As we shall discover, the answer is an unequivocal yes.

One such outlook that helps referees cope with abuse is *what* they attribute the abuse to.

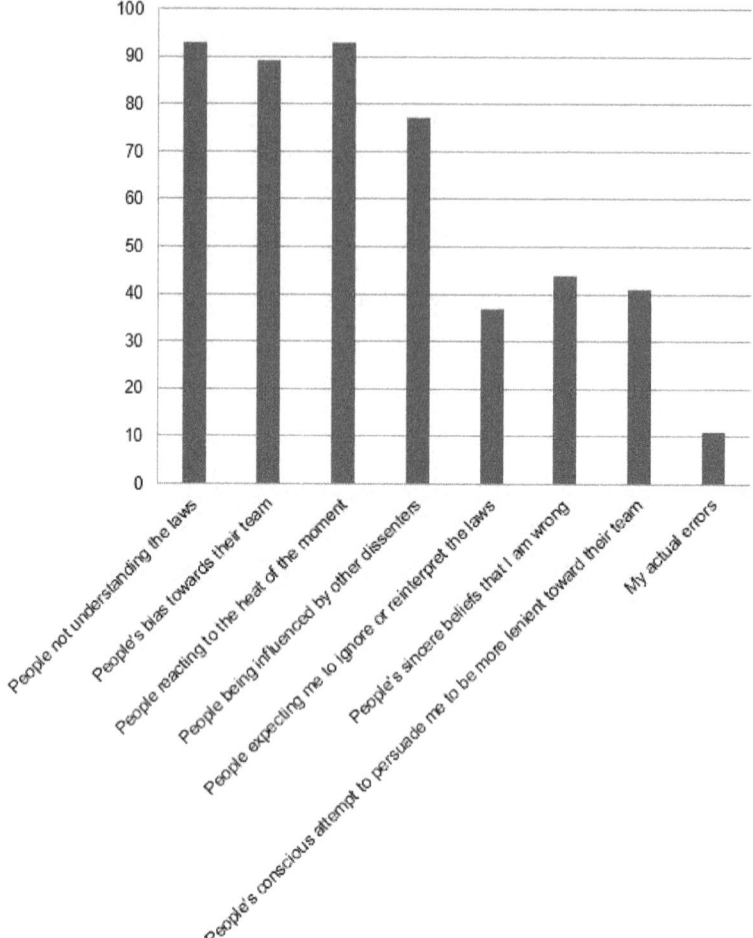

**Perceived reasons for dissent and abuse
(% of referee endorsement)**

People not understanding the laws

People's bias towards their team

People reacting to the heat of the moment

People being influenced by other dissenters

People expecting me to ignore or reinterpret the laws

People's sincere beliefs that I am wrong

People's conscious attempt to persuade me to be more lenient toward their team

My actual errors

**Figure 16.1: The percentage of referees who endorse a
particular reason for dissent and/or abuse (adapted from
Wolfson & Neave, 2007).**[274]

As shown in figure 16.1, referees attribute dissent and abuse to a
number of causes. First up, it appears that referees are quick to
point out that abuse is down to others and not to their own
shortcomings. But, let's flash back, for a moment, to Weiner's
Attribution Theory (see chapter five).

If we recall, coaches and players tend to blame external factors (e.g., things that are nothing to do with their own ability or effort) and unstable factors (e.g., things that can change such as luck or the referee) when they lose. This is to protect their view that they will succeed in the future. It appears referees do the same, as the two most endorsed reasons for dissent and abuse – people reacting to the heat of the moment and people not understanding the laws of the game[275] – are out of their control and non-permanent. Referees adopt these views to protect their beliefs that they can meet the demands of the role. If they felt that abuse was justified and that they were incompetent, they would be much more likely to quit. Would you continue participating in an activity you felt you were useless at?! Additionally, a referee who feels that they cannot meet the demands of the role may experience negative emotions, such as anger or depression.[276]

Referees attribute failures to factors outside their control that can change over time – just like players and coaches! This reinforces their belief that they'll succeed in the future.

Referees do not do this as a result of arrogance, especially in light of previously discussed research into the importance of self-belief. After all, if a player was to attribute a poor performance to 'not being good enough' it would be safe to assume that they would not have a long career.

Additionally, referees acknowledge that there are occasions when dissent occurs as a result of an actual error, much like a player would accept criticism for a scuffed shot or misplaced pass. So what happens when a referee accepts that they made a mistake and does this help them cope with the stress of errors and consequent criticism?

Response to error	% of referees endorsing this response
Try to learn something from it	100
Analyse what happened so I can understand it better	96
'Replay' the situation in my mind and imagine what I could have done	96
Remind myself that I tried my best	89
Talk to fellow officials about what happened	93
Remind myself that errors are rare	90
Enjoy the comfort and company of my family and/or friends	74
Remind myself of the good games I've had	69
Remind myself of the difficulties in getting every decision right	70
Try to think of other things rather than dwell on it	63
Feel a temporary loss of pride	67
Feel embarrassed	32
Nothing – just ignore it	29

Worry that it might happen again	22
Toss and turn over it	12
Have a stiff drink	22
Worry that my 'superiors' will hold it against me	15
Worry that I might get a bad reputation	7

Figure 16.2: Responses to errors (Wolfson & Neave, 2007).

Looking at the most commonly endorsed responses shown in figure 16.2 (e.g., 'try to learn something from it', 'analyse what happened so I can understand it better' and 'replay the situation in my mind and imagine what I should have done'), they are all helpful approaches that will lead to improved performance. For example, 'replaying the situation in my mind' is a good example of psychological preparation that can improve performance.[lv] The other responses are great examples of a 'growth mindset'…

The Growth Mindset

A 'growth mindset' is when an individual believes they can improve their ability. It contrasts to a 'fixed mindset' where an individual believes that their ability is pre-determined.

For example, a footballer may think, 'I can't take penalties' after missing one. If so, this is an example of a fixed mindset: they are assuming they cannot change or improve and this is obviously unhelpful for performance.

So how do you change this approach?

By encouraging the attitude of 'I can't take penalties *yet*' or 'I can get better at penalties *if* I keep practicing'. A great example can be found in the attitude of former England captain David Beckham who practiced juggling the ball in his garden as a child.

[lv] This will be discussed in more detail in chapter seventeen.

At first, Beckham could only achieve two or three touches before the ball dropped. However, with practice, Beckham managed to improve his ability. Beckham states that he stopped practicing at over 1,000 and then moved onto free kicks.[277] It is clear, then, why our responses to failure are so important to performance and referees are no different.

A growth mindset is not only beneficial to performance but also to mental health. After all, if a referee believes that they cannot improve on an error, or that they will never improve, such negative self-appraisal leads to negative emotions.

Good referees show a 'growth mindset', which helps them improve performance and cope with errors.

The responses in figure 16.2 also reveal two coping strategies to errors that *cannot* be associated with growth mindset. The first of these can be seen in the statements 'talk to fellow officials about what happened' and 'enjoy the comfort and company of my family and/or friends'. These are examples of 'social support'.

Social Support

93% of referees said that when they made an error, they would talk to fellow officials about what happened. Social support is not only important when coping with anxiety and depression,[278] but it is also seen as an essential coping strategy for dealing with the demands of refereeing.[279] To underline its value, it is also important for job satisfaction amongst English football referees. For example, one referee explained:

"If you didn't have anyone to talk to, there would be a lot of down moments… I knew from the people around me that I was good enough to referee so I gave it another go."[280]

But does social support help everyone? As one level 4 referee said: "I feel the benefit of a coach [social support person for a referee] is for someone who is younger."[281] While the importance of mentoring novice referees is endorsed by former FIFA referee Sonia Denoncourt,[282] the coping process and responses to issues such as abuse are the same regardless of age.[283] Therefore for all referees – young and old – social support is an important coping tool.

Referees cite social support as an important coping strategy.

Although some feel it is more beneficial for younger referees, social support can help people deal with anxiety and depression regardless of age.

The second strategy for coping with errors is rationalisation. This is the process of allowing our beliefs to be logical, non-extreme and, above all else, flexible. For example, 90% of sampled referees stated that they remind themselves that 'errors are rare'[lvi] and 70% endorsed the reasoning that 'it is difficult to get every decision right'. This is rational thinking. These officials are being logical by stating that they cannot get every decision right – much like a player cannot execute every skill perfectly – and also by being flexible. They give themselves leeway by accepting that they do not have to be right all the time, despite best intentions.

Rational Thinking

If you were officiating a game of football and a player shouted at you – perhaps swearing at you in the process – what would you do? Perhaps you would send them off, perhaps not. Now, don't just think about *what* you would do, think about *why* you would do it. Are you simply following procedure, or are you reacting to an event emotionally? Does a player swearing at you have a meaning that goes beyond the laws of the game?

In chapter 14, the topic of emotional regulation was discussed. It is often assumed that people will react to the same demands with the same emotions, but this is not the case. Our emotional reaction is dependent upon the label we attach to the event, not the event itself.[284] For example, a player swearing at a referee may cause some officials to feel belittled or disrespected personally, which would lead to anger or sadness. However, another referee may dismiss the action as a 'heat of the moment' comment, and a release of frustration from the player (not a personal attack), leading to emotions such as patience and tolerance. How we

---

[lvi] This is a statement of fact. Analysis showed that after the first 48 games of the 2018 FIFA World Cup referees recorded a 95% success rate regarding decisions, which improved to 99.3% with the intervention of VAR (Sky Sports, 2018c. Pierluigi Collina says World Cup VAR has proved successful.
http://www.skysports.com/football/news/12098/11421135/pierluigi-collina-says-world-cup-var-has-proved-successful. Cited on 13/08/18 from the World Wide Web).

perceive events and rationalise their meaning is fundamental to our mental health.

The importance of rational thinking on mental health was established by Albert Ellis in 1957. Ellis found that rational beliefs result in helpful behaviours, whereas irrational beliefs lead to unhelpful ones.[285] For instance, a referee that *would like* to perform well in an important match may experience 'concern' over their performance. This is helpful. It directs attention and motivates the official to prepare for the match. However, a referee that feels they *must* perform well is likely to experience 'anxiety' about their forthcoming fixture. This is likely to lead to unhelpful behaviours, such as a lack of concentration or withdrawal from relevant activities. Put simply, irrational beliefs result in unhealthy emotions which limit the achievement of our goals, while rational beliefs enable success and help produce healthy emotions.[286]

Before we discuss the difference between healthy and unhealthy emotions and behaviours, let's establish where they come from.

Both irrational and rational thoughts stem from one primary belief.[287] The primary view that leads to irrational beliefs is *inflexible demands*, whereas the primary view that leads to rational beliefs is preferences.

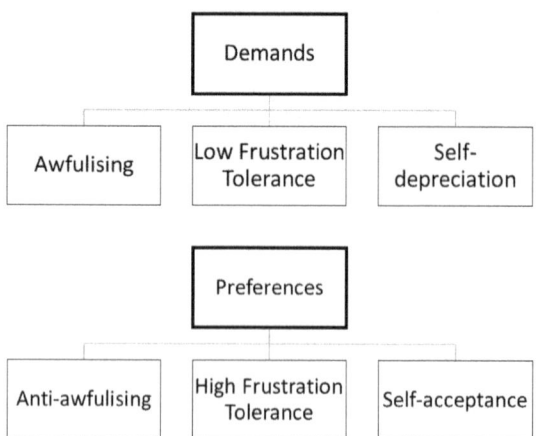

Figure 16.3: Primary and secondary irrational beliefs (Dryden, 2012).

A demand is an inflexible expectation made upon oneself, meaning that anything other than meeting this demand is unacceptable. For example, a footballer that states 'I *must* win this game' or a referee claiming that 'I *must* get every decision correct' is placing an inflexible demand upon themselves. What if our footballer plays incredibly well and does their absolute best but does not win? What if our referee gets 99% of their decisions correct? Is this not enough? With a demand comes secondary irrational beliefs.

Awfulising: when the consequences of the demand not being met are exaggerated (e.g., "It is the end of the world if we lose" or "I can't stand not playing well")

Low frustration tolerance: when an individual cannot bear their demand not being met and so reacts with frustration or aggression (e.g., if an individual believes that they must always be treated with respect then they will feel angry if someone does not meet this standard)

Self-depreciation: when an individual is overly critical of themselves (e.g., an individual who labels themselves 'useless' because they have not met their demand).

Alternatively, an individual may hold the primary belief of *preferences*. For example, a footballer would very much like and want to win the game but, if they do not, it does not devalue them as an individual; they will cope with this disappointment. This view leads to anti-awfulising, high frustration tolerance, and self-acceptance.

Rational thinking may be beneficial for mental health, but does it help performance? Yes, it does. This may shock those who see irrational belief as some sort of 'Faustian trade' for excellent performance. Surely it would be better for John Stones or Marcus Rashford to say "we *must* win this game" before an important fixture, rather than "we'll try our best but if we lose, we'll get over it"? This statement would be motivating and performance enhancing, wouldn't it? We must be clear on this: *it is not*.

Firstly, traditional 'wall-banging' battle cries may increase arousal, resulting in a 'pumped-up' team, but it is actually pre-game speeches or statements that centre on game plans and focus (such as "it is important that we play to our strengths" or "concentration will be very important in this match") that are the most effective for improving performance.[288]

Secondly, it is highly doubtful that athletes actually believe such statements. Although we often hear performers talk about the importance of winning a competition or reaching a final, it has been suggested that it is difficult for an athlete *not* to think about the 'absolute outcome', especially in pinnacle events (such as the Olympics or World Cup). Therefore their attention and comments automatically lean towards their ultimate goal (e.g., winning the gold medal or lifting the trophy). This may not be what they actually believe. They may simply wish to progress as far as possible as a team or to develop as a performer.

As fans, we don't hear this view as an athlete may see that valuing anything less than winning as a "betrayal of what it means to compete".[289] Let's look at an example. On March 10th, 2019, Tottenham Hotspur captain Hugo Lloris stated that Spurs must win all eight of their remaining games in the Premier League in order to finish in the top four (and thus qualify for the following season's Champions League campaign).[290]

However, this statement is not true. Firstly, Tottenham lost four of their remaining games (Liverpool, Manchester City, West Ham United and Bournemouth) and drew another (Everton), claiming only nine points with wins against Crystal Palace, Huddersfield Town and Brighton. Yet they still finished fourth. Secondly, and this is the real issue, Tottenham didn't *have* to finish in the top four. It would be better for them if they did, but if they didn't they would have another attempt next season. And it certainly doesn't define the players as individuals. So why didn't Lloris say this? Why not state, 'We would like to finish in the top four but, if we don't, we'll do our best next year'?

There are two possible answers.

The first is that it wouldn't go down well with fans. Supporters of clubs want to know that results mean everything to players and nothing less than their absolute best and total dedication is good enough. The second is that, perhaps, Lloris means it. It is possible he has placed an inflexible demand on himself and his team by stating that they must finish in the top four. No excuses.

There is evidence however, that this demand led to some of the negative outcomes shown in figure 16.3. For instance, Lloris himself made an obvious error in the following game away at Liverpool, when he dropped the ball instead of making a routine catch, resulting in a goal for the home side and a 2-1 defeat for Tottenham. Was this the outcome of increased anxiety due to inflexible demands? During the penultimate game of the season, away to Bournemouth, Spurs' Player of the Year, Heung-Min Son, was shown a straight red card for uncharacteristically shoving Bournemouth player Jefferson Lerma in a game that Son's side were dominating but failing to score in. Inflexible demands lead to low-frustration tolerance.

But what about referees? Do they hold such beliefs? Do they see games as 'must-win' in light of their own performance and, consequently, suffer from negative emotional outcomes? The conclusions presented in table 16.2 suggest that referees hold preferences regarding making correct decisions rather than absolute demands. This is illustrated perfectly by a referee who said:

> "I might be a controversial here, but the mass brawl we talk about is a joke...I've had loads of mass confrontations and it's just all about men trying to look hard, but it doesn't affect my mindset...You don't really have control over that part of it. It's really up to the players how the game will continue, it's not something I can control, so I just think, 'let them get on with it, and then take control when it calms down'. All I can control is making correct decisions as I see them, so I do that and it doesn't affect me." [291]

This is a good example of rational thinking. It would be understandable for a referee to believe, "I must not lose control of the game" when, in fact, the behaviour of 22 other people is not something a referee can always control.

Finally, irrational beliefs do not result in behaviours that benefit sports performance.[292] The actions that both irrational and rational beliefs lead to are shown in figure 16.5.

Emotion	Healthy or Unhealthy	Type of Belief	Adversity[lvii]	Action Tendency (Behaviour)
Anxiety	Unhealthy	Irrational	Threat/Danger	Withdraw mentally and physically and/or seek reassurance
Concern	Healthy	Rational	Threat/Danger	Face up to threat and/or take constructive action to minimise danger
Unhealthy Anger	Unhealthy	Irrational	Goal obstruction and/or threat to self-esteem	Attack others physically and/or verbally and/or passive aggressively
Healthy Anger	Healthy	Rational	Goal obstruction and/or threat to self-esteem	Assert self with other and/or request behavioural change from other
Depression[lviii]	Unhealthy	Irrational	Loss and/or failure	Withdraw into oneself and/or attempt to terminate feelings in self-destructive ways
Sadness	Healthy	Rational	Loss and/or failure	Express and talk about feelings to significant others

Table 16.5: Behavioural benefits of rational beliefs (adapted from Dryden & Branch, 2008).

[lvii] Based on inference about an event and therefore subjective.

[lviii] Non-clinical.

Let's look at these actions to see how they may help or hinder performance.

An individual experiencing anxiety, for example, would 'mentally or physically withdraw' from the activity whereas an athlete showing a healthy concern about performance 'faces up to threat and takes action to minimise danger'. A referee who 'mentally withdraws' from the activity (e.g., they cease concentrating on the game) would not perform well. So what do good officials do? A Level 3 referee put it best, "I relish the challenge. I don't shy away."[293]

This attitude is echoed by elite referees, who don't perceive nerves as anxiety, but as a 'healthy concern about performance'. This can be seen in practice in the comments made by former referee Howard Webb, who stated that if he felt nerves, he perceived them as a good thing as he was ready for the challenge ahead.[294]

Let's look at another example. Picture a player who is verbally insulting an official. A referee who experiences irrational anger and attacks the player verbally or physically is not one who is performing well; whereas a referee who asserts themselves and requests behavioral change from the offender is doing their job to a high standard.

Irrational beliefs are harmful to our mental health, leading to awfulising, low frustration tolerance, and self-depreciation.

Not only this, but irrational beliefs also harm performance.

Elite referees demonstrate rational beliefs.

The evidence provided in part two has indicated how difficult it is to ascertain if, and to what extent, individual differences impact both performance and mental health problems with referees.

In order to deal with both threats to performance and their own well-being, referees must adopt a number of coping strategies. How effective these strategies are have a huge impact on how a referee performs, and how they cope with the demands of the role.

It is with both performance and health in mind that we approach the final part of this book. How do we take what we have learned and apply them to improve things for referees? Additionally, who is responsible for doing this and can it be done? This shall be our focus in part three.

PART THREE

PRACTICAL APPLICATIONS FOR
IMPROVEMENT

17: Knowledge Without Practice Makes But Half the Artist: Can a Referee Practice Psychological Skills?

When referees in the English Premier League turned professional in 2001, many thought the main consequence would be increased fitness. This would benefit performance as, typically, many individuals attribute refereeing errors to a lack of fitness (e.g., poor positioning).

However, despite the fitness levels of officials being higher than ever, it seems that some people are still not convinced that referees are good enough to warrant the label of 'professional'. For example, on the 13th of January, 2018, referee Andy Haines turned down a penalty appeal from Doncaster in their League One match against Plymouth Argyle. In his post-match interview, then Doncaster manager Darren Ferguson stated: "The referees are part-time and the standard is appalling, their fitness levels are a disgrace, I've had enough of it."[lix][295]

Fitness is, undoubtedly, an important aspect of refereeing performance and physical skills are the primary focus of training plans involving deliberate practice and sports performance.[296] Such plans are often built from frameworks; simplified diagrams that are designed to point out all the necessary parts of successful performance. However, frameworks involving deliberate practice have been developed to accommodate other key qualities that contribute to success in a sporting context, such as mental attributes. Put simply, it is not enough to only improve physical skills. This belief has led to academics acknowledging the difference between physical effort and mental effort.[297] Seeing as we have established the importance of psychological skills and effort in relation to refereeing performance, incorporating mental skills training into practice must be considered especially important.

[lix] Ferguson also suggested that poor officials should be 'shot'.

Fortunately, elite referees are aware of the importance of mental skills. For example, Premier League referee Michael Oliver recently made clear that referees train throughout the summer at St George's Park in order to prepare for both the physical and mental demands of officiating Premier League football.[298] This is important; when sports officials are asked what underpins a successful performance, cognitive skills are seen as more important than physical ones.

In rugby league, by way of comparison, officials identified 24 attributes as important for optimum performance, with the top six qualities being exclusively psychological.[299] These were:

- Decision-making (e.g., accuracy),
- Reading the game,
- Communication,
- Game understanding (e.g., empathy/perception),
- Game management (e.g., knowing when to intervene to benefit the game)
- Knowing the laws

Fitness (remember that this was seen as the most important area to improve) was ranked 9th, and it suggests that match day officials should be striving to improve their cognitive skills.

Of course, the Professional Game Match Officials Limited (PGMOL) group already employs sport psychologists to aid referees in this area. While being interviewed for this book, former head of the PGMOL, Keith Hackett, said that Premier League referees have meetings to discuss subjects such as dealing with stress and conflict and the effective use of body language, for example. Referees are also offered private, one-to-one sessions. This is to be admired. Former New Zealand All-Black and Rugby World Cup winner Dan Carter said it best when he claimed:

"When I started my career, if you said you were going to see a psychologist, everyone would ask if you were all right. Now they say that if you don't." [300]

However, and this is an important issue, psychological support appears to only be available to referees at the highest level. According to several grassroots referees interviewed for this book, there is 'absolutely no guidance' regarding the psychological aspects of the game at the lower levels.

This is a fundamental mistake because it is at this level that referees may be affected the most. For instance, the FA have difficulty retaining referees between the ages of 20 and 24, with this age group experiencing a significant numbers decrease between 2007 and 2010.[301]

Don't be fooled into thinking this is just about age. It is also to do with experience. For example, age has no bearing on self-control, but this important aspect of refereeing *is* influenced by experience.[302] Therefore to offer only elite referees guidance in this area seems misguided. Psychological preparation is not about age, but practice.

Referees can benefit from psychological training.

Psychological skills make up the six most important skills a referee can have.

Although everyone can benefit, only elite referees are given help in this area despite younger, inexperienced officials having the most to gain from it.

Deliberate Practice

Training improves performance. This is one of the fundamental truths in sport. The role of coaches is to enable best practice in order to aid the athletes in their charge to meet their potential; therefore, improvements into *how* we practice will result in better performance. This notion is what the study of sports science is built upon and with good reason. Advances in practice have seen measurable gains in athletic triumphs. For example, at the 1956 Olympic Games, in Melbourne, the winning time in the men's 100m final was 10.5 seconds, while at the 2016 Olympic Games in Rio de Janeiro the race was won in 9.81 seconds. Such improvement can also be seen in professional football, with the game being 20% faster in 2012 than it was in 2007.[303]

It is safe to assume that such improvement stems from the quality and quantity of practice. Key researchers in the field of coaching and skill acquisition have made clear that the relationship between practice and performance is 'monotonic' (e.g., the amount of time spent practicing is related to the increased skill of an individual); the following illustration shows what main factors affect deliberate practice (figure 17.1).[304]

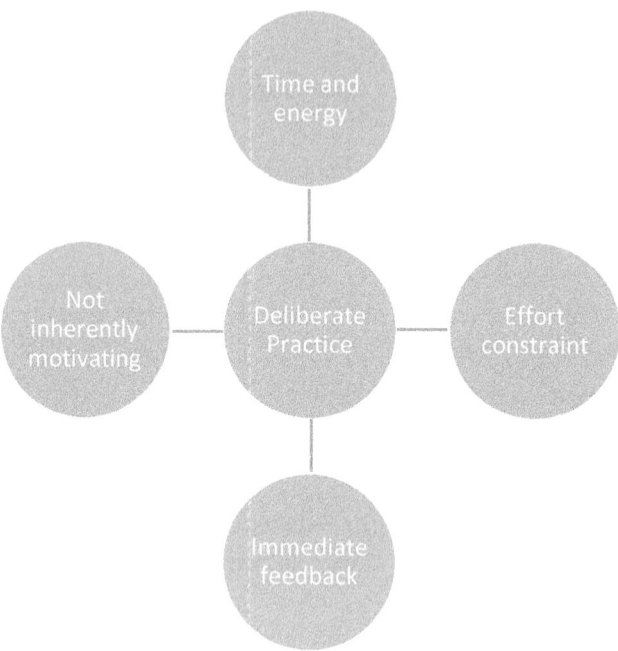

Figure 17.1: The deliberate practice framework (adapted from Ericsson et al., 1993 and MacMahon et al., 2007).[305]

This framework states that *for practice to improve performance*, an individual must invest time and energy into the practice. Simply put, it cannot be done casually; it must be purposeful.

Time must be dedicated to practice but this time is limited due to both the energy expended during the activities and the need to prevent an individual from suffering from 'burn-out'. This can be physical, such as not being physically capable of carrying out the activity because of fatigue, and mental, such as not being able to concentrate sufficiently on the task for it to be worthwhile.

Feedback must be provided immediately, and the practice itself cannot be inherently motivating.

So what sort of practice do referees do? Figure 17.2 shows what elite referees do to practice, and compares the time spent doing it in their first year of officiating, then 1998, and 2003.

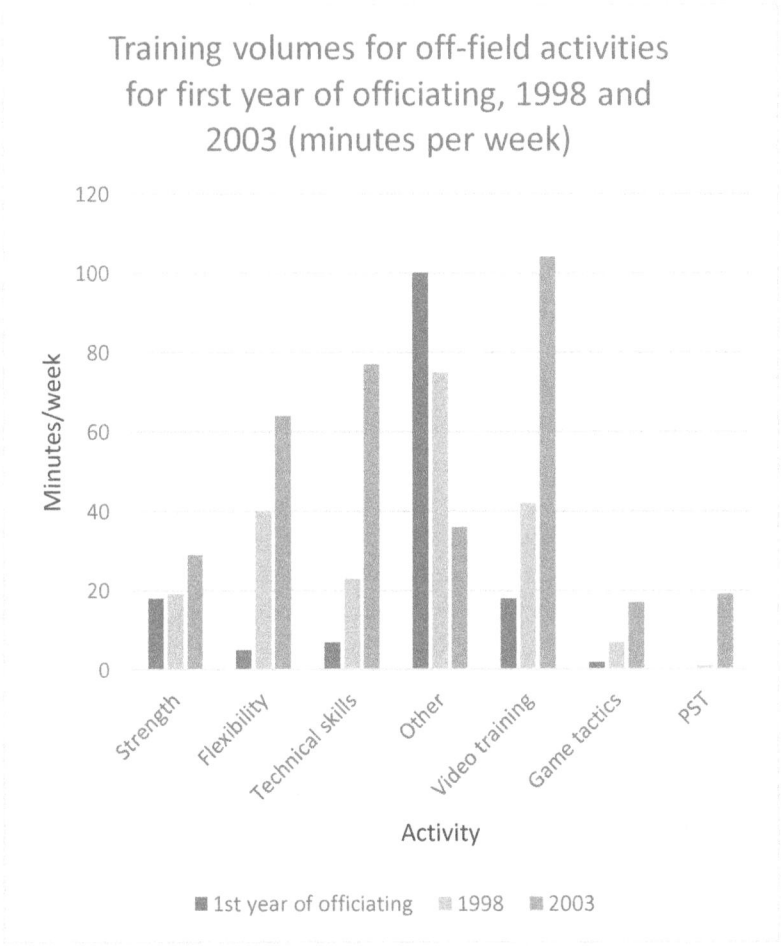

Figure 17.2: Training volumes for elite referees at three different time periods (taken from MacMahon et al., 2007). NOTE: PST = psychological skills training.

Although the study is an older one, it shows that officials spend an increased amount of time per week developing psychological skills. And that is a finding which carries through to the present day. One Level 3 referee interviewed said that psychological skills training is "far more important than the standard training." Most notably, psychological skills development comes in the form of video training.

How important is it? What evidence is there that video training improves performance by improving psychological skills? Recently, there has been some excellent work in this area. Dr Lee Moore and his colleagues have looked extensively at perceptual-cognitive expertise in rugby union officials.[306] Basically, this means 'are the referees looking at the right things and, in turn, making the correct decisions based on what they saw'?

The answer is yes, provided the referee is trained and experienced.

In the study, it was the elite officials (e.g., those that referee in the top flight of the game and/or internationally) that not only made more accurate decisions than trainee referees and players but, importantly, spent more time looking at *the correct visual cues*.

For instance, rather than looking at contact points or the front row of the scrum (which are the most relevant areas for an official during this action) one player was recorded not only looking at the advertising hoardings, but actually reading the name of the tea brand that had paid for the privilege! This is certainly refreshing for referees who are told that you have to have played the game to be a good referee. We know that football officials get more decisions right than players when tested (see the introduction to this book) and this research helps explains why this is. Simply put, psychological skills training is important and officials share this view.

To illustrate this, the next graph reveals how relevant or important off-field activities are to referees (figure 17.3).

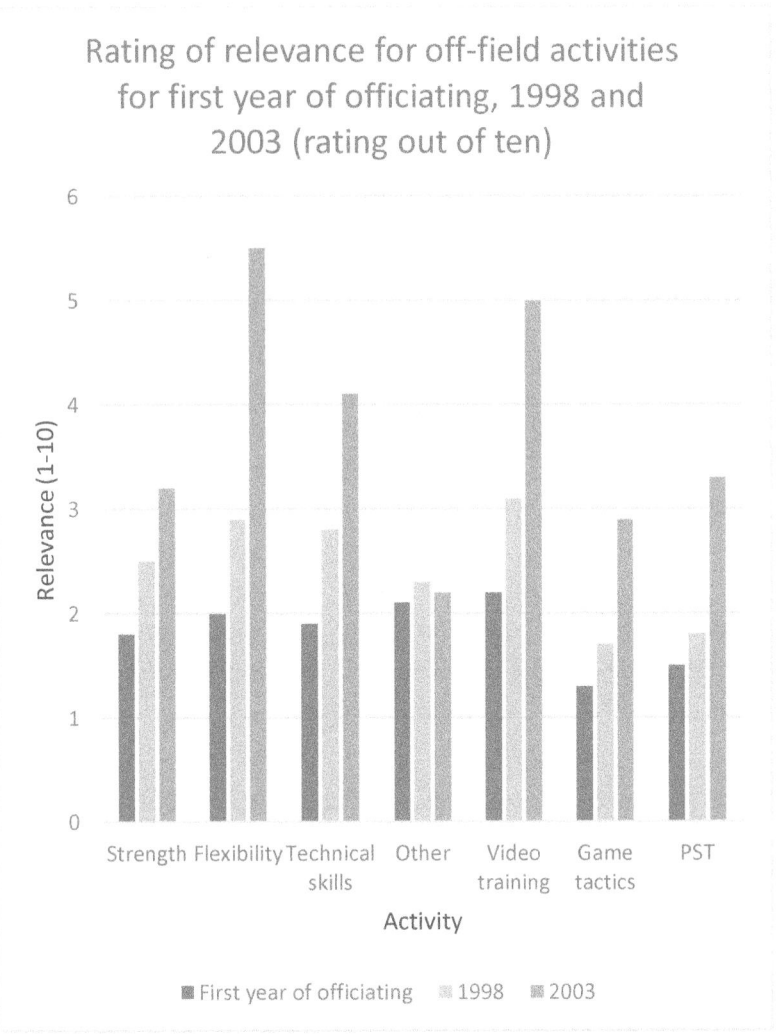

Figure 17.3: Mean ratings of relevance for off-field activities for elite referees over three time periods (adapted from MacMahon et al., 2007). NOTE: PST = psychological skills training.

The referees' responses reveal that flexibility training and video training were seen as the most relevant activities. Importantly, all types of training were seen as more important in the final year of the study when compared to officials' first years of refereeing, suggesting that officials wish to develop and acknowledge the role of practice in achieving this end.

Two other conclusions can be drawn from this chart. The first is that perceptual-cognitive decision-making skill, developed through video training, is seen as incredibly relevant to today's referees. A possible explanation of this is the increased speed of modern football. Faster play gives officials less time to make decisions, and ways to improve decision-making skills were therefore seen as important.

The second conclusion is that as the culture of professionalism has become more established, the importance of training and deliberate practice is better understood and appreciated. Preparation is key for *all* sports performers, and many in professional football are quick to underline its value. Former Manchester United and England full-back Gary Neville, for example, stated:

> *"I would say preparation for a match has been the key to my career. If that's wrong, any element of it is wrong, I'm in trouble. My biggest lesson in life was preparation costing me and I never took that risk again... you just don't know what is going to happen."* [307]

As we have previously established that referees should be considered performers, and also have a number of unpredictable and uncontrollable possibilities to deal with, preparation coupled with deliberate practice is a key focus for improved performance.

Deliberate practice is a must to improve performance, especially since the game gets ever faster.

To be the best, referees have to train more and more.

This training is not only physical, but psychological too.

So what can a referee do to practice? In the next chapter we will establish a framework that referees can use to aid their psychological preparation for games.

18: Prior Planning Prevents Poor Performance: How Can a Referee Prepare Psychologically?

Football fans are no doubt aware of the meticulous preparation that many players undertake. Diet, dossiers, and the dissection of their opponents (not literally!) is par for the course. But what about the referees?

In the previous chapter, we established the importance of practice and preparation for referees. But how can they do this? Referees need a model to help them in this area; a framework to guide them. Researcher Roy Samuel[308] – as can be seen in figure 18.1 – offers one; a model that has been designed with elite referees in mind. The framework presented here has been adapted to be clearer and applicable to referees of all levels.

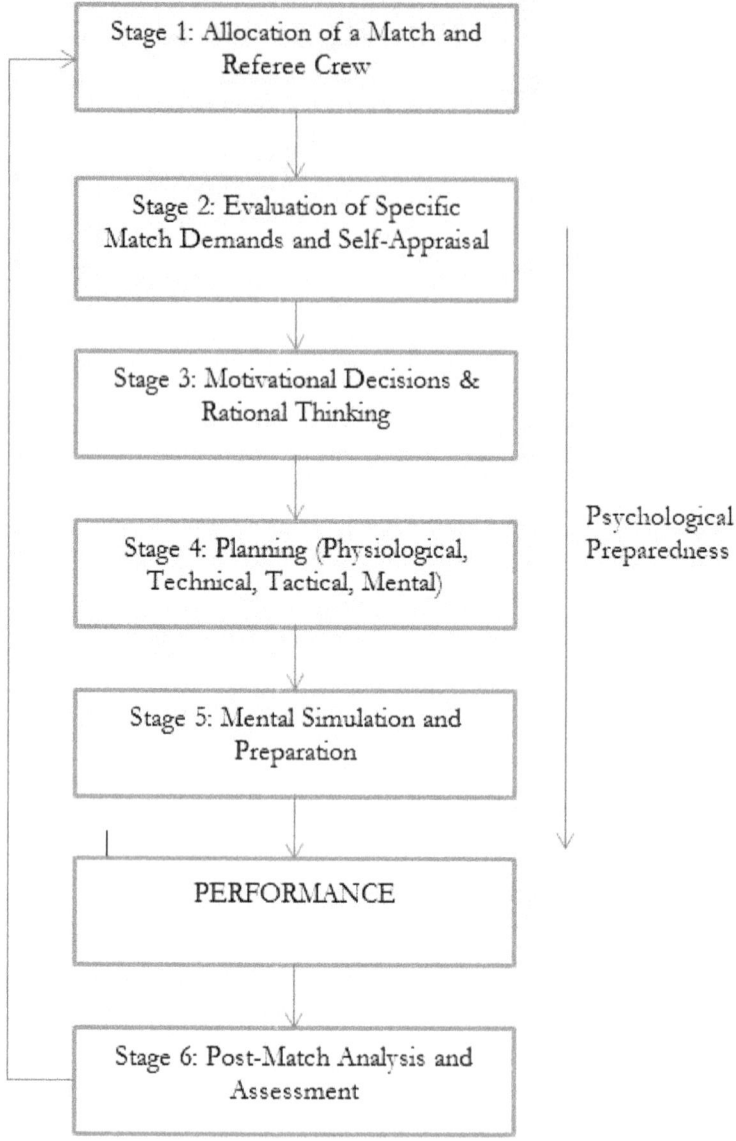

Figure 18.1: An adapted framework for football referees' psychological preparation (adapted from Samuel, 2015).

Obviously, there are some psychological influences that a referee cannot influence and which will never change (e.g., a biased crowd), so officials, therefore, must focus on what they can do to help protect themselves from such pressures.

Our goal for this chapter is to discuss each stage of the model to clarify how a referee and their associations can do this.

Allocation of a Match and Referee Crew

Once a referee has been assigned a match, they should immediately begin the planning process. At this stage, planning should focus on logistics. How long does it take to arrive at the venue? What time will you need to be there by? At what time will you be free to leave? Is it possible the game could go into extra-time?

These time pressures – not just travel time but also administrative issues – are cited as sources of job dissatisfaction in referees.[309] Keith Hackett even had to sacrifice a European final because he couldn't get the time off work!

At the highest level, officials will meet in a hotel near the ground and normally eat together on the morning of the match. While this is not necessarily possible at lower levels, the importance of liaising with assistant referees, pre-match, cannot be underestimated. Doing this allows the officials to discuss potential situations, such as preferred methods of communications or protocol for events that may arise,[lx] and can be done at all levels (even when the assistants are volunteers).

For example, the referee may ask their assistants not to give any fouls for the first ten minutes so they can see what he or she perceives as a foul, thus improving consistency. Alternatively, a referee may wish for their assistants to be in total control of their area of the pitch and be solely responsible for awarding fouls. This makes sense as it is in the 'lateral areas' (e.g., the corners of the pitch nearest to the assistant referees) where the most mistakes are made (17% versus 13% in the middle of the pitch).[310]

[lx] You may remember we discussed this in chapter thirteen and labelled it 'situation modification'.

Finally, when working with others, it is important to establish an open and honest line of communication. Successful leaders have a respect that is volunteered rather than demanded.[311] Therefore, while the referee's decision may be final, they must accept the guidance of their assistants and encourage their input. This is achieved by the following principles of communication set out by Professor Kevin Burke: [312]

- Speak freely, honestly and forthrightly
- Don't explain brief statements (although they can be discussed further if needed)
- Don't openly react to statements
- Always keep an open mind

Such open and honest communication in sport holds such importance that former performance manager for Australia Rugby Union, Wayne Goldsmith, believes coaches and sport scientists should be trained in this skill.[313] This would also be beneficial to referees. After all, they are not alone in running a football match; there are two assistant referees and a fourth official there to aid them.

There are benefits to having others providing perspective on an event (e.g., an alternative view may prompt an official to 'reframe' or re-evaluate the information).

In his 2009 book, *Outliers: The Story of Success,* [314] the popular science writer Malcolm Gladwell recounts the tale of a Korean aircraft crash in 1997. The crash, Gladwell states, had two causes: first, the respect for hierarchy that is fundamental to Korean culture and, second, the indirect nature of the Korean language. Essentially, the crash could have been averted if more direct language was used by the co-pilot towards the pilot (he had identified the problem but, according to the black box footage, was struggling to share that knowledge overtly with the captain); and if those in charge were more accepting of criticism or feedback from those beneath them in the chain of command.

While pooling information is a valuable process to help an individual obtain a fair and balanced view, especially if there are alternatives that they haven't considered,[315] the process is no guarantee of a successful outcome. This is because new information that is unpopular with the majority view is 'downplayed' or ignored.[316] Consequently, group discussion is more likely to result in the original view of the group or group leaders being retained.[lxi] Therefore, as you would expect, a discussion system that is anonymous significantly outperforms face-to-face discussions.[317] Referees and their assistants, however, have to discuss events face-to-face; and the referee has the final decision.

Diving into the dynamic between referees and their assistants is not easy, as viewers are not privy to their conversations. However, in the game between Liverpool and Tottenham Hotspur on the 4th of February 2018, there was a consultation between the referee, Jon Moss, and his assistant, Eddie Smart, that was picked up very clearly by cameras and microphones broadcasting the game. The conversation went as follows:

Smart: "All I need to know is, did Lovren touch the ball?"

Moss: "I don't know."

Smart: "If he's not touched the ball, it is offside, so you're chalking off the penalty. It has to be offside if Lovren has not touched the ball."

[At this point two players participate in the conversation]

Tottenham's Christian Eriksen: "He did touch the ball."

Liverpool's Emre Can: "He didn't touch the ball."[lxii]

Moss [to Smart]: "Just talk to me again."

Smart: "You know what I'm asking; I need to clarify, has Lovren touched the ball? If he has, it's a deliberate action and, therefore, it's a penalty. If he has not, it is offside."

Moss: "I have no idea whether Lovren touched the ball, to be honest with you. [To his microphone]: Martin [Atkinson, who is watching on TV] have you got anything from TV?"

---

lxi This may explain why, despite the fact that the referee is not alone, their absolute authority makes them vulnerable to the effects of conformity (see chapter three).

lxii Both players are trying to reframe the information to the referee. This is why group discussion is important: it *should* help an individual frame information correctly provided the discussion is open and hierarchy can be challenged.

[Then, immediately after asking the question] **Moss**: "I'm giving the penalty."[318]

This conversation highlights that although group discussion should minimise the impact of phenomena such as schema theory and confirmation bias, the hierarchy of an organisation may limit its benefits. In this instance, Eddie Smart is advising the referee that a penalty should only be awarded if Lovren touched the ball. The referee cannot answer the question (which is acceptable – it is folly to expect a referee to see every detail of a football match), and so, probably because a decision has to be made, states 'I'm awarding the penalty'. It is important to note that this was his original view, supporting the view that face-to-face discussion, where there is a clear hierarchy, will result in the 'leader' – in this case the referee – simply retaining their original view.

This does not mean that the official was necessarily wrong in his decision. In fact, what this transcript shows is that elite level officials are open in their communication, just as Goldsmith recommends. Smart has no qualms in requesting a conversation with Moss to clarify a decision. Referees should therefore make it clear to assistants that they are free to voice their own views and challenge a decision if they feel something has been missed.

Finally, referees should also be aware of their own motivation. For instance, are they focussing too much on officiating as many matches as they can (a characteristic of obsessive passion)? Referees are advised to monitor this and acknowledge when they need a break.[319]

Preparation Tip 1: when given a game, plan travel times in advance, allowing for all contingencies.

Preparation Tip 2: Encourage an open and honest relationship with assistants. Even volunteer assistants at grassroots. Tell them to discuss things with you to prevent problems.

Evaluation of Specific Match Demands and Self-Appraisal

How a referee perceives the demands of the role – and the stress it entails – is important (see figure 14.1). Stress can be heightened by the prospect of officiating a challenging team or being observed by an assessor. Referees are therefore encouraged to focus on their skills; the skills that will help them overcome these demands.[320] In particular, referees should attempt to improve their self-efficacy (see figure 10.1).

If we recall, self-efficacy is someone's self-belief in their ability to perform a task and has four elements. Therefore a referee should:

- Concentrate on previous performances that went well
- Observe other referees at a similar level[lxiii]
- Engage with others, and get others to engage with them, using verbal encouragement
- Examine and practise ways of preparing for matches psychologically

While the final two points will be addressed later, the first two are practical interventions a referee can do; by appraising their resources positively, in dealing with demands, a referee is less likely to experience negative performance behaviours (see figure 14.1).[321]

Preparation Tip 3: Referees should spend some time prior to a match thinking about successful previous performances and why they were good.

Preparation Tip 4: Where possible, spend time watching referees at a similar level.

[lxiii] It is worth reinforcing that a former Level 3 referee and current FA referee coach stated in an interview for this book that watching others at a similar level is the best thing a developing referee can do.

Motivational Decisions and Rational Thinking

Before a match, a referee may experience "inner conflicts and apprehension."[322] Even though many referees, including elite referees, possess a strong self-belief in their abilities (see chapter ten) it is important to remember that an individual may still experience doubt in their performance. It is therefore advised that referees make four conscious decisions:[323]

1. Invest uncompromising effort
2. Dare to make difficult decisions
3. Control themselves
4. Choose to rely (or not) on their assistants

How can referees achieve all of these decisions? One solution is to practice rational thinking.

In chapter sixteen, we established that rational thinking is a key coping strategy for referees. However, thinking rationally *after the event* is not likely to improve performance. What would be more effective is for a referee to practise rational thinking always, and particularly pre-match, using rational-emotive behaviour therapy (REBT).

Leading REBT researcher, Dr Martin Turner, stated in an interview for this book that "performance is just an indication of how someone is functioning". In other words, a referee who believes they must get every decision right may believe that they are motivating themselves but in reality they are revealing that they possess unrealistic demands and expectancies. Officiating perfectly is as improbable as a player going through a game without making one mistake, regardless of severity.

Individuals carry their beliefs with them when entering a sporting context and real referee testimony reveals how such demands can negatively affect performance. For instance, one level 6 referee explained that he finds it difficult to deal with players disrespecting him because, in his own words, "I was brought up to be respectful to others." This is a good example of an inflexible demand (e.g., 'people *must* be respectful to me') leading to negative performances (see figure 18.2). In this case, a player shouting at a referee is an action that leads to an irrational belief (e.g., this is awful), creating a consequence that is not helpful to performance (e.g., anxiety or anger).

So what can a referee do?

Appraising the causes of feelings is integral to emotional regulation, leading to improved performance and it is recommended by the British Association of Sport and Exercise Science.[324] Therefore, referees should practice rational thinking.

While age is a significant factor that decreases irrational beliefs,[325] younger and less experienced referees can motivate themselves by establishing rational beliefs. This can be done on three fronts:

Truth: is your motivational statement true? For instance, a referee may say to themselves, "I must get every decision right or I am a poor referee." This is not true; much like a striker doesn't have to score every chance they get in order to avoid negative evaluation. Instead, a referee could state, "I would like to get as many decisions as possible right."

Logic: does your motivational statement make logical sense? If, for example, a referee states, "Good referees don't make mistakes. Therefore if I make a mistake, I am a bad referee." This is not a logical conclusion because there has not been a referee that hasn't made a mistake. A more logical statement would be, "All referees make mistakes. Therefore although I do not want to make one, it would not make me a bad referee."

Pragmatism: is your statement helpful? Let's assume that, in order to motivate themselves, a referee says to themselves, "If I don't get a good evaluation from my observer today then I am useless at this." Would this lead to a good performance? The evidence says not (see chapter sixteen). A more practical, helpful statement would be: "All I can do is my best and that is what I will do."

Therefore a referee reinforcing rational beliefs will be more likely to see a benefit in performance instead of using more traditional, motivational statements before a game. It is hoped that this will help referees generate the self-awareness that is encouraged for improved performance.[326]

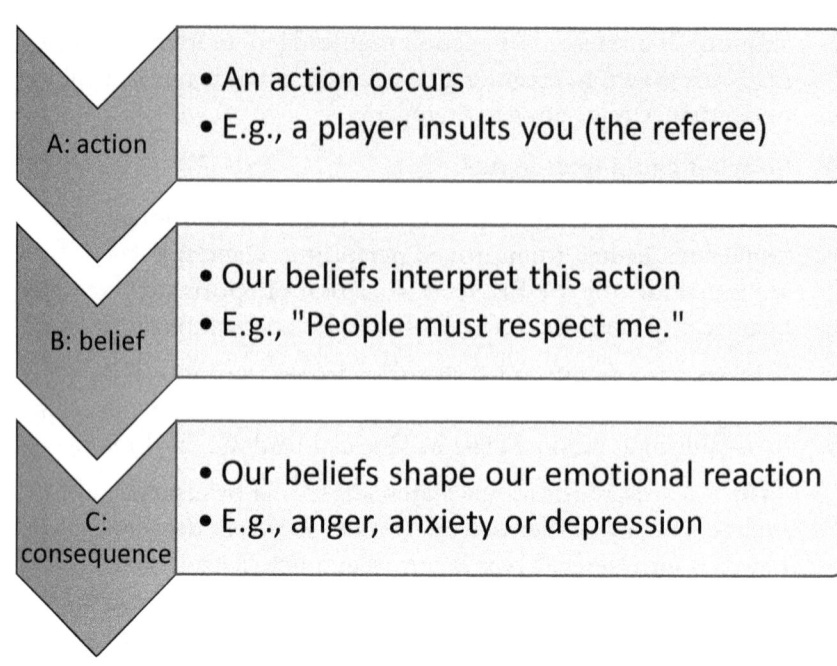

Figure 18.2: The 'ABC' model of REBT (adapted from Dryden & DiGiuseppe, 1990).[327]

Preparation Tip 5: Referees should practice the principles of rational thinking.

1. Is your belief going into a game true?

2. Is your belief going into a game logical?

3. Is your belief going into a game useful?

Planning

There are four types of planning that underpin best performance.[328] The first is physiological planning.

Physiological planning

Although this book is concerned with the psychological preparation of referees, awareness of physiological demands has been shown to help with mental skills. For instance, extreme temperatures (hot or cold) which affect the comfort of a referee can have a negative impact on decision-making[329] and hydration is also important for performance (most referees are dehydrated post-game).[330]

Technical planning

The second area of planning is technical planning. This applies to referees at all levels, even though elite referees have much more experience in this area. Technical planning refers to preparing communication systems (see allocation of a match and referee crew), ensuring all equipment is in place, and designing a warm-up.[331]

Good referees implement good technical planning. We have already seen how Michael Oliver establishes communication systems with his assistants pre-match (and why) in chapter thirteen, and Howard Webb reinforces the importance of checking equipment as part of his preparation for a match (an area that will be covered in more detail in the next chapter).[332] But there is more to technical planning than communicating with assistants.

Technical planning extends to going over a checklist of protocols for game situations. For instance, where to stand at free-kicks[lxiv] or how to control emotions if the crowd become aggressive. Another part of this checklist is to prepare for 'what if' situations. A superb example comes from an article written about the events at Stamford Bridge on 20th October, 2018.

After Chelsea scored a late equaliser against Manchester United, United, manager Jose Mourinho was taunted by a Chelsea coach resulting in a potentially violent situation near the tunnel. Although the situation looked out of control, the officials knew exactly what to do because of technical planning. The article states:

> *"It [the planning] would have started around 75 minutes before kick-off when Mike Dean [the referee] sat down with the match delegate, the police and the head of security to discuss all manner scenarios. One of*

---

lxiv Referees are often advised to be in a position where they can see the wall to observe any potential handball, for example.

those would have been what to do if it all kicked off in spectacular style between the two benches." [333]

This shows the importance of planning and how, as Sun-Tzu states in *The Art of War*, [334] 'every big problem begins as a little problem.' By anticipating events and how they would deal with them, referees are better placed to take appropriate action.

Tactical planning

A referee needs to consider the playing styles of a team. For example, if a team always plays the ball short at goal-kicks then a referee must position themselves closer to the penalty box than they would should the team always kick the ball long. Although it is suggested that a team's aggressiveness should be considered,[335] this may lead to adverse effects on performance (see chapters five, six and seven). Therefore this is better prepared for by sufficient mental planning.

Mental planning

This final aspect relates to the referee using planning to create a helpful pre-performance state in order to avoid unhelpful states (such as a lack of concentration).[336]

It is hoped that the earlier suggestion of practicing REBT would help in areas such as stress control and emotional regulation, particularly as rational-thinking has been shown to help referees cope with the demands of their role (see chapter sixteen).

Additionally, referees should discuss with others how they approach certain games and individuals. This allows referees to benefit from the experience of others (which, if we recall, is an important foundation of self-efficacy) and also builds a catalogue of strategies to help deal with potentially damaging situations. For example, former FIFA referee Keith Hackett revealed that he always smiled when he met the players before the game to try to establish trust. Additionally, he possessed a large number of pre-planned phrases to help him deal with situations, such as:

- "I am looking for an improvement, please."
- "Don't shout; I can hear you."

- "You two need to sort yourselves out or I will have to intervene officially."

Planning such responses helps an official respond quickly and efficiently, and enables them to switch attentional focus appropriately, while maintaining a consistent approach.

Preparation Tip 6: Get to know your body. What can you do physically to perform to your best? (e.g., how much sleep do you need and how much fluid should you drink before a match?)

Preparation Tip 7: Create a checklist of situations (both on and off the field) that you may need to deal with. What is the best way to react to them, and who might you need to discuss this with beforehand?

Preparation Tip 8: Consider tactical approaches to a game. At elite levels, referees can research teams easily. At lower levels, a referee must observe the tactics of a team and adjust their approach accordingly.

Preparation Tip 9: Consider what you can do to develop psychological skills such as concentration (see the next section for guidance). Additionally, pre-plan actions, for a number of scenarios, using the help of other referees.

Mental Simulation and Preparation

An individual may train or practice well but still perform poorly if they are not psychologically prepared for an activity. Simply put, how someone feels before a game has an impact on refereeing performance.[337]

This is endorsed by what actual referees think about the importance of the pre-performance routine (PPR). For example, Howard Webb stated that before a match, "you get your kit out... check everything... You want all your mental energy and focus to be on the game."[338] The view that mental preparation is important is not exclusive to elite referees, though. One level 6 referee explained:

> "For me, being ready is like being in a trance. It's you and that inner voice inside you. It kind of blurs out everything else – the players, the sidelines, so when you focus on one thing it's just you and the voice telling you what to do, and nothing else can influence you. The times I've reached this during games have been some of my best games as a ref. But if you get this wrong, it can badly affect performance. [Like] not taking challenges into context and not recognising the game as not just incident after incident but more of a flow."

So how does a referee achieve this 'flow'? One way is to implement a PPR.

What is a pre-performance routine and what are the benefits?

Many people who have taken part in sport have practiced a PPR. Provided that you repeat the same actions before each competition – such as listening to the same music or doing the same warm-up – then you have exercised a routine to help prepare you for a contest.

A PPR is "a sequence of task-relevant thoughts and actions which an athlete engages in systematically prior to his or her performance of a specific sports skill."[339]

Let's break this definition down.

First, a PPR must be *task relevant*. Many may believe going for a jog is an effective warm-up in football, for example, but it is not relevant. After all, footballers (and referees) tend to 'stop-and-go' as opposed to move at one speed consistently. Second, a PPR combines both *thoughts* and *actions*. It is not enough to simply perform a physical action; an individual's preparation must also involve thinking about performance. Finally, it must be *systematic*. Whatever is done, it must be done regularly.

If all of the above criteria are met, a referee may see a substantial improvement in performance. PPR's have been suggested to have the following benefits:

- Decrease the effect of distractions[340]
- Increased ability to focus attention[341]
- Improve concentration[342]
- Increase consistency in performance[343]

As if these benefits weren't enough, PPR also benefits self-efficacy[344] (see chapter ten) and prevents individuals from 'over-thinking' their skills, thus reducing the likelihood of acting 'automatically'. (If we recall, this was a contributing factor to why referees punish teams with an aggressive reputation more – see chapter five).[345]

It is clear, then, why a referee should incorporate a PPR. So how is it done?

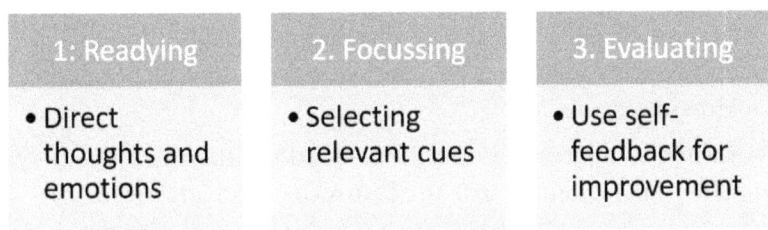

1: Readying	2. Focussing	3. Evaluating
• Direct thoughts and emotions	• Selecting relevant cues	• Use self-feedback for improvement

Figure 18.3: Suggested phases for PPR (adapted from Lidor & Mayan, 2005).[346]

Phase one: Readying

There are two key aims here. The first is to feel comfortable and generate positive thoughts about performance. This can be done by readying kit and talking to colleagues in order to relax. A discussion of previous, positive performances is also encouraged to develop confidence. As some officials state that certain venues have distinguishing characteristics that can challenge positive performance[347] (e.g., a low stand that allows sunlight to obscure vision), discussing this with colleagues may help develop an awareness which is encouraged.[348] For grassroots referees, who may be alone when they officiate, visualising best performance pre-warm up is good practice. Although imagery does not necessarily improve decision-making, it can help promote competition-related thoughts and emotions which is an important characteristic of this phase.[349]

The second aim of this phase is to develop an awareness of relevant body parts. Simply put, to have an effective and relevant warm-up. During the 2002 FIFA World Cup, for instance, offside errors were highest during the first fifteen minutes of the match because assistant referees needed time to adjust to the movement, depth and speed of the players.[350]

Phase two: Focussing

In this stage, it is important for a referee to select relevant cues to aid performance. This means minimising the effect of irrelevant cues such as how the official is feeling, or a team's reputation. Realistically, this stage should be completed in the dressing room after a physical warm-up. Referees should watch video clips of fouls to hone in on relevant cues. Because of its practical nature, clips can be watched using a mobile phone in the dressing room.

As shown in figures 17.2 and 17.3, video training is a valued practice. This endorsement is reinforced by research. For example, one contemporary study[351] with less-experienced referees revealed a significant improvement in decision making post-training. The use of video analysis is recommended for officials at all levels, not just the Select Group 1 who currently receive this type of training courtesy of the PGMOL.[352]

The major criticism of the use of video training is that it is artificial (e.g., it does not accurately represent the experience of refereeing). However, this may not be that important. *All* practice is conditioned, including that of the players themselves. For instance, consider the claim that there is no point practising penalties as it is impossible to replicate the environment and pressure of the real thing. If this is the case, then why practice anything?!? No-one would suggest that a footballer who develops their skills on a training field (instead of in front of 60,000 people) is not helping their game. Therefore the deliberate practice of cognitive-perceptual skills is advised, particularly when applied to specific roles such as refereeing.

It is important to note that it is not suggested that video training should stop once an official attains a certain level, despite inexperienced referees experiencing greater benefits. Even at the highest level, there is a difference in cognitive skills amongst football officials. For example, it has been demonstrated that internationally (FIFA) accredited assistant referees assess offside decisions correctly more often than national (country FA) accredited assistant referees (76.4% v 67.5%).[353]

Phase three: Evaluating

After the game, the referee should assess their routine and establish whether it helped achieve the aims of the three phases. Each routine is individual and so the officials have some responsibility to reflect and monitor the effectiveness of what they are doing before a game. That said, it is important to note that a PPR may take months to establish.[354] Referees should be patient in this process.

Preparation Tip 10: All referees (especially younger or less experienced ones) should use video training as a method of practice.

Preparation Tip 11: When doing physical training, referees should try to simulate real-life situations as much as possible.

Preparation Tip 12: Referees should establish their own PPR using the following phases: readying, focussing, evaluating.

Performance

During the game, the referee will be exposed to the influences (e.g., crowd noise) that were established in part one of the book. It is hoped that sufficient practice and adherence to the preparation framework in figure 18.1 will help insulate the referee as much as possible from these influences. However, there are two practical interventions that can help to maximise best performance.

The first is positive self-talk.[355] Simply put, this is the practice of talking to one's self (internally or out loud) to reinforce positive behaviour or interrupt negative thoughts. Self-talk can help an individual with attentional control,[356] changing mood[357] and controlling effort.[358] Successful referees have been known to use this method. For example, Keith Hackett has said:

> *"I used to talk to myself mentally, giving myself encouragement when the game was tough. I would often say, "Come on, focus. GO…keep up with play."*

Figure 18.4 shows some suggested self-talk when negative events or thoughts may occur.

Negative event or thought	Positive self-talk suggestion
The crowd hate me	Their feelings are irrelevant to my performance
I'm behind the play	GO! Keep up with them
This is getting heated	Stay calm. Control what you can.
I don't want to fail	As long as I give my best, I cannot fail
I'm nervous	That's OK. It's only because I want to do well. I've done this before
I think I've made a mistake	I can't change it. Forget about it and focus on the next decision

Figure 18.4: Suggested positive self-talk comments for dealing with negative events or thoughts

The second intervention is to have a genuine break at half-time. Short-breaks restore the ability to control emotions,[359] which has a significant impact on performance (see chapter twelve). Referees should therefore avoid unnecessary discussion of the game, which may also lead to a decrease of sequential effects (see chapter eleven).

> Performance Tip 13: Practise positive self-talk throughout the game.
>
> Performance Tip 14: Have a genuine break. Avoid unnecessary discussion about the game at half-time.

Post-Match Analysis and Assessment

A referee should focus their assessment not on the outcome but on their performance. They should analyse their decision-making processes, game-management, and refereeing style.[360] Referees should also evaluate their PPR.

The purpose of this process is to increase self-awareness which can lead to greater resilience in the face of criticism from the media and other external sources.[361] If possible, this should be done with colleagues (social support has been shown to be a key coping strategy for many referees (see chapter sixteen)).

> Post-Performance Tip 15: Avoid focussing on the outcome of the game; focus on your performance (e.g., your decision-making and style).
>
> Post-Performance Tip 16: Acknowledge areas you can develop and accept that failures are positive if you learn from them. Discuss these with colleagues where possible.

This chapter has established many ways that a referee can improve their performance, from planning to PPRs to analysis. By implementing these tips, an official can help negotiate the psychological hurdles that impede performance.

However, the responsibility for performance does not lie purely with the individual. After all, a football club would not expect its players to know the best way to train, prepare, or rest. Similarly, we cannot expect a referee to do it all. The next chapter will reveal how we all can make little differences to help a referee. We all want referees to do a fantastic job, so what can we do to help them help us?

19: Help Them Help Us: What Can We Do to Assist Referees?

It would be easy to focus on the abuse of referees and the claims that football's governing bodies, at all levels, do not do enough to prevent it. 2018, for instance, saw the 'worst assault on a match official on British soil'[362] and Martin Cassidy, the chief executive of Ref Support UK (a charity that helps referees cope and deal with abuse) stated:

> *"People of all ages have been phoning us. There's been an increase this season – I don't know why – but there's definitely been a difference.*
>
> *You can't blame the FA when a player headbutts a referee or gives abuse but we do think the time is right to have a **wholesale look at the process**. [emphasis mine]"* [363]

It is only by looking at the entire process surrounding the development and treatment of referees that valid recommendations for progress become possible. These developments are not just about how we treat referees, but are also significant in helping them improve. This is what we *all* want. So let's establish what can be done.

Six Areas to Help Referees

An evaluation of everything covered in this book leads to the identification of six areas that may impact a referee's performance, all of which can be addressed by the game's governing bodies, the media, and the fans. These areas can be seen in figure 19.1.

Figure 19.1: The six areas of change to improve refereeing in football.

Lack of training

A Level 6 referee interviewed for this book was asked whether or not they had ever received any psychological training or education across their career or when attending courses. Their answer was "never." When pushed on this, they said that the concept of confidence, for example, was only "touched upon, but not in depth." This isn't the nondescript answer of an amateur referee that wasn't paying attention. When asked if there is any psychological skills training for grassroots referees, one Referees' Association employee said: "not to my knowledge."

This highlights a worrying lack of education into the important psychological features of refereeing, particularly when (if we cast our mind back to chapter seventeen) the six most important attributes a referee can possess are mental, not physical.[364]

If referees are not given adequate training or guidance in this area then they will become more susceptible to the influences discussed in part one, and more vulnerable to poor performance. So what can be done?

The FA need to introduce and reinforce the importance of psychological skills training into their courses for training referees. Age and experience are established factors that help a referee. For instance, it has been shown how the influence of home advantage is minimised with experience. Regarding age, a Level 3 referee stated that "communication... becomes easier with maturity."[365]

It is not just communication that improves with age, but also other areas such as tolerance. For instance, the FA have difficulty retaining referees between the ages of 20 and 24, with numbers decreasing between 2007 and 2010.[366] As age reduces the susceptibility of anxiety and depression,[367] this could explain the drop-out rate in the 20-24 age group; are they best equipped to tolerate the relentless demands placed upon the officials? The FA need to do more to help younger referees in this area.

As it stands, only Select Group referees are given access to sport psychologists and receive psychological training. This makes little sense. While all referees will benefit from this kind of support, if anyone needs it then it's developing referees. It's giving the board a pay rise when the employees can't afford their commute.

County FAs, who are responsible for administering courses for grassroots referees, should enlist the help of psychologists who can help construct a learning curriculum. Topics should include:

- Psychological preparation
- Pre-performance routines
- Positive self-talk
- Relaxation techniques

In addition to the traditional psychological 'canon' already suggested, REBT should also be incorporated. Negative emotions are part of life and part of refereeing. It would be foolish to avoid them when not only is this impossible but, as shown in chapter sixteen, rationalising events is an effective coping strategy for referees. Additionally, REBT encourages self-acceptance, which contributes to greater resilience to criticism[368] and, let's face it, referees will always receive criticism! These sessions should be offered during preseason in workshops for referees; training programmes that develop mental toughness in referees have reported improvements in performance.[369]

Burton Albion player Marvin Sordell has suggested that clubs should employ full-time counsellors, after his own battle with depression.[370] In light of the fact that officials are under similar pressures and demands (see chapter fourteen), county FAs could do a lot worse than to employ psychologists to assist in the training and counselling of referees.

In addition to employing psychologists, governing bodies and refereeing associations should also employ and encourage the use of mentors to a greater extent. Former FIFA referee Sonia Denoncourt says:

> "[mentoring is] Very important. Within two years, around 80% of referees have quit from the time they started. Why? A lack of mentorship and support… A mentorship programme at the beginning of an official's career gives them the tools to become more competent and reach two years which drastically improves their chances of officiating long-term."[371]

Finally, the FA need to distribute video training exercises to its members. In the technological age, this would be a cheap, efficient, and practical tool to improving refereeing performance. This application would also tackle the problem that referees, at a lower level, do not receive adequate time to practise and that the match itself is the only opportunity to practise.[372] Therefore video training can help satisfy this element whilst improving the culture of practice in officiating.

Action Point 1 – Embed psychological skills training, employ counsellors, recruit more mentors, and promote the use of video training for all developing referees

To neglect the training and supervision of grassroots referees is short-sighted. The greater the pool of talent, the more we can draw from the well, which contributes to the next area of development that is focussed on officiating at the highest level.

Lack of numbers

At the time of writing, there are 17 Select Group referees and 28 assistant referees. Is this enough to help protect officials from the variety of psychological influences that can harm performance, such as the halo effect or player reputation? Frankly, no.

Every weekend there are ten Premier League fixtures.[lxv] Bearing in mind that each fixture requires two referees (one to officiate the game and one to act as the fourth official and potential replacement referee) then that means that some referees *must* be at two games per weekend. When we also consider that most Premier League clubs play cup games midweek (or the occasional league fixture) that need elite officials, and that five of the current Select Group are UEFA referees who may be required to oversee Champions League or Europa League games from Tuesday to Thursday, it is clear to see that referees have a busy schedule. Especially when we see that an elite referee must stay with their assistants near the game location the evening before the match. But what implications does this have?

The first is related to the mental health of the referee. As discussed previously, lack of time due to travelling, training, and administration is a severe concern for referees that impacts job satisfaction. Having more referees means each individual will not be needed as often, giving them more time to switch-off and enjoy other pursuits. Enjoying activities that are not specific to your sport has been shown to aid the development of decision-

---

[lxv] I appreciate that occasional cup games and television schedules mean that this isn't always true due to rescheduled matches, but let's not argue semantics.

making,[373] and anecdotal evidence supports this conclusion. Keith Hackett enjoyed walking and playing golf, for instance.

Allowing officials to have more time away from the game will also help decrease obsessive passion which has a negative impact on performance (see chapter nine).

The second implication is performance-related. Referees are highly likely to come across the same players often because of their low numbers, resulting in them being more likely to be influenced by individual or team reputations, the halo effect, and possible sequential effects. It also puts extra pressure on a referee, (as if they need more), because fans or players may think an official 'doesn't like them' or favours another team. For instance, Howard Webb was repeatedly mocked by fans for being a 'Manchester United' fan. Although it is doubtful that such accusations significantly impact a referee (if at all), they certainly don't help things and just invite unwanted controversy.

A possible solution is for nations to 'share' officials. Could Germany and England 'swap' officials every other weekend, for instance? However, this is not without its own problems. Let's refer back to an example used in chapter seven: the criticism of the American referee Mark Geiger for tolerating dissent from Columbia's players following the decision to award a penalty kick to England in the 2018 FIFA World Cup. If we recall, it was claimed that Geiger did the right thing by understanding that – culturally – South American countries do not perceive dissent to be as serious as in Northern European countries. Hence sending a player off would have made matters worse. Therefore, would refereeing talent 'translate' well? In other words, would English fans be happy with a game being refereed with Italian, Spanish, or Portuguese expectations?

One solution might be to standardise the behaviour and training of referees. However, leading researcher in referees and officials Dr Tom Webb contests this on the grounds that it is over-simplistic, and his research suggests that accepting cultural differences, opposed to fighting them, actually leads to improved performance over time. Of course, that is not to say that officials should ignore flagrant law-breaking (some Columbian players were seen 'scuffing up' the penalty spot in an attempt to sabotage Harry Kane's chance of success – their efforts were in vain), but instead officials and fans should "try to find the right balance" between cultural tolerance and law-enforcement.

Action Point 2 – Examine methods to promote and train more Select Group referees, and trial UEFA-qualified referees in other nations to create a wider pool of officials to select from.

Law changes

On October 26th, 2018, *The Times* printed an article about the FA potentially banning substitutions in injury time in an attempt to stop coaches wasting time.[374] At first glance, the logic seems clear as this is what normally happens in such a scenario:

A coach makes a substitution when their team is winning.

The player being replaced is apparently so tired they cannot move faster than a slow walk (they normally have to do up their laces, remove their shin-pads or pull their socks up in the process).

This angers the opposition players (who would probably do the same thing) and the fans of the losing side.

The referee gets shouted at for not making the offender move faster.

The referee either doesn't add on sufficient time, resulting in criticism from the losing team and their fans, or allows so much time that a goal is scored resulting in criticism from the side who were winning.

The referee is now discussed and/or criticised regardless of their action.

So, it is understandable why change is on the agenda. However, it is a classic example of the tail wagging the dog. If the problem is that time is being wasted, then remove the responsibility of timekeeping from the official. Referees already have an incredible number of demands placed upon them; timekeeping is a simple one to remove. The fourth official (or independent timekeeper) can be responsible for the playing time and can stop the clock when a substitution is made. If fans are aware of this then it makes no difference how often the replaced player has to pull up their socks on their way to the touchline and the playing time is one less thing that an official can be criticised for.

Law changes have already been made to help officials. In fact, on March 2nd, 2019, a law was implemented to help officials in the scenario referenced above. From the 2019/20 season, substitutes will be required to leave from the nearest touchline, rather than making their way to the technical area. A step in the right direction to helping referees.

Another upcoming change is that 'sin-bins' (e.g., temporary dismissals from the field of play for a set time limit) will be mandatory in all adult county leagues.[375] This is to minimise verbal abuse towards referees as an official may not wish to send-off a player for dissent, deeming the punishment too harsh or fearing the consequences of such an action. This seems a positive step, but what others could be implemented?

A law that is under constant scrutiny is the handball law. One former Level 3 referee interviewed stated that the handball law "helps no one." For those that need reminding, the laws of the game – at the time of writing – state that a handball must be deliberate and therefore, in the words of this referee, the law asks officials to be "mind-readers." Perhaps changing the law so that any time the ball strikes the arm or hand, a free-kick or penalty is given would help the referee?

An interesting example comes from Manchester United's epic comeback against Paris St-Germain in the 2018/19 Champions League first knockout round. With United needing a goal to avoid elimination, Slovenian referee Damir Skomina awarded a stoppage-time penalty to the British side after VAR (video assistant referees) showed PSG defender Presnel Kimpembe's arm deflect an attempt on goal. Was it a penalty? The subsequent discussion and conflicting views by ex-referees demonstrated two things.[376]

First, we're back to the subjective nature of many decisions. Second, the exact wording of the law promotes confusion. Think about it, how many 'deliberate' handballs have you seen in your lifetime? Diego Maradona and Luis Suarez both have clear examples from FIFA World Cup fixtures and Thierry Henry deliberately handled to prevent the Republic of Ireland from qualifying for the tournament. Beyond that, it becomes difficult.

Yet, handballs are given frequently. It is for this reason that the law has changed, stating that if the arms extend beyond the body's "natural silhouette" then a handball will be given, regardless of intent. Does this change help officials? Possibly not. What is 'natural' and what is 'not'?

Kimpembe was jumping at the time of the contact and so his arms were outstretched further than if he was standing still, but still in a rather 'natural' position. We can safely assume that this law change – while a step in the right direction – will not eliminate controversy. Perhaps the outcome should be reviewed, rather than the cause. For instance, if the ball strikes the hand, but a player has not been deemed to deliberately move their arm towards the ball, an indirect free-kick could be awarded (even if inside the penalty box). This may remove some of the difficulty – and subsequent controversy – for the officials.

In the future, perhaps the law regarding penalty kicks may be reviewed, too. As discussed in part one, penalty kick decisions are vulnerable to sequential effects due to their importance. Put simply, a game can turn on the awarding (or refusal) of a penalty kick. The likelihood of scoring a penalty (77%) is much greater than scoring a goal from open play (12%)[377] and, importantly, they are becoming more common.

By March 18th, 2019, there were more penalties awarded in the Premier League than the 2017/18 season in its entirety.[378] Essentially, penalties are becoming a frequent and likely method of winning games. This puts added pressure on referees, who are often accused of 'costing' teams games with their decisions to award spot kicks. But are all fouls in the box equal? If a player has their back to goal, for instance, or if a shot that is not on target is stopped by an opponent's hand, should a penalty be awarded? This is not to say that they should or shouldn't, but to illustrate that fans need to be aware that, should the laws remain the same in this area, then the referee has not won or lost them the game. We all need to accept that, sometimes, football can just be cruel.

A final law change being suggested by many is to allow referees to wear body-cams. This would not only help protect lower level referees from abuse or violence by deterring potential offenders but, at elite level, it would aid in the understanding of the demands a referee must meet in a game.

Action Point 3 – Review the laws of the game in light of assisting referees; determine and review which laws referees find particularly difficult or stressful to implement.

Lack of understanding

It is amazing to consider that, in a world of documentaries covering the changing rooms and inner-sanctums of the world's richest clubs, there seems to be a genuine lack of understanding into the role and duties of a referee. Of course, it is hoped that books such as this will help such understanding but much more can be done. Why not make – and market more effectively – more documentaries such as *Ref: Stories from the Weekend* [379] and *Match 64: The Inside Story of the 2010 Final* [380], that provide tremendous insight into how officials do their jobs?

For instance, if the briefing featured in *'Match 64'* between referee Howard Webb and FIFA officials regarding empathy for potentially nervous players before the 2010 FIFA World Cup Final was transparent, perhaps Webb could have been spared a stadium booing him as he collected his medal for officiating the match? Additionally, the discussion and release of a video showing Michael Oliver communicating to players and his assistant during the 2018 FA Cup Final led to a genuine appreciation of the challenges facing a referee by fans.[381] More of this is required!

Action Point 4 – The FA should release more information about the matchday experience of a referee. Transparency leads to understanding and appreciation.

Challenging convention

An increase in transparency will also influence this next area of change; an area that we are all responsible for. Let's look at some issues in other sports before we talk about convention.

It is often assumed that rugby players are a bastion of virtue and therefore do not argue with the referee because they understand it is immoral. This is wrong. Sports people demonstrate immoral behaviour regardless of the sport they are playing. Rugby, for example, has a higher number of anti-doping rule violations than athletics despite athletes being tested more[382] and former director of rugby at Harlequins, Dean Richards,[lxvi] told previous head of discipline at the Rugby Football Union Jeff Blackett in 2009:

> *"The use of fake blood, cutting players, re-opening wounds, feigning injury in the front row, jabbing players with anaesthetic all occur regularly throughout the game."*[383]

In cricket, Steve Smith, the former Australian captain, received a 12-month ban for ball-tampering and NFL quarter-back Tom Brady was suspended for four games after 'Deflategate' – a scandal involving releasing pressure from American footballs in order to make them easier to grip.

What's the point of all this? It is to illustrate that all sports are susceptible to immoral actions. In short, sometimes sportspeople cheat. But it is *how* they cheat that is important. It is a question of morality versus convention; are they cheating because they are bad people or are they cheating because it is *expected* or *accepted?*[lxvii] When footballers cheat, they don't do it by tampering with the match ball or by taking performance-enhancing substances (although that has happened on occasion), they do it by trying to influence the referee with appeals, arguments and foul or injury simulations.

---

lxvi Richards was found guilty of being the man behind the 'bloodgate' scandal of 2009 – where Harlequins' Tom Williams used a fake 'blood-capsule' in order for his team to be able to use a replacement player – and was banned for three years.

lxvii Our previously discussed example of the behaviour of cricket players v baseball players is a good illustration of this concept.

Some FA's have tried to change this convention. For example, in 2018, the Jersey FA released a plan to assist referees. The points in this plan included:

- Referees have been asked to be firmer with players but mindful of respecting them
- Stricter application of the laws, particularly around dissent, meaning sin-bins will be used more frequently
- A lower tolerance on foul and abusive language
- Managers, coaches, and club officials will be reminded of their responsibility to manage the behavior of players, spectators, and technical areas
- Referees will speak to managers before games to ensure their individual style of refereeing is understood and communicated to players
- Managers and coaches will be asked to attend Respect education training. This could be expanded to include persistent offending players
- Clubs will be asked to punish or exclude serious offenders and trouble-makers
- Action will be taken against participants who use social media to abuse referees, clubs, the league, and the JFA
- Schools and youth football to take a tougher line on abusive parents and spectators

These points are all designed at challenging the convention in football that it is acceptable to abuse the referee.

An interesting point in this plan is the penultimate one, which threatens action against individuals who use social media to abuse referees. On October 21st, 2018, the official Twitter account of Portsmouth FC Women posted a video of their coach reflecting on a defeat. The coach states:

> "You've got to control the controllables, again the officiating is appalling at this standard. I'll happily say it wasn't the main benefactor [sic] for the result…but I think if people are going to start to take the women's game seriously and taking this level seriously the officiating needs to be of a good enough standard and the FA and local counties have got to see

that. Today you've got a referee who's blatantly refereed this team [the opposition] before and home bias and it's appalling." [384]

We've established that referees are influenced by the crowd and location (although normally with large attendances in sold-out stadiums) but to suggest that the referee is deliberately biased is tantamount to calling them a cheat. Until clubs realise this and stop this behaviour, the convention of challenging, harassing, and criticising the referee will continue to be accepted by players, coaches, and fans.

There is also a responsibility of the mainstream media to help change this convention. This isn't a new problem. Founding Father of the United States of America, Alexander Hamilton, said:

> *"It is the press which has corrupted our public morals – and it is to the press we must look for the means of our... regeneration."*

Does the press corrupt our morals regarding referees? Absolutely, and this isn't a new problem for football. In 1979, Brian Clough told John Motson that media treatment of referees – most notably the BBC programme 'Match of the Day' – is "nothing short of criminal" (e.g., that they give referees far too hard a time).[lxviii] More modern examples of the media giving referees a tough ride are readily available. Swiss referee Urs Meier reportedly went 'into hiding with police protection' following criticism from an English tabloid after England's Euro 2004 defeat to Portugal. Meier said:

> *"I'm absolutely shocked by the media campaign against me... I always thought the spirit of fair play was important in England, with respect for officials. But the English newspapers... have caused a big problem. I have security problems and this is not the right way to handle referee's decisions, whether they are right or wrong."* [385]

---

lxviii Like anything involving Clough, it's captivating viewing and can be seen at https://www.youtube.com/watch?v=Kd8wKQo2M6U.

This treatment goes also goes beyond tabloids. In December, 2018, *The Times* featured an article that claimed referee Lee Mason 'joined in the celebrations' after the official held his arms up to signal an advantage to Liverpool's Mo Salah during his second goal against Bournemouth.[386] Of course, it is possible the article was written tongue-in-cheek, but this is not the point: it calls into question the integrity of the referee who actually made an excellent decision at the time.[lxix]

The problem extends further than the written press. On the 5th of January, 2019, former player and TV pundit Robbie Savage criticised the decision of a referee not to order a retake of a penalty taken by Chelsea's Cesc Fabregas due to his 'stuttering' run-up. Savage proceeded to read out the Laws of the Game in an attempt to justify his view. However, ex-Premier League official Peter Walton correctly pointed out that the law Savage referred to was outdated – it was written in 2014 – and had since been changed. It is clear that those – such as Savage – in such public positions in the media must be clear regarding the laws of the game. Their opinions influence the attitudes of many watching viewers.

In a world of data and instant information, it would be hoped that the truth always comes out. Unfortunately, online sources are not much better. On January 29th, BBC 5 Live Sport tweeted:

Should #MCFC [Manchester City] be 2-0 up? Aguero's strike ruled out as De Bruyne took the free-kick too quickly. The Belgian [De Bruyne] gets a yellow for his troubles...

@5liveSport

This tweet is followed by a quote from pundit and ex-England international Danny Mills, who said:

[lxix] For the record, Mason did appear to hold his arms up for a prolonged amount of time to signal the advantage; however, it seemed to me, at least, that he just wanted to illustrate that it was his excellent decision to let play go on that led to a goal.

"What is the referee doing? It is unbelievably quick thinking by De Bruyne… it's not a bookable offence."

The problem here is that, well, it is! If a referee informs the player to wait until the whistle is blown before taking a free-kick and the player ignores this instruction then a referee should caution them.[lxx] Of course, it is possible that De Bruyne was not told to wait. Only the referee and the player know that. But the point is that Mills does not know either.

Even clearer examples of the law not being fully understood by those in the media are made every day. For instance, during the Women's FIFA World Cup match between France and Nigeria in June, 2019, France were given the opportunity to retake a penalty after an intervention from VAR (video assistant referee). The Nigerian goalkeeper was deemed to have moved off her line before the kick was taken, with the Laws of the Game stating at least one foot has to be in contact with the goal line when the ball is struck. The issue here is how the incident was presented in the media. For example, in response to the decision and that a number of French players were in the penalty box when the kick was taken, former USA international and BBC pundit Hope Solo tweeted:

We need eyes on everyone in these scenarios,
not just the goalkeepers!
@hopesolo, 18th June, 2019

This prompted many responses from the public, mainly inferring that this incident highlights the inconsistency of referees in enforcing one law but not the other. But, here's the rub: the law states that encroaching in the penalty box is only punished if a player gains an advantage from it (e.g., scoring a rebound from a missed kick). Here is what the law actually says regarding VAR and penalties:

[lxx] For those that are interested, Lee Markwick of the Referees' Association says that this action would come under FA Caution Code C1 – 'Unsporting Behaviour'.

LAW 2: Penalty Kick Decisions

The role of the VARs is to ensure that no clearly wrong decisions are taken in conjunction with awarding or not awarding a penalty kick. This includes:

g) encroachment by an attacker or defender who becomes directly involved in play if the penalty kick rebounds from the goalpost, crossbar or goalkeeper.

It's there in plain black and white. There was no controversy, error or inconsistency. But, in the eyes of the public, this was not the case and their fire was fuelled by those in the media. BBC Sport, in their report of the game for instance, ran the headline: "VAR continued to cause controversy at the #FFAWWC when France were allowed to retake a missed penalty." Of course, not all in the media are quite as quick to jump on the anti-referee bandwagon. Sky Sports football commentator Gary Taphouse replied to the BBC regarding their headline:

The correct headline should be something like: 'Players bizarrely ignorant of recent law change – VAR helps ref get decision spot on.'
@garytaphouse, 18th June, 2019

His view is refreshing but alarmingly rare.

To be blunt, the media must be more responsible and make sure they have all relevant information before passing judgement and essentially labelling an official incompetent. The media also need to be aware of how they evaluate referees. They can draw attention to, and reinforce, a culture and acceptance of referee abuse. Referees understand that they make mistakes and accept criticism, but criticism often crosses the line and questions the official's competence and/or integrity. Whether this happens or not depends on whether those in the media care more about their 'angle' or about presenting the facts.

The silver lining, however, is that the FA and other governing bodies could always use the media to defend their referees. To show where a governing body could have stepped in, for instance, Australian referee Ben Williams believed that, despite making the 'right call' in sending off a player in Australia's top flight A-League for violent conduct, the media outcry was so great he was removed from the Melbourne derby the following weekend. In his own words, "no one backed me up."[387] The media is clearly a powerful tool in damaging a referee's reputation and health, why not use it as a vehicle for the opposite?

Action Point 5 – Challenge the convention of abusing the referee. Clubs must set an example and the FA should punish those that do not. The media must accept their responsibility and improve their understanding of the role. The FA must be more vocal in the media, defending their referees.

Of course, it will take time to change this convention and, even if successful, there will be occasions when referees are abused verbally or physically. So, the final part of this chapter looks at what can change when this occurs.

Support

Clearly, referees don't think enough is done when abuse rears its ugly head. 60% of referees report an experience of abuse every couple of games, and 19% say they have experienced physical abuse resulting in the conclusion that "there remains a need to implement stronger sanctions and show greater support when dealing with cases of misconduct."[388] What exactly does this statement reveal?

First, that sanctions are not strict enough. The FA and County FAs must adopt a stronger and more consistent stance regarding referee abuse. The use of sin-bins is a step in the right direction, allowing a referee to remove a player for a set amount of time as opposed to sending them off for what may be a heat-of-the-moment comment. The FA have also introduced a mandatory five-year suspension from football for anyone found guilty of assault. Referees must be supported by their FAs when reporting such incidents. If not, we will see more and more action taken by referees. For instance, in response to one league proposing a 'no ref day' to highlight the importance of officials, author and researcher Dr Tom Webb tweeted:

It will keep happening until abuse towards referees is properly addressed. People forget that the vast majority of referees at most levels of the game are volunteers. As a volunteer, they simply don't need the hassle. The environment has to change for any difference to be made.

@DrTomWebb

How could it be 'properly addressed'? Perhaps the FA could take abuse towards referees as seriously as changing room dimensions? This isn't a joke. Registered charity Ref Support UK revealed that, on October 29th, 2018, the FA sent a letter to all Step 3 and 4 clubs (a classification system in non-league football in England) stating that if their changing rooms did not meet minimum size requirements they would be relegated to Step 5. By way of comparison, if a club and/or its players abuse, threaten, or attack a referee they will be fined, but not relegated.[lxxi]

Secondly, governing bodies need to show greater commitment and enthusiasm in enforcing their policies. In 2018, match day officials in Australia's A-League planned to cover up the 'Respect' logo on their shirts following the refusal of Football Federation Australia (FFA) to sanction Wellington Phoenix coach Mark Rudan for his comments regarding referee Adam Kersey. Rudan, whose side had a player sent-off and conceded late in the game to draw 1-1, stated:

[lxxi] There has been an important update in this area, however. In June, 2019, the FA proposed to the government that officials be given 'public service' status, meaning that those who assault referees would be more likely to expect a prison sentence. See Wilson, J. (2019b). Exclusive: FA wants threat of prison sentences for referee assaults. https://www.telegraph.co.uk/football/2019/06/18/exclusive-fa-wants-threat-prison-sentences-referee-assaults/. Cited on 19/06/19 from the World Wide Web.

"I've never seen anything like it. It got to the point where I had to laugh. I turned around to my coaching staff. It was hilarious, a joke, an absolute joke. If he can sleep well at night, good on him." [389]

Many feel that this quote targets Kersey's competence as a referee and should have been punished if the FFA were serious about encouraging a respectful culture towards officials.

Finally, referees must be given specialist, psychological support. As shown in chapter sixteen, social support is a vital crutch for referees. They need support from their employers and colleagues. A Level 6 referee interviewed for this book said that referees and County FAs need to show more support for each other:

"I suppose it's second nature to judge others but really we are all refs and we should stick together."

This support comes not only in communication but in provision. The FA must educate, train, and appoint individuals to oversee the mental health of referees in their charge. The Referees' Association Welfare, Representation and Partnership lead, Lee Markwick, would like to see the FA's Referee Development Officers evolve into 'Referee Welfare & Development Officers'. Their purpose, to:

"Provide full support, help and guidance to all referees following any physical, mental or verbal abuse. This must also include welfare support to any referee facing an FA misconduct charge. Support, help and guidance means regular contact and advising on any FA Discipline or Police process when a crime has been committed. Everyone must also take into account the other 'victims' affected by the incident (e.g., family members and friends). At this current moment in time, evidence reveals that FA safeguarding and welfare is mainly confined to only U18s."

Things are moving slowly, but moving all the same.

Action Point 6 – The FA must promote a more consistent, rigid, and strict 'Respect' campaign as well as training or appointing individuals to oversee the mental health of their referees.

Conclusion

We started this book by discussing the 2018 FIFA World Cup in Russia and how very few people would know the name of the individual who refereed that game. One aspect of officiating that all football fans would have taken note of, however, was the use of a video assistant referee (VAR).

Whether or not you agree with the use of VAR is as subjective as the referees' interpretations of events that are being reviewed. However, its introduction reveals that football may finally be embracing the concept of 'idea sex': the notion of utilising and combining innovations from other areas. This term was used in an article in *The Times* in 2018 to highlight why football often fails to evolve. As the article made clear:

> *"Coaches in football often say that they are following 'best practice'. But shouldn't best practice be regarded as temporary rather than permanent? The question should be: how can we improve upon best practice?"* [390]

The most successful leaders in the sport, such as Rinus Michels, Johan Cruyff, Brian Clough, Arrigo Sacchi, Sir Alex Ferguson, Arsene Wenger, Jose Mourinho and Pep Guardiola, have been the innovators. Innovators need problems. They need something to fix or improve. Therefore to develop, we must always ask 'how can we do this better?' One way is to draw inspiration from other sports.

England manager, Gareth Southgate, is a great example of someone who does this. When watching a basketball game in the United States of America, for example, Southgate wished to talk to one of the team's owners to find out how players find space in such a small area, demonstrating how Southgate "deliberately gathered information from other sports – tactical, technical but also psychological – and applied them to football."[391] The FA *need* to do this with regards to referees.

Let's briefly return to the ball-tampering scandal in Australian cricket. While many will point the finger at the culprits – Steve Smith, David Warner and Cameron Bancroft – an independent report accused Cricket Australia, the sport's governing body, of creating a culture of "winning without counting the costs".[392] Is the FA equally guilty of not doing enough to understand the demands of the referee's role and not acting strongly enough in the event of abuse? Responsibility for all areas of English football lies at the door of the FA and they must accept their responsibility for referee development and welfare. Simply put, they must learn from other sports and from all disciplines involved in sports science, such as strength and conditioning, nutrition, sociology and psychology. In doing so, they can best understand how to improve the conditions for referees, and subsequent performances.

While no approach trumps another, it is clear that many leading sport scientists see psychological skills and training as a key pathway behind improvement. For instance, former Head of Performance at Manchester United, and current Head of Performance at the Welsh FA, Tony Strudwick has said:

"The next biggest development will be in the area of cognitive research. As the game of football becomes ever faster, we will reach a plateau in terms of physical preparation. The ability of athletes to make quicker decisions – in high-pressure environments – and the development of tools to stimulate areas of the brain that facilitate these processes will take the game on to another level. Therefore, I envisage a number of technological advancements in the areas of vision and cognition." [393]

This book has highlighted ways of doing this through the psychological influences on a referee. These influences exist because referees are human. Mistakes are just that: mistakes. There has never been a proven incident of deliberate bias or outright cheating regarding officials in England, unlike in other European nations.

It is hoped that this book will promote understanding of the influences on a referee and help explain why some things that appear to happen, happen. On one level, it is understandable why some people appear frustrated with referees. A football match can have thousands of events within it. During the 2010 UEFA Champions League Final between Inter Milan and Bayern

Munich, football statistics company Opta recorded 2,842 events (e.g., passes, interceptions, shots).[394] Of these events, two counted at the final whistle: Diego Milito's pair of goals for the Italian side.

Consequently, a lot goes into scoring a goal. So when the decision of an official can directly influence the scoring of one, its importance is often overstated (e.g., 'the referee cost us a goal!'). It is hoped that our improved understanding results in the officials' influence being more readily accepted.

Additionally, greater understanding may also prevent what some believe to be inevitable: strike action from referees and serious injury. On January 31st 2019, referees from grassroots football met with the chief executive of the FA to discuss abuse suffered by officials. This meeting coincided with strike action being called for by Ref Support UK, with their chair Janie Frampton stating:

"My fear is that it's going to take something very serious, or a death, before anyone will take it seriously." [395]

Worryingly, referee abuse seems to be a trend that is crossing both cultural and sporting divides. In the United States, officials are reporting such a high level of abuse in baseball and basketball that there are more referees over 60 than under 30 years of age.[396] Who is going to replace the officials when they retire? Without officials there would be no game, so why is this culture growing?

An American group, the National Association of Sports Officials (NASO), researched this area by surveying over 17,000 sports officials from all sports, across all levels of their respective games.[397] The main cause of poor sportsmanship, they believe, came from parents, with the epidemic getting worse (see figures 20.1 & 20.2).

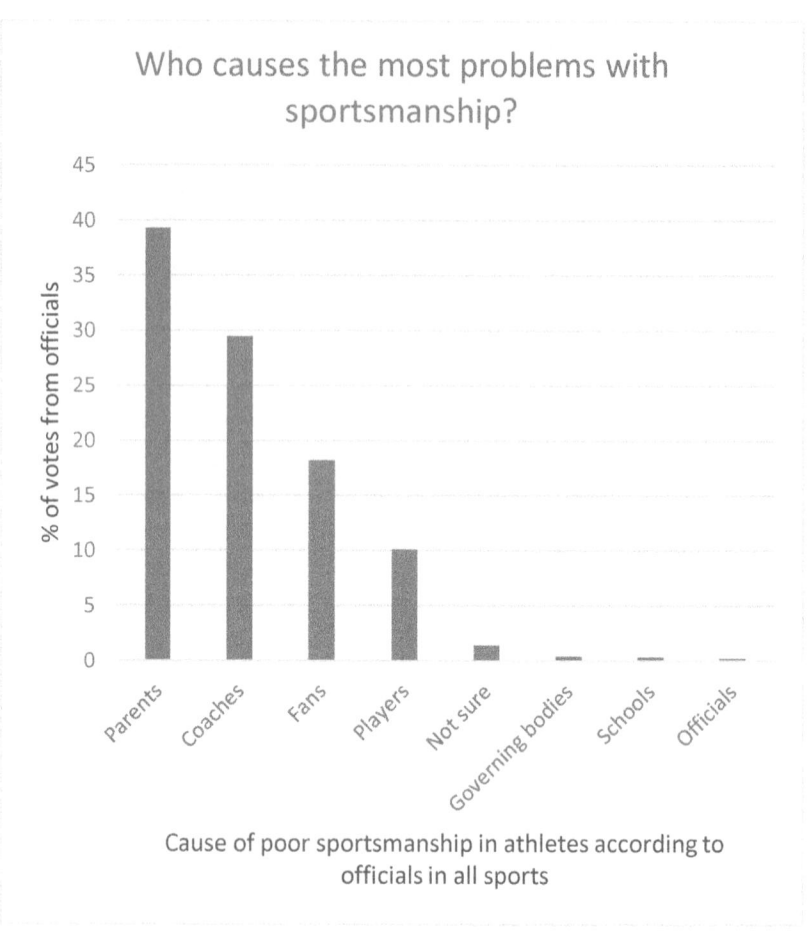

Figure 20.1: Survey of over 17,000 officials, in all sports, on the causes of bad sportsmanship (NASO, 2017).

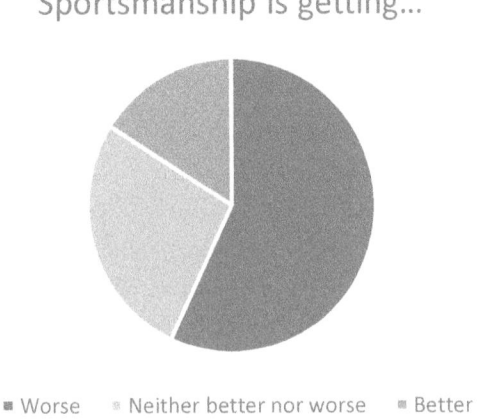

Sportsmanship is getting...

■ Worse ■ Neither better nor worse ■ Better

Figure 20.2: Survey of over 17,000 officials in all sports who were asked if sportsmanship was getting worse, better or staying the same (NASO, 2017).

Could this be a consequence of a growing perception in the importance of sport? A lot boils down to what we think makes a 'good' coach; is a good coach one that is technically gifted and 'gets results' or one that acts in a morally correct way? Aristotle labelled these qualities *techné* (being technically good at something) and *phronesis* (doing things in the right way) and it's important to note that these are not mutually exclusive: a good coach is one that does both. For instance, notable sport psychologist Dr Steve Peters says that not accepting a decision made by the referee once it's been made often doesn't help players.[398] Therefore, coaches should seek to encourage their players to accept decisions more readily and exploit opponents that don't.

A superb example came in the second leg of the Champions League semi-final between Liverpool and Barcelona at Anfield in May, 2019. Liverpool's coaching staff instructed the ballboys to give their players the ball back as quickly as possible to restart the game. This was due to them noticing in the first leg that the Barcelona players – who won the game 3-0 – disputed every decision made by the officials.[399] Could this mean that they were not fully focussed on the game while they voiced their objections? It sure did. Liverpool scored their fourth (and winning) goal after some quick thinking by a ball boy; full-back Trent Alexander-Armstrong exploiting Barcelona players unprepared to defend a corner.

Simply put, teams do better when they are focussed on the game and not on the referee.

Hence, a good coach should encourage players to accept decisions more readily and also appreciate the impact they have in doing this. Figure 20.3, for example, shows how officials believe that coaches are the most responsible individuals for player conduct across all sports.

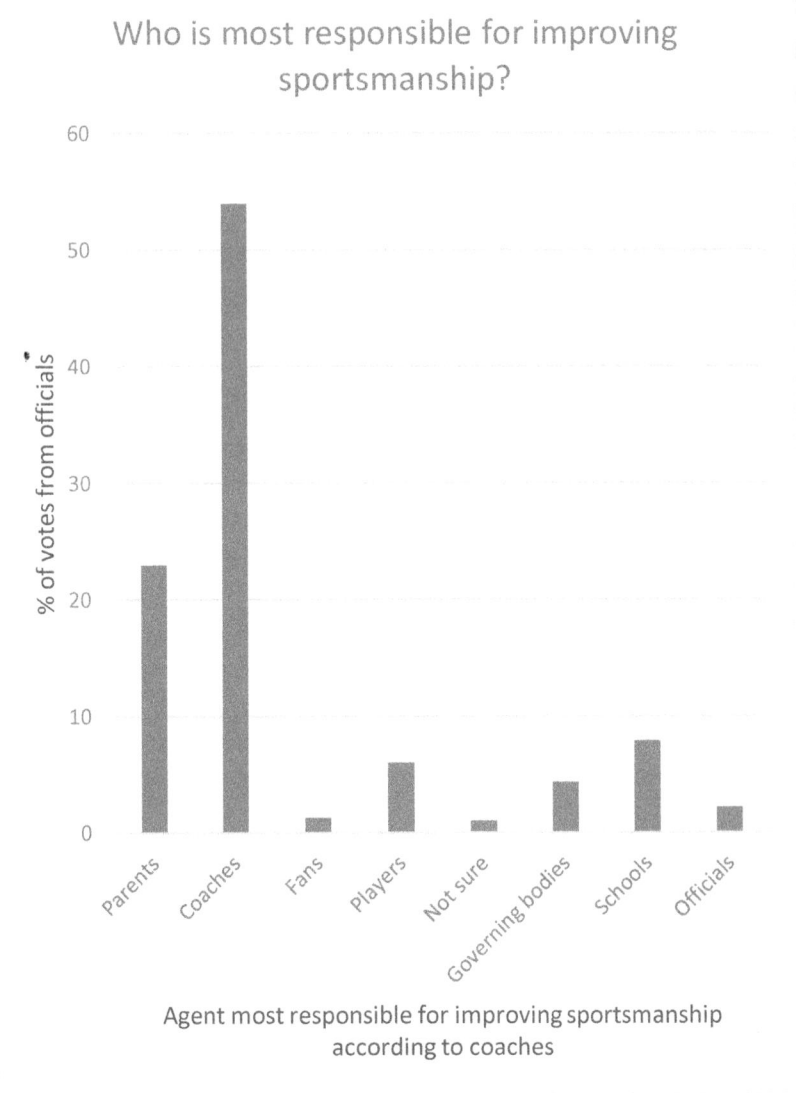

Figure 20.3: Survey of officials in all sports on who is most responsible for improving sportsmanship (NASO, 2017).

It is hoped that an increased understanding of how and why referees make decisions will assist coaches in promoting tolerance when they perceive they have been wronged. At the time of writing, a better example could not have been provided than during the Burnley v Southampton match on February 2nd 2019 in the English Premier League. After Burnley's Ashley Barnes appears to be fouled by Alex McCarthy (the Southampton goalkeeper), referee Anthony Taylor books Barnes for simulation (e.g., diving). The decision seems to have come after advice from Taylor's assistant which so enraged Barnes that he proceeded to barrage the assistant with verbal abuse.[lxxii] For the record, it seemed like a mistake. But this is to miss the point. After the match, Burnley manager Sean Dyche focussed only upon the mistake and not on his player's reaction.

In this book, we've looked at reasons that may explain why the penalty wasn't given, and why the officials did not send Barnes off for verbal abuse (for instance, were they regulating their emotions to show they can 'relate' to a player's passion and frustration?) But why did Dyche ignore the behaviour of his player? Why does the abuse of officials still appear to be 'fair game', even amongst those within the refereeing fraternity? Former referee Chris Foy not only failed to condemn the actions of Barnes, he supported them by stating:

> "Having had the benefit of seeing the incident more than once, however, it was a clear-cut penalty. No wonder Barnes was furious." [400]

Well, that's alright then! Why not focus on the first part, the privilege of seeing the incident more than once? As Brian Clough informed us at the start of the book, it is incredibly difficult to referee a football match. If there is one thing this book has, hopefully, accomplished, it is reinforcing his point.

Another reason for our collective refusal to blame officials (and not the players) is that we focus too much on the result and not enough on the people who entertain us by playing and running

---

[lxxii] You don't have to be a good lip-reader (or have a lively imagination) to understand exactly what Barnes says.

the game. As former Welsh international Lewin Nyatanga says about being a player:

> *"I think in the fans' eyes you become non-human. People see you as a footballer and not a person... People think they [players] just stay in a cardboard box until next Saturday."* [401]

Again, this book has sought to address that, at least with regards to officials. The outcome of such a veracious will to win often results in a contradictory position for fans to occupy. Author Tim Parks describes this paradox best:

> *"Everyone wants their team to win at all costs and everyone earnestly wishes the world to be fair."* [402]

Invariably, it is when our team loses that the will to win often trumps our sense of fairness and understanding. The referee, more often than not, is the chief conspirator: the architect of our players' downfall. For instance, reflecting on why Chelsea did not make the Women's Champions League final, manager Emma Hayes said:

> *"I am going to take a fine for it – I thought the referee was horrendous."* [403]

The referee may (or may not) have made mistakes but the point is why do coaches never attribute success to refereeing decisions? Has a coach ever said that getting to a Final was the result of favourable decisions from the decisions? Of course not. It is not human nature. As has been shown in this book, we seek to protect ourselves from failure by blaming others. We attribute successes to ourselves.

Hayes went on to say that the referee was influenced by their opponents, Lyon ("she was scared of them"). Let's assume that this is true. This book shows that any influence on a referee is not because of bias, but because of human nature. So, what happens if we try to change our nature and the perception that the final score is the only thing that matters?

Interestingly, in the summer of 2018 something other than the FIFA World Cup occurred in the sporting world. UK Sport conducted a public consultation that exposed the importance of mental health in sport.[404] This shift in philosophy – away from medals and towards well-being – should be replicated by the FA at all levels. Importantly, it must be understood that this perspective is not in competition with winning. On the contrary, it can help enable success. Sport should be fun and it should be for all. That is not to say winning at the highest level is not important. It is. But by appreciating the bigger picture and accepting that there is more to sport than what is shown on the scoreboard we will actually see more people participate and, as a result, experience greater creativity in those sports. This innovation is the ally, not nemesis, of winning.

Perhaps fans, deep down, believe football needs controversy. Perhaps they even want it. It thrives off the element of chance and the whim of someone in the middle who may (or may not) have been influenced by a reaction, or piece of exquisite deception. We, as fans, must consider what we want: a perfect game or a perfect storm. Accepting this element of chance – that comes from having an arbiter – will result in greater tolerance and understanding towards officials.

The term 'it's just a game' doesn't seem to apply to football. It's easy to see why. How can it, when it has such universal appeal and the power to unite (and divide) so readily? But in order for us to have it, we need the men and women in the middle. Refereeing is about learning. It is about continual development and the accumulation of experience to deal with events in the best way. Likewise, spectators, players and coaches must reciprocate this approach and learn about referees. They are not perfect, they are human. Let us both treat and understand them as such.

Endnotes

[1] McFee, G. (2013). Officiating in aesthetic sports. *Journal of the Philosophy of Sport, 40,* 1-17.

[2] Brand, G. (2018). Referee myth-busting: How many decisions do officials get right? http://www.skysports.com/football/news/11096/10808860/referee-myth-busting-how-many-decisions-do-officials-get-right. Cited on 16/03/18 from the World Wide Web.

[3] Football Association, The. (2018). Law 5: The Referee. www.thefa.com/football-rules-governance/lawsandrules. Cited on 16/03/18 from the World Wide Web.

[4] MacMahon, C., Helsen, W. F., Starkes, J. L., & Weston, M. (2007). Decision-making skills and deliberate practice in elite association football referees. *Journal of Sports Sciences, 25,* 65-78.

[5] Kelso, P. (2013). West Ham manager Sam Allardyce charged by FA over comments after Manchester United defeat. https://www.telegraph.co.uk/sport/football/teams/west-ham/9812243/West-Ham-manager-Sam-Allardyce-charged-by-FA-over-comments-after-Manchester-United-defeat.html. Cited on 02/09/18 from the World Wide Web.

[6] Jamieson, J. P. (2010). The home field advantage in athletics: A meta-analysis. *Journal of Applied Social Psychology, 40,* 1819-1848.

[7] Pollard, R. (2006). Worldwide regional variations in home advantage in association football. *Journal of Sports Sciences, 24,* 231-240.

[8] Runciman, D. (2008). Home sweet home? *The Guardian,* February 3rd, 2008.

[9] FourFourTwo Australia (2016). How important is the 12th man? January 1st, 2016.

[10] Dohmen, T. J. (2008). The influence of social forces: Evidence from the behaviour of football referees. *Economic Inquiry, 46,* 411-424; Riedl, D., Strauss, B., Heuer, A., & Rubner, O. (2015). Finale furioso: referee-biased injury times and their effects on home advantage in football. *Journal of Sports Sciences, 33,* 327-336; Sutter, M. & Kocher, M. G. (2004). Favouritism of agents – the case of referees' home bias. *Journal of Economic Psychology, 25* (4), 461-469.

[11] Boyko, R. H., Boyko, A. R., & Boyko, M. G. (2007). Referee bias contributes to home advantage in English Premiership football, *Journal of Sports Sciences, 25,* 1185-1194; Buraimo, B., Forrest, D., & Simmons, R. (2010). The 12th Man?: Refereeing bias in English and German soccer. *Journal of the Royal Statistical Society: Series A, 173,* 431-449.

[12] Cited in Pritchard, C. (2012). Fergie time: Does it really exist? www.bbc.co.uk/news/magazine-20464371. Cited on 28/02/18 from the World Wide Web.

[13] Sky Sports (2017a). Remembering Sergio Aguero's Man City title-winning goal, five years on. www.skysports.com/football/news/11679/10871583. Cited on 28/2/18 from the World Wide Web.

[14] Anderson, C., & Sally, D. (2014). *The Numbers Game: Why Everything You Know About Football is Wrong*. London: Penguin (p22).

[15] See Sutter & Kocher, 2004

[16] Riedl et al., 2015

[17] Riedl et al., 2015

[18] Sutter & Kocher, 2004.

[19] Magee, W. (2018). *'Why do you want more time?' Fourth official could not believe Arsene Wenger wanted no end to League Cup suffering*. *The Telegraph*, February 25th, 2018.

[20] Delaney, M. (2018). Unai Emery accuses referee of Real Madrid bias after PSG's last-16 first-leg defeat. *The Independent*, February 14th, 2018.

[21] Boyko et al., 2007 (p.1188)

[22] Winter, J. (2006). *Who's the B*****d in the Black?: Confessions of a Premiership Referee*. London: Ebury Press.

[23] World Football. (2018). Premier League 2016/17 attendance. www.worldfootball.net/attendance/eng-premierleague. Cited on 15/2/18 from the World Wide Web.

[24] Williams, O. (2010). Let's choose the music and dance. www.bbc.co.uk/blogs/olliewilliams/2010/02/ice_dance_music.shtml. Cited on 05/02/18 from the World Wide Web.

[25] BT Sport Films (2017). *Ref: Stories from the weekend*. First aired on April 4th, 2017.

[26] Sky Sports (2018a). Ref Watch: Dermot Gallagher's verdict on Tottenham's penalties. www.skysports.com/football/news/11661. Cited on 16/2/18 from the World Wide Web.

[27] Balmer, N. J., Nevill, A. M., & Lane, A. M. (2005). Do judges enhance home advantage in European championship boxing? *Journal of Sports Sciences, 23*, 409-416.

[28] Balmer, N. J., Nevill, A. M., & Williams, A. M. (2001). Home advantage in the Winter Olympics (1908-1998). *Journal of Sports Sciences, 19*, 129-139.

[29] Unkelbach, C. & Memmert, D. (2010). Crowd noise as a cue in referee decisions contributes to the home advantage. *Journal of Sport & Exercise Psychology, 32*, 483-498.

[30] MacInnes, P. (2016). West Ham feeling far from home after London Stadium teething problems. *The Guardian*, September 11th, 2016.; Steinberg, J. (2016). Nine decades of memories of Upton Park as West Ham prepare to depart. *The Guardian*, May 7th, 2016.

[31] Dohmen, T. J. (2008). The influence of social forces: Evidence from the behaviour of football referees. *Economic Inquiry, 46*, 411-424.

[32] Goumas, C. (2014). Home advantage and referee bias in European football. *European Journal of Sports Science, 14*, 243-249.

[33] Goumas, 2014

[34] Boyko, R. H., Boyko, A. R., & Boyko, M. G. (2007). Referee bias contributes to home advantage in English Premiership football, *Journal of Sports Sciences, 25*, 1185-1194.

[35] Unkelbach and Memmert, 2010

[36] Football Association, The. (2018). Law 5: The Referee. www.thefa.com/football-rules-governance/lawsandrules. Cited on 16/03/18 from the World Wide Web.

[37] Taylor, D. (2012a). Referee Mike Dean demoted after Manchester United v Chelsea errors. *The Guardian*, April 7th, 2010.

[38] Taylor, 2012a

[39] Kaya, A. (2014). Decision making by coaches and athletes in sport. *Social & Behavioural Sciences, 152*, 333-338.

[40] Nevill, A. M., Balmer, N. J., & Williams, A. M. (2002). The influence of crowd noise and experience upon refereeing decisions in football. *Psychology of Sport & Exercise, 3*, 261-272.

[41] Palmer, K. (2018). Exclusive: Former referee accuses Anthony Taylor of 'weakness' after FA Cup chaos at Wigan. www.uk.sports.yahoo.com/news. Cited on 26/03/18 from the World Wide Web.

[42] Asch, S. E. (1955). Opinions and social pressure. *Scientific American, 5*, 31-35 (p35).

[43] See Tamir, M. (2016). Why do people regulate their emotions? A taxonomy of motives in emotion regulation. *Personality & Social Psychology Review, 20*, 199-222.

[44] Boyko, R. H., Boyko, A. R., & Boyko, M. G. (2007). Referee bias contributes to home advantage in English Premiership football, *Journal of Sports Sciences, 25*, 1185-1194.

[45] Mann, D. T. Y., Williams, A. M., Ward, P., & Janelle, C. M. (2007). Perceptual-cognitive expertise in sport: A meta-analysis. *Journal of Sport & Exercise Psychology, 29*, 457-478.

[46] Morris, G., & O'Connor, D. (2017). Key attributes of expert NRL referees. *Journal of Sports Sciences, 35*, 852-857.

[47] Syed, M. (2018a). Why an ancient need to defend territory gives home team a sporting advantage. *The Times*, April 9th, 2018.

[48] Landin, D. (1994). The role of verbal cues in skill learning. *Quest, 46*, 299-313 (p299).

[49] see Abernathy, B. (1993). Attention. In R. N. Singer, M. Murphey, & L. K. Tennant (Eds.), *Handbook of research on sport psychology* (pp.127-170). New York: MacMillan; Abernathy, B. & Russell, D. G. (1987). Expert-novice differences in an applied selective attention task. *Journal of Sport Psychology, 9*, 326-345.

[50] Abernathy, 1993:p127

[51] Nideffer, R. N. (1981). *The ethics and practice of applied sport psychology*. Ithaca, NY: Mouvement; Nideffer, R. N. (1993). Attention control training. In R. N. Singer, M. Murphey, & L. K. Tennant (Eds.), *Handbook of research on sport psychology* (pp.542-556). New York: MacMillan.

[52] Wrisberg, C. A. (1993). Levels of performance skill. In R. N. Singer, M. Murphey, & L. K. Tennant (Eds.), *Handbook of research on sport psychology* (pp.61-72). New York: MacMillan.

[53] Wrisberg, 1993

[54] Loftus, E. F. & Palmer, J. C. (1974). Reconstruction of automobile destruction: An example of the interaction between language and memory. *Journal of verbal learning and verbal behaviour, 13*, 585-589.

[55] Lex, H., Pizzera, A., Kurtes, M., & Schack, T. (2014). Influence of players' vocalisations on soccer referees' decisions. *European Journal of Sport Science, 5,* 424-428.

[56] Chaiken, S. & Trope, Y. (1999). *Dual-process theories in social psychology.* New York, NY: Guilford Press.

[57] Sky Sports (2018b). Bournemouth v Everton live. www.skysports.com/football/bmouth-vs-everton/live/390778. Cited on 25/08/18 from the World Wide Web.

[58] Ready to Go (2010). Owen Coyle – f**king nob. https://www.readytogo.net/smb/threads/owen-coyle-f-ing-nob.550109/. Cited on 14/05/18 from the World Wide Web.

[59] Syed, M. (2018b). Sir Alex Ferguson and José Mourinho helped nurture shameful idea that referees are biased. *The Times,* April 16th, 2018.

[60] Idessane, K. (2018). Scottish referees: 'Abuse culture' needs to stop, says John Mckendrick. https://www.bbc.co.uk/sport/football/46513470. Cited on 12/12/18 from the World Wide Web.

[61] Szczepanik, N. (2009). Ancelotti enjoys warm glow of a Cole-fired performance. *The Times,* October 26th, 2009.

[62] Johansen, B. T. (2015). Reasons for officiating soccer: the role of passion-based motivations among Norwegian elite and non-elite referees. *Movement & Sport Sciences, 87,* 23-30.

[63] Sky Sports (2018c). Pierluigi Collina says World Cup VAR has proved successful. http://www.skysports.com/football/news/12098/11421135/pierluigi-collina-says-world-cup-var-has-proved-successful. Cited on 13/08/18 from the World Wide Web

[64] Davis, M. (2018). Sunday morning referee quits after alleged assault by player. http://www.bbc.co.uk/sport/football/43736236. Cited on 25/04/18 from the World Wide Web; Folkesson, P., Nyberg, C., Archer, T., & Norlander, T. (2002). Soccer referees' experience of threat and aggression: Effects of age, experience, and life orientation on outcome of coping strategy. *Aggressive Behaviour, 28,* 317-327.

[65] Weiner, B. (1972). Attribution theory, achievement motivation, and the educational process. *Review of educational research, 42,* 203-215.

[66] New Zealand Institute of Health & Fitness (2018). Personal Training Attribution Theory. https://nzihf.ac.nz/personal-training/attribution-theory/. Cited on 04/05/18 from the World Wide Web.

[67] Van Kleef, G. A., De Dreu, C. K. W., & Manstead, A. S. R. (2004). The interpersonal effects of anger and happiness in negotiations. *Journal of Personality & Social Psychology, 86,* 57-76.

[68] Jones, M. V., Paull, G. C., & Erskine, J. (2002). The impact of a team's aggressive reputation on the decision of association football referees. *Journal of Sports Science, 20,* 991-1000.

[69] Fitts, P. M., & Posner, M. I. (1967). *Human Performance.* Belmont: Brooks/Cole.

[70] Andersen, J. R. (1982). Acquisition of cognitive skill. *Psychological Review, 89,* 369-406; Andersen, J. R. (1993). *Rules of the mind.* Hillsdale, NJ: Erlbaum.

[71] Schmidt, R. A. (2003). Motor Schema Theory after 27 years: Reflections and implications for a new theory. *Research Quarterly for Exercise and Sport, 74,* 366-375.

[72] Bernstein, N.A. (1967). *The co-ordination and regulation of movements.* Oxford: Pergamon Press.

[73] Masters, R. S. W., Lo, C. Y., Maxwell, J. P., & Patil, N. G. (2008). Implicit motor learning in surgery: Implications for multi-tasking. *Surgery, 14,* 140-145; Masters, R. S. W., Poolton, J. M., & Maxwell, J. P. (2008). Stable implicit motor processes despite aerobic locomotor fatigue. *Consciousness and Cognition, 17,* 335-338; Poolton, J. M., Masters, R. S. W., & Maxwell, J. P. (2007). Passing thoughts on the evolutionary stability of implicit motor behaviour: Performance retention under physiological fatigue. *Consciousness and Cognition, 16,* 456-468.

[74] Ellis, J. (2009). David Elleray. http://metro.co.uk/2009/10/27/david-elleray-3423877/. Cited on 30/04/18 from the World Wide Web.

[75] Pinker, S. (1999). *How the Mind Works.* London: Penguin.

[76] Fiske, S. T., Neuberg, S. L., Beattie, A. E., & Milberg, S. J. (1987). Category-based and attribute-based reactions to others: Some informational conditions of stereotyping and individuating processes. *Journal of Experimental Social Psychology, 23,* 399-427.

[77] Plessner, H. (1999). Expectation biases in gymnastics judging. *Journal of Sport & Exercise Psychology, 21,* 131-144.

[78] Kahneman, D. (1973). *Attention and effort.* Englewood Cliffs, NJ: Prentice Hall; Fiske, S. T., & Taylor, S. E. (1991). *Social cognition.* Reading, MA: Addison-Wesley.

[79] BT Sport Films (2017). *Ref: Stories from the weekend.* First aired on April 4th, 2017.

[80] Moskowitz, G. B. & Carter, D. (2018). Confirmation bias and the stereotype of the black athlete. *Psychology of Sport & Exercise, 36,* 139-146.

[81] Rada, J. (1996). Color blind-sided: Racial bias in network television's coverage of professional football games. *The Howard Journal of Communications, 7,* 231-240.

[82] Kuper, S. & Szymanski, S. (2009). *Why England Lose & Other Curious Football Phenomena Explained.* London: Harper Collins.

[83] Nakrani, S. (2019). Paul Pogba's 'pace and power' stresses need for rethink over BAME coverage. *The Guardian,* January 21st, 2019.

[84] Moskowitz & Carter, 2018

[85] Ellis, 2009

[86] Plessner, 1999.

[87] Guardian, The. (2018). Manchester City fended off a brief West Ham revival to win 4-1 at the London Stadium and continue David Moyes's relegation concerns. https://www.theguardian.com/football/live/2018/apr/29/west-ham-v-manchester-city-premier-league-live. Cited on 30/04/18 from the World Wide Web.

[88] Rudd, A. (2018). Clinical Manchester City leave West Ham in trouble. *The Times,* April 30th, 2018.

[89] Jones, M. V., Paull, G. C., & Erskine, J. (2002). The impact of a team's aggressive reputation on the decision of association football referees. *Journal of Sports Science, 20,* 991-1000.

[90] MacMahon, C. & Mildenhall, B. (2012). A practical perspective on decision making influences in sports officiating. *International Journal of Sports Science & Coaching, 7,* 153-165 (p.154).

[91] Plessner, H. (1999). Expectation biases in gymnastics judging. *Journal of Sport & Exercise Psychology, 21,* 131-144.

[92] Findlay, L. C., & Ste-Marie, D. M. A. (2004). Reputation bias in figure skating judging. *Journal of Sport & Exercise Psychology, 26,* 154-166.

[93] Plessner, H. & Haar, T. (2006). Sports performance judgments from a social cognitive perspective. *Psychology of Sport & Exercise, 7,* 555-575 (p.563).

[94] Syed, M. (2018c). Mark Clattenburg: 'People say my tattoos mean I'm an egotist. Why should they tell me how to live my life?' *The Times,* May 12th, 2018.

[95] Biernat, M., & Vescio, T. K. (2002). She swings, she hits, she's great, she's benched: Implications of gender-based shifting standards for judgment and behaviour. *Personality & Social Psychology Bulletin, 28,* 66-77.

[96] Akerlof, G. A. (1997). Social distance and social decisions. *Econometrica, 65,* 1005-1027; Arkelof G. A., & Kranton, R. E. (2000). Economics and identity. *The Quarterly Journal of Economics, 115,* 715-753.

[97] Jacobs, J. E., & Eccles, J. S. (1992). The impact of mothers' gender-role stereotypic beliefs on mothers' and children's ability perceptions. *Journal of Personality & Social Psychology, 63,* 932-944.

[98] Coulomb-Cabagno, G., Rascle, O., & Souchon, N. (2005). Players' gender and male referees' decisions about aggression in French soccer: A preliminary study. *Sex Roles, 52,* 547-553.

[99] Rejer, P. (2018). Geiger deserves much praise. https://theref.online/paul-rejer-geiger-deserves-much-praise/. Cited on 25/07/18 from the World Wide Web.

[100] Hagemann, N., Strauss, B., & Leißing, J. (2008). When the referee sees red... *Psychological Science, 19,* 769- 771.

[101] See Steinfeldt, J. A., Foltz, B. D., Mungro, J., Speight, Q. L., Wong, Y. J., & Blumberg, J. (2011). Masculinity socialisation in sports: Influence of college football coaches. *Psychology of Men & Masculinity, 12,* 247-259, for an excellent review of the socialisation of American Football players and coaches.

[102] Sharpe, J. (2017). How good a signing is Harry Maguire for Leicester City? https://www.hinckleytimes.net/sport/football/how-good-signing-harry-maguire-13194288. Cited on 23/05/18 from the World Wide Web.

[103] Sheldon, W. H. (1954). *Atlas of Men: A Guide for Somatotyping the Male at All Ages.* New York: Harper.

[104] Ogden, J. (2010). *The Psychology of Eating: From Health to Disordered Behaviour (2nd Ed).* New Jersey: Wiley-Blakwell; Staffieri, J. R. (1967). A study of social stereotype of body image in children. *Journal of Personality and Social Psychology, 7,* 101-104.

[105] Van Quaquebeke, N., & Giessner, S. R. (2010). How embodied cognitions affect judgments: Height related attribution bias in football foul calls. *Journal of Sport & Exercise Psychology, 32,* 3-22.

[106] van Quaquebeke & Giessner, 2010

[107] van Quaquebeke & Giessner, 2010

[108] Akawor, I. (2017). Stoke are difficult. https://www.aclsports.com/stoke-difficult-mourinho/. Cited on 10/07/19 from the World Wide Web.

[109] Peach, S. (2014). Kelvin Davis defends Adam Lallana over Mark Clattenburg referee complaint. https://www.independent.co.uk/sport/football/premier-league/kelvin-davis-defends-adam-lallana-over-mark-clattenburg-referee-complaint-9052748.html. Cited on 08/12/18 from the World Wide Web.

[110] BBC Sport (2018a). Mark Halsey: Former Premier League referee says player asked to be booked. https://www.bbc.co.uk/sport/football/44647718. Cited on 09/10/18 from the World Wide Web.

[111] Hackett, K. (2018a). Referees – Being confident not arrogant earns respect. https://www.soccertoday.com/referees-being-confident-not-arrogant-earns-respect/. Cited on 09/10/18 from the World Wide Web.

[112] Syed, M. (2018d). Why Pep Guardiola gets an easier ride than Jose Mourinho. *The Times,* February 21st, 2018.

[113] Gibson, J. L., & Gore, J. S. (2016). Is he a hero or a weirdo? How norm violations influence the Halo Effect. *Gender Issues, 33,* 299-310; Thorndike, E. L. (1920). A constant error in psychological ratings. *Journal of Applied Psychology, 4,* 25-29.

[114] Gibson & Gore, 2016

[115] McFee, G. (2013). Officiating in aesthetic sports. *Journal of the Philosophy of Sport, 40,* 1-17.

[116] Syed, 2018d

[117] Cited from Metro News (2018). Manchester United fans demand Pep Guardiola ban following Jose Mourinho's suspension for kicking water bottle. https://metro.co.uk/2018/02/20/manchester-united-fans-demand-pep-guardiola-ban-following-jose-mourinhos-suspension-kicking-water-bottle-7326556/. Cited 18/05/18 from the World Wide Web.

[118] Cited in Syed, M. (2018c). Mark Clattenburg: 'People say my tattoos mean I'm an egotist. Why should they tell me how to live my life?' *The Times,* May 12th, 2018.

[119] Coulomb-Cabagno, G., Rascle, O., & Souchon, N. (2005). Players' gender and male referees' decisions about aggression in French soccer: A preliminary study. *Sex Roles, 52,* 547-553.

[120] Cited in Neil, R., Bayston, P., Hanton, S., & Wilson, K. (2013). The influence of stress and emotions on association football referees' decision-making. *Sport & Exercise Psychology Review, 9,* 22-41(p35).

[121] Jones, M. V., Paull, G. C., & Erskine, J. (2002). The impact of a team's aggressive reputation on the decision of association football referees. *Journal of Sports Science, 20,* 991-1000.

[122] Cited in Neil et al (2013pp.34)

[123] Moskowitz, G. B. & Carter, D. (2018). Confirmation bias and the stereotype of the black athlete. *Psychology of Sport & Exercise, 36,* 139-146.

[124] Kelso, P. (2013). West Ham manager Sam Allardyce charged by FA over comments after Manchester United defeat. https://www.telegraph.co.uk/sport/football/teams/west-

ham/9812243/West-Ham-manager-Sam-Allardyce-charged-by-FA-over-comments-after-Manchester-United-defeat.html. Cited on 02/09/18 from the World Wide Web.

[125] Abrams, D., Randsley de Moura, G., & Travaglino, G. A. (2013). A double standard when group members behave badly: Transgression credit to ingroup leaders. *Journal of Personality & Social Psychology, 105,* 799-815.

[126] BBC Sport (2018b). Neymar: PSG striker needs 'special treatment', says new boss Thomas Tuchel. https://www.bbc.co.uk/sport/football/44191348. Cited 25/05/18 from the World Wide Web.

[127] ITV (2006). *The Truth About Referees.* First aired March 7th, 2006.

[128] Abrams, Randsley de Moura & Travaglino, 2013

[129] Greenwald, A. G., McGhee, D. E., & Schwartz, J. L. K. (1998). Measuring Individual Differences in Implicit Cognition: The Implicit Association Test. *Journal of Personality & Social Psychology, 34,* 1464-1480.

[130] Page, K., & Page, L. (2010). Alone against the crowd: Individual differences in referees' ability to cope under pressure. *Journal of Economic Psychology, 31,* 192-199.

[131] Sports Law Scotland. (2018). A look at the relationship between referees and governing bodies. http://www.sportslawscotland.co.uk/2018/11/referees-appointment-management-and.html#.XAmMyWZ1TIU. Cited on 06/12/18 from the World Wide Web.

[132] Men in Blazers. (2017). Mark Clattenburg podcast special. https://soundcloud.com/meninblazers/men-in-blazers-120117-mark-clattenburg-pod-special. Cited on 24/08/18 from the World Wide Web.

[133] Bird, J. (2018). Why would anyone want to be a Sunday league referee? The love of the game. https://www.theguardian.com/football/2018/aug/30/sunday-league-referee-hackney-marshes-love-of-the-game. Cited on 30/08/18 from the World Wide Web.

[134] Wolfson, S. & Neave, N. (2007). Coping under pressure: Cognitive strategies for maintaining confidence among soccer referees. *Journal of Sport Behaviour, 30,* 232-247.

[135] Duda, J. L., & Treasure, D. C. (2010). Motivational processes and the facilitation of quality engagement in sport. In J. M. Williams (Ed.) *Applied Sport Psychology: Personal Growth to Peak Performance* (pp.267-304). London: McGraw-Hill.

[136] McClelland, D. C., Atkinson, J. W., Clark, R. W., & Lowell, E. L. (1953). *The achievement motive.* New York: Appleton-Century-Crofts.

[137] Vallerand, R. J., Blanchard, C. M., Mageau, G. A., Koestner, R., Ratelle, C., Léonard, M., Gagne, M., Marsolais, J. (2003). Les passions de l'âme: On obsessive and harmonious passion. *Journal of Personality & Social Psychology, 85,* 756-767.

[138] Bense, K. (2018). 'It doesn't keep me up at night': Rory McIlroy says the hunt to win another major doesn't weigh on him. https://www.golf.com/tour-news/2018/07/05/rory-mcilroy-it-doesnt-keep-me-night-hunt-win-another-major-doesnt-weigh-him. Cited on 22/09/18 from the World Wide Web.

[139] Phillipe, F. L., Vallerand, R. J., Andrianarisoa, J., & Brunel, P. (2009). Passion in referees: Examining their affective and cognitive experiences in sport situations. *Journal of Sport & Exercise Psychology, 31*, 77-96.

[140] Samuel, R. D. (2015). A psychological preparation framework for elite soccer referees: A practitioner's perspective. *Journal of Sport Psychology in Action, 0*, 1-18.

[141] Johansen, B. T. (2015). Reasons for officiating soccer: the role of passion-based motivations among Norwegian elite and non-elite referees. *Movement & Sport Sciences, 87*, 23-30.

[142] Nicholls, J. (1989). *The competitive ethos and democratic education.* Cambridge, MA: Harvard University Press.

[143] Cox, R. H. (1998). *Sport Psychology: Concepts and Applications (4th Ed).* New York: WCB/McGraw-Hill.

[144] Duda, J. L. (2001). Goal perspective research in sport: Pushing the boundaries and clarifying some misunderstandings. In G. C. Roberts (Ed.), *Advances in motivation in sport and exercise* (pp.129-182). Champaign, IL; Human Kinetics.

[145] Duda & Treasure, 2010

[146] Duda & Treasure, 2010

[147] BBC Sport. (2015). Ricardo Moniz: Notts County boss says referee are 'arrogant'. https://www.bbc.co.uk/sport/football/34062441. Cited on 29/08/18 from the World Wide Web; Hunt, S. (2017). 'He's probably the most arrogant man I've met on a football pitch': Stephen Hunt on Premier League referee Mike Dean. https://www.independent.ie/sport/soccer/premier-league/hes-probably-the-most-arrogant-man-ive-met-on-a-football-pitch-stephen-hunt-on-premier-league-referee-mike-dean-35333847.html. Cited on 29/08/18 from the World Wide Web.

[148] Thakare, A. E., Mehrotra, R., & Singh, A. (2017). Effect of music tempo on exercise performance and heart rate among young adults. *International Journal of Physiology, Pathophysiology and Pharmacology, 9*, 35-39.

[149] Wolfson, S. & Neave, N. (2007). Coping under pressure: Cognitive strategies for maintaining confidence among soccer referees. *Journal of Sport Behaviour, 30*, 232-247.

[150] Hackett, K. (2018b). Referees need to display presence. https://www.soccertoday.com/referees-need-to-display-presence/. Cited on 23/12/18 from the World Wide Web.

[151] Eurosport. (2014). Thierry Henry retires: Why France will never love its record scorer. https://www.eurosport.com/football/thierry-henry-retires-why-france-will-never-love-its-record-scorer_sto4718482/story.shtml. Cited on 21/09/18 from the World Wide Web.

[152] Kendall, C. (2018). Truthful & honest from referee Danny Guest: "We are normal guys...why shouldn't we have a voice!" http://thebootifulgame.co.uk/2018/10/24/truthful-honest-by-referee-danny-guest-we-are-normal-guys-why-shouldnt-we-have-a-voice/. Cited on 27/10/18 from the World Wide Web.

[153] Anderson, C., & Sally, D. (2014). *The Numbers Game: Why Everything You Know About Football is Wrong.* London: Penguin.

[154] Sutcliffe, S. (2019). Mistakes, abuse and VAR: What are the pressures like on a Premier League referee?
https://www.bbc.co.uk/sport/football/47690634. Cited on 24/04/19 from the World Wide Web.

[155] Seyle, H. (1950). *Stress*. Montreal: Acta.

[156] Lazarus, R.S. & Folkman, S. (1984). Stress, appraisal, and coping. New York: Springer.

[157] Webb, T. (2019). How to improve your officiating association.
http://reflive.com/blog/tom-webb-interview. Cited on 25/01/19 from the World Wide Web.

[158] Endler, N. S. (1978). The interaction model of anxiety: Some possible implications. In D. M. Landers & R. W. Christina (Eds.), *Psychology of motor behaviour in sport – 1977* (pp.332-351). Champaign, IL: Human Kinetics.

[159] Webb, T. (2017). *Elite Soccer Referees: Officiating in the Premier League, La Liga and Serie A*. London: Routledge.

[160] Webb, T. (2019).

[161] Both cited in Neil, R., Bayston, P., Hanton, S., & Wilson, K. (2013:pp33-34). The influence of stress and emotions on association football referees' decision-making. *Sport & Exercise Psychology Review, 9*, 22-41.

[162] Syed, M. (2018e). Referee intoxicated by power – like a nightclub bouncer. *The Times*, April 2nd, 2018.

[163] Syed, M. (2018c). *Mark Clattenburg:* 'People say my tattoos mean I'm an egotist. Why should they tell me how to live my life?' *The Times*, May 12th, 2018.

[164] Law, M. (2015). Leicester City news: Nigel Pearson blasts referee Mike Dean as 'arrogant' after penalty decision.
https://www.telegraph.co.uk/sport/football/teams/leicester-city/11487920/Leicester-City-news-Nigel-Pearson-blasts-referee-Mike-Dean-as-arrogant-after-penalty-decision.html. Cited on 06/06/18 from the World Wide Web.

[165] Fifield, D. (2015). Jose Mourinho: referee was 'weak and naïve' in Chelsea's draw at Dynamo Kyiv.
https://www.theguardian.com/football/2015/oct/20/dynamo-kyiv-chelsea-champions-league-match-report. Cited on 06/06/18 from the World Wide Web.

[166] See Bruner, M. W., & Spink, K. S. (2010). Evaluating a team building intervention in a youth exercise setting. *Group Dynamics: Theory, Research & Practice, 14*, 304-317; Curren, T., Hill, A. P., Hall, H. K., & Jowett, G. E. (2015). Relationships between the coach-created motivational climate and athlete engagement in youth sport. *Journal of Sport & Exercise Psychology, 37*, 193-198; Surujlal, J., & Dhurup, M. (2012). Athlete preference of a coach's leadership style. *African Journal for Physical, Health Education, Recreation & Dance, 18*, 111-121.

[167] Nideffer, R. N. (1981). *The ethics and practice of applied sport psychology*. Ithaca, NY: Mouvement; Nideffer, R. N. (1993). Attention control training. In R. N. Singer, M. Murphey, & L. K. Tennant (Eds.), *Handbook of research on sport psychology* (pp.542-556). New York: MacMillan.

[168] Williams, J. M., Nideffer, R. M., Wilson, V. E., Sagal, M., & Peper, E. (2010). Concentration and strategies for controlling it. In J. M. Williams (Ed), *Applied Sport Psychology: Personal Growth to Peak Performance* (pp.336-360). New York: McGraw-Hill.

[169] Fraser, S. (2018). Johanna Konta delivers angry outburst and storms off after defeat in Nottingham final. https://www.thetimes.co.uk/article/johanna-konta-delivers-angry-outburst-and-storms-off-after-defeat-in-nottingham-final-8ll8tgl30. Cited on 18/06/18 from the World Wide Web.

[170] Lazarus, R. S. (2000:p229). How emotions influence performance in competitive sports. *The Sport Psychologist, 14,* 229-252.

[171] Syed, M. (2018f). Karius was too focused to think clearly. *The Times,* May 30th, 2018.

[172] Easterbrook, J. A. (1959). The effect of emotion on cue utilisation and the organisation of behaviour. *Psychological Review, 66,* 183-201.

[173] Parsons, T., & Bairner, A. (2015). You want the buzz of having done well in a game that wasn't easy: A sociological explanation of the job commitment of English football referees. *Movement & Sport Sciences, 87,* 41-52.

[174] Hull, C. L. (1943). *Principles of behaviour.* New York: Appleton Century.

[175] Spence, J. T., & Spence, K. W. (1966). The motivational components of manifest anxiety: Drive and drive stimuli. In C. D. Spielberger (Ed.), *Anxiety and Behaviour* (pp.291-326). New York: Academic Press.

[176] BT Sport Films (2017). *Ref: Stories from the weekend.* First aired on April 4th, 2017.

[177] Jordet, G. (2009). When superstars flop: Public status and choking under pressure in international soccer penalty shootouts. *Journal of Applied Sport Psychology, 21,* 125-130.

[178] BBC Sport. (2006). Ref Poll sent home from World Cup. http://news.bbc.co.uk/sport1/hi/football/world_cup_2006/5108722.stm. Cited 11/06/18 from the World Wide Web.

[179] Slater, M. J., Haslam, S. A., & Steffens, N. K. (2018). Singing it for "us": Team passion displayed during national anthems is associated with subsequent success. *European Journal of Sport Science, 18,* 541-549.

[180] See Schwarz, N., & Bless, H. (1992). Constructing realities and its alternatives: Assimilation and contrast effects in social judgment. In L/ L/ Martin & A. Tesser (Eds.), *The Construction of Social Judgment* (pp.217-245). Hillsdale, NJ: Erlbaum; Stapel, D. A., & Winkielman, P. (1998). Assimilation and contrast as a function of context-target similarity, distinctness, and dimensional relevance. *Personality & Social Psychology Bulletin, 24,* 634-646.

[181] Sky Sports (2017b). *The Referees: Onside with Carragher & Neville.* First aired 7th April, 2017.

[182] Joyce, P. (2019a). Klopp facing charge over claim of referee bias. *The Times,* February 6th, 2019.

[183] Sutcliffe, S. (2019).

[184] Plessner, H. & Betsch, T. (2001). Sequential effects in important referee decisions: The case of penalties in soccer. *Journal of Sport & Exercise Psychology, 23,* 254-259.

[185] Endler, N. S. (1996). Stress, anxiety and coping: The multidimensional interaction model. *Canadian Psychology, 38*, 136-153.

[186] Prenderville, L. (2018). Graham Poll hails Michael Oliver's "courage" over Real Madrid penalty – 'it's a pity he isn't going to the World Cup'. *The Mirror*, April 12th, 2018.

[187] Gilis, B., Helsen, W., Catteeuw, P., & Wagemans, J. (2008). Offside decisions by expert assistant referees in Association Football: Perception and recall of spatial positions in complex dynamic events. *Journal of Experimental Psychology, 14*, 21-35.

[188] ESPN. (2018). Referee suspended, apologies for tripping Nantes player in PSG game. http://www.espn.co.uk/football/nantes/story/3349068/referee-suspended-apologises-for-tripping-nantes-player-in-psg-game. Cited on 11/10/18 from the World Wide Web.

[189] Hanin, Y. L. (Ed., 2000). *Emotions in sport.* Champaign, IL: Human Kinetics.

[190] Lazarus, R. S. (1999). *Stress and emotion: A new synthesis.* London: Free Association.

[191] Lazarus, R. S. (2000). How emotions influence performance in competitive sports. *The Sport Psychologist, 14*, 229-252.

[192] Cited in Neil, R., Bayston, P., Hanton, S., & Wilson, K. (2013:p.28). The influence of stress and emotions on association football referees' decision-making. *Sport & Exercise Psychology Review, 9*, 22-41.

[193] Cited in Neil et al (2013:pp.28)

[194] Folkesson, P., Nyberg, C., Archer, T., & Norlander, T. (2002). Soccer referees' experience of threat and aggression: Effects of age, experience, and life orientation on outcome of coping strategy. *Aggressive Behaviour, 28*, 317-327.

[195] Cited in Neil et al (2013:pp.29)

[196] Plessner, H. & Betsch, T. (2001). Sequential effects in important referee decisions: The case of penalties in soccer. *Journal of Sport & Exercise Psychology, 23*, 254-259.

[197] BT Sport Films (2017). *Ref: Stories from the weekend.* First aired on April 4th, 2017.

[198] Tamir, M. (2016). Why do people regulate their emotions? A taxonomy of motives in emotion regulation. *Personality & Social Psychology Review, 20*, 199-222.

[199] Tamir (2016:pp.199)

[200] Jordet, G. (2009). When superstars flop: Public status and choking under pressure in international soccer penalty shootouts. *Journal of Applied Sport Psychology, 21*, 125-130.

[201] Gohm, C. L. (2003). Mood regulation and emotional intelligence: Individual differences. *Journal of Personality & Social Psychology, 84*, 594-607.

[202] Kay, O. (2019). No wonder referees live in fear when players' abuse goes unpunished. *The Times*, February 9th, 2019.

[203] Nevill, A. M., Balmer, N. J., & Williams, A. M. (2002). The influence of crowd noise and experience upon refereeing decisions in football. *Psychology of Sport & Exercise, 3*, 261-272.

[204] Sky Sports (2017c). Clattenburg: I let Spurs self-destruct against Chelsea at Stamford Bridge in 2016.

http://www.skysports.com/football/news/11661/11156272/mark-clattenburg-let-tottenham-self-destruct-against-chelsea-at-stamford-bridge-in-2016. Cited on 04/12/17 from the World Wide Web.

[205] Neil, R., Bayston, P., Hanton, S., & Wilson, K. (2013:p34). The influence of stress and emotions on association football referees' decision-making. *Sport & Exercise Psychology Review, 9*, 22-41.

[206] Fischer, A. H., Manstead, A. S. R., Evers, C., Timmers, M., & Valk, G. (2004). Motives and norms underlying emotion regulation. In P. Philoppot & R. S. Feldman (Eds.), *The regulation of emotion* (pp.187-210). Mahwah, NJ: Lawrence Erlbaum.

[207] Sky Sports (2017d). Mark Clattenburg game-plan comments are 'nonsense', says Dermot Gallagher. http://www.skysports.com/football/news/11095/11157862/mark-clattenburg-game-plan-comments-are-nonsense-says-dermot-gallagher. Cited on 06/12/17 from the World Wide Web.

[208] Anshel, M. H., & Weinberg, R. S. (1999). Re-examining coping among basketball referees following stressful events: Implications for coping interventions. *Journal of Sport Behaviour, 22*, 141-161.

[209] Gross, J. J. & Thompson, R. A. (2007). Emotion Regulation: Conceptual Foundations. In J. J. Gross (Ed.), *Handbook of Emotion Regulation* (pp.3-24). New York: Guilford Press.

[210] Gross & Thompson, 2007

[211] BT Sport Films (2017). *Ref: Stories from the weekend*. First aired on April 4th, 2017.

[212] Zeqiri, D. (2018). Fascinating video highlights the difficulties of being a top-flight referee – and the need for VAR. https://www.telegraph.co.uk/football/2018/08/27/fascinating-video-highlights-difficulties-top-flight-referee/. Cited on 16/09/18 from the World Wide Web.

[213] Haselton, M. G., & Nettle, D. The paranoid optimist: An integrative evolutionary model of cognitive biases. *Personality & Social Psychology Review, 10*, 47-66.

[214] BBC Sport. (2018c). Chelsea VAR controversy: Referee should have been told to watch video – Antonio Conte. https://www.bbc.co.uk/sport/football/42727541. Cited on 27/06/18 from the World Wide Web.

[215] BT Sport Films (2017). *Ref: Stories from the weekend*. First aired on April 4th, 2017.

[216] Lazarus, R. S. (1993). From psychological stress to the emotions: A history of changing outlooks. *Annual Review of Psychology, 44*, 1-21.

[217] Guillen, F., & Feltz, D. (2011). A conceptual model of referee efficacy. *Frontiers in Psychology, 2*, 1-5.

[218] Samuel, R. D. (2015). A psychological preparation framework for elite soccer referees: A practitioner's perspective. *Journal of Sport Psychology in Action, 0*, 1-18.

[219] Mellick, M. C., Fleming, S., Bull, P., & Laugharne, E. J. (2005). Identifying best practice for referee decision communication in association and rugby union football. *Football Studies, 8, 42-57.*

[220] Slack, L. A., Maynard, I. W., Butt, J. & Olusoga, P. (2013). Factors underpinning football officiating excellence: Perceptions of English football referees. *Journal of Applied Sport Psychology, 25,* 298-315.

[221] Brand, R. & Neß, W. (2004). Regelanwendung und Game-Management – Qualifizierende Merkmale von Schiedsrichtern in Sportspielen. *Zeitschrift für Sportpsychologie, 11*(4), 127-136.

[222] BT Sport (2016). Howard Webb on when to book a player. https://www.youtube.com/watch?v=nunux4SWk_E. Cited on 29/06/18 from the World Wide Web.

[223] Fifield, D. (2010). World Cup final: Howard Webb's dream job descends into nightmare. https://www.theguardian.com/football/2010/jul/12/howard-webb-final-nightmare-yellow-cards. Cited on 29/06/18 from the World Wide Web.

[224] FIFA TV (2012). *Match 64: The inside story of the 2010 Final.* https://www.youtube.com/watch?v=47yOv3MS20M. Cited on 25/06/18 from the World Wide Web.

[225] Folkesson, P., Nyberg, C., Archer, T., & Norlander, T. (2002). Soccer referees' experience of threat and aggression: Effects of age, experience, and life orientation on outcome of coping strategy. *Aggressive Behaviour, 28,* 317-327.

[226] Folkesson et al (2002:pp.326)

[227] Hackett, K. (2019). Card-happy Mike Dean should try a quiet word rather than going to war with misbehaving players. https://www.telegraph.co.uk/football/2019/02/04/card-happy-mike-dean-should-try-quiet-word-rather-going-war/. Cited on 06/02/19 from the World Wide Web.

[228] PsychRef. (2019). The referee as game-manager. http://www.psychref.org/2018/01/the-referee-as-game-manager.html. Cited on 06/02/19 from the World Wide Web.

[229] Raghunathan, R., & Pham, M. T. (1999). All negative moods are not equal: Motivational influences of anxiety and sadness on decision making. *Organisational Behaviour & Human Decision Processes, 79,* 56-77.

[230] Lane, A. M., Beedie, C. J., Jones, M. V., Uphill, M., & Devonport, T. J. (2012). The BASES expert statement on emotion regulation in sport. *Journal of Sports Sciences, 30,* 1189-1195.

[231] Lane et al, 2012

[232] Tamir, M. (2016). Why do people regulate their emotions? A taxonomy of motives in emotion regulation. *Personality & Social Psychology Review, 20,* 199-222.

[233] Bauman, N. J. (2016). The stigma of mental health in athletes: are mental toughness and mental health seen as contradictory in elite sport? *British Journal of Sports Medicine, 50,* 135-136.

[234] BBC Sport. (2018d). Ellie Soutter death: Father criticises pressure on athletes. https://www.bbc.co.uk/news/uk-england-surrey-45023187. Cited on 31/07/18 from the World Wide Web.

[235] Roan, D. (2018). How big a problem is football facing? And what is being done? https://www.bbc.co.uk/sport/football/45135228. Cited on 10/08/18 from the World Wide Web.

[236] Taylor, D. (2012b). Michael Carrick: 'Depression over a game sounds extreme but I felt in a very dark place'. *The Guardian*, October 12th, 2018.

[237] Hytner, D. (2018). Chris Kirkland: 'I didn't want to wake up in the morning. It just starts again.' *The Guardian*, October 11th, 2017.

[238] Kelner, M. (2018). Danny Rose open up about depression after tragedy and tough year at Spurs. *The Guardian*, June 6th, 2018.

[239] Dixon, M. & Turner, M. J. (2018). Stress appraisals of UK soccer academy coaches: an interpretive phenomenological analysis. *Qualitative Research in Sport, Exercise and Health, 10*, 620-634.

[240] BT Sport Films (2017). *Ref: Stories from the weekend*. First aired on April 4th, 2017.

[241] Cited in Neil, R., Bayston, P., Hanton, S., & Wilson, K. (2013:p.33). The influence of stress and emotions on association football referees' decision-making. *Sport & Exercise Psychology Review, 9*, 22-41.

[242] Parsons, T., & Bairner, A. (2015). You want the buzz of having done well in a game that wasn't easy: A sociological explanation of the job commitment of English football referees. *Movement & Sport Sciences, 87*, 41-52.

[243] Parsons & Bairner (2015:pp.47)

[244] Parsons & Bairner (2015:pp.48)

[245] Bauman, 2016

[246] Gleeson, S., & Brady, E. (2017). When athletes share their battles with mental illness. https://eu.usatoday.com/story/sports/2017/08/30/michael-phelps-brandon-marshall-mental-health-battles-royce-white-jerry-west/596857001/. Cited on 06/08/18 from the World Wide Web.

[247] BBC Sport. (2018e). Matt Cecchin: NRL referee quits over 'vile abuse and death threats'. https://www.bbc.co.uk/sport/rugby-league/45055588. Cited on 03/08/18 from the World Wide Web.

[248] BBC Sport. (2013). Mark Halsey fears an under-pressure official could take own life. https://www.bbc.co.uk/sport/football/24105438. Cited on 30/07/18 from the World Wide Web.

[249] Voborný, J., Zeman, T., Blahutková, M., & Václaviková, D. (2013). Factor analysis of pre-match and post-match subjective psychological experiences and mental states of football referees. *British Journal of Sports Medicine, 47*, 12.

[250] Folkesson, P., Nyberg, C., Archer, T., & Norlander, T. (2002). Soccer referees' experience of threat and aggression: Effects of age, experience, and life orientation on outcome of coping strategy. *Aggressive Behaviour, 28*, 317-327.

[251] See Blascovich, J., & Mendes, W. B. (2000). Challenge and threat appraisals: The role of affective cues. In J. P. Forgas (ed), *Feeling and Thinking: The role of affect in social cognition* (pp.59-82). Paris: Cambridge University Press; Dixon, M. & Turner, M. J. (2018). Stress appraisals of UK soccer academy coaches: an interpretive phenomenological analysis. *Qualitative Research in Sport, Exercise and Health, 10*, 620-634.

[252] Folkesson et al, 2002

[253] Tayeb, M. (2013). Geert Hofstede. In M. Witzel & M. Warner (Eds.), *The Oxford Handbook of Management Theorists* (pp.427-447). Oxford: Oxford University Press.

254 Sky Sports (2017b). *The Referees: Onside with Carragher & Neville*. First aired 7th April, 2017.

255 Idessane, K. (2018). Scottish referees: 'Abuse culture' needs to stop, John McKendrick. https://www.bbc.co.uk/sport/football/46513470. Cited on 14/12/18 from the World Wide Web.

256 Parks, T. (2003). *A Season with Verona: Travels Around Italy in Search of Illusion, National Character and Goals*. Vintage: London (p4).

257 BBC Sport. (2018f). 'Bullets sent in post to three key figures at Italian Referees' Association'. https://www.bbc.co.uk/sport/football/43662117. Cited on 14/11/18 from the World Wide Web.

258 Wilson, J. (2019a). Referees charity calls on FA to reboot Respect campaign after rise in reports of abuse of officials. http://www.telegraph.co.uk/football/2019/01/23/referee-reports. Cited on 28/01/19 from the World Wide Web.

259 Pitchford, A. (2005). *Referee training & development in England: A report for The Football Association*. Unpublished MSc thesis, Gloucester: University of Gloucestershire.

260 BBC Sport. (2012b). Chelsea regret handling of Mark Clattenburg racism allegation. https://www.bbc.co.uk/sport/football/20507362. Cited on 30/07/18 from the World Wide Web.

261 Folkesson, P., Nyberg, C., Archer, T., & Norlander, T. (2002). Soccer referees' experience of threat and aggression: Effects of age, experience, and life orientation on outcome of coping strategy. *Aggressive Behaviour, 28*, 317-327.

262 BBC Sport. (2018g). Being an amateur referee: your stories of threats and attacks, but a love of the game. https://www.bbc.co.uk/sport/football/46208857. Cited on 30/11/18 from the World Wide Web.

263 Barnard, P. (1968). Are we too tough on our referees? *Goal Magazine*, September 28th, 1968.

264 Papineau, D. (2017:p.73). *Knowing the Score: How sport teaches us about philosophy (and philosophy about sport)*. London: Constable.

265 Williams, B. (2018). The problem with chasing perfection. https://www.playersvoice.com.au/ben-williams-problem-with-chasing-perfection/. Cited on 16/11/18 from the World Wide Web.

266 Referees' Association. (2012a). Background and Formation. www.refereesassociation.co.uk/index.asp?page=become-a-referee. Cited 08/08/18 from the World Wide Web.

267 Parsons, T., & Bairner, A. (2015). You want the buzz of having done well in a game that wasn't easy: A sociological explanation of the job commitment of English football referees. *Movement & Sport Sciences, 87*, 41-52.

268 Referees' Association. (2012b). Background and Formation. www.refereesassociation.co.uk/index.asp?page=ra-history. Cited 08/08/18 from the World Wide Web.

269 Webb, T. (2016). 'Knight of the Whistle': W.P. Harper and the impact of the media on an Association Football referee. *The International Journal of the History of Sport, 33*, 306-324.

[270] BBC Sport. (2018h). Russia 2018: What will happen if there is racist chanting during the World Cup? https://www.bbc.co.uk/sport/football/44405889. Cited on 07/06/18 from the World Wide Web.

[271] Jacob, G. (2018). Rule change allows managers to watch TV replays during matches. https://www.thetimes.co.uk/article/rule-change-allows-managers-to-watch-tv-replays-during-matches-b8sxh036s. Cited on 02/08/18 from the World Wide Web.

[272] Wilson, J. (2017). FA relaunches Respect campaign amid referee strike threat over increasing abuse at grassroots. https://www.telegraph.co.uk/football/2017/01/17/referee-strike-threat-triggers-fa-action-abuse-grassroots-match/. Cited on 13/08/18 from the World Wide Web.

[273] Parsons & Bairner, 2015

[274] Wolfson, S. & Neave, N. (2007). Coping under pressure: Cognitive strategies for maintaining confidence among soccer referees. *Journal of Sport Behaviour, 30,* 232-247.

[275] Wolfson and Neave, 2007

[275] Dixon, M. & Turner, M. J. (2018). Stress appraisals of UK soccer academy coaches: an interpretive phenomenological analysis. *Qualitative Research in Sport, Exercise and Health*, 10, 620-634.

[277] Syed, M. (2016). *Black Box Thinking: Marginal Gains and the Secrets of High Performance*. London: John Murray.

[278] Roohafza, H. R., Afshar, H., Keshteli, A. H., Mohammadi, N., Feizi, A., Taslimi, M., & Adibi, P. (2014). What's the role of perceived social support and coping styles in depression and anxiety? *Journal of Research in Medical Sciences, 19,* 944-949.

[279] Parsons, T., & Bairner, A. (2015). You want the buzz of having done well in a game that wasn't easy: A sociological explanation of the job commitment of English football referees. *Movement & Sport Sciences, 87,* 41-52.

[280] Parsons & Bairner (2015:pp.48)

[281] Parsons & Bairner (2015:pp.49)

[282] RefLIVE. (2018). How to recruit and retain more female officials: A Q&A with Sonia Denoncourt. www.reflive.com/blog/how-to-recruit-and-retain-more-female-officials/. Cited 11/10/18 from the World Wide Web.

[283] Wolfson & Neave, 2007

[284] Goldfried, M. R., & Sobocinski, D. (1975:p.509). Effect of irrational beliefs on emotional arousal. *Journal of Consulting & Clinical Psychology, 43,* 504-510.

[285] Ellis, A. (1994). The sport of avoiding sports and exercise: A rational emotive behaviour therapy perspective. *The Sport Psychologist, 8,* 248-261.

[286] Ellis, A., Gordon, J., Neenan, M., & Palmer, S. (1997). *Stress counselling: A rational emotive behaviour approach*. London: Cassell.

[287] Dryden, W. (2012). The 'ABCs' of REBT I: A preliminary study of errors and confusions in counselling and psychotherapy textbooks. *Journal of Rational-Emotive and Cognitive-Behaviour Therapy, 30,* 133-172.

[288] Vargas, T. M., & Short, S. E. (2011). Athletes' perceptions of the psychological, emotional, and performance effects of coaches' pre-game speeches. *International Journal of Coaching Science, 5,* 27-43.

[289] Hermansson, G., & Hodge, K. (2012:p.128). Uncontrollable outcomes: Managing expectations at the Olympics. *Journal of Sport Psychology in Action, 3,* 127-138.

[290] Sky Sports (2019). Hugo Lloris says Tottenham must win remaining Premier League games in top-four bid. https://www.skysports.com/football/news/11675/11661639/hugo-lloris-says-tottenham-must-win-remaining-premier-league-games-in-top-four-bid. Cited on 13/05/19 from the World Wide Web.

[291] Cited in Neil, R., Bayston, P., Hanton, S., & Wilson, K. (2013:p.33). The influence of stress and emotions on association football referees' decision-making. *Sport & Exercise Psychology Review, 9,* 22-41.

[292] Dryden, W., & Branch, R. (2008). *The fundamentals of rational-emotive behavioural therapy.* West Sussex: Wiley.

[293] Kendall, C. (2018). Truthful & honest from referee Danny Guest: "We are normal guys…why shouldn't we have a voice!" http://thebootifulgame.co.uk/2018/10/24/truthful-honest-by-referee-danny-guest-we-are-normal-guys-why-shouldnt-we-have-a-voice/. Cited on 27/10/18 from the World Wide Web.

[294] BT Sport Films (2017). *Ref: Stories from the weekend.* First aired on April 4th, 2017.

[295] BBC Sport. (2018i). Darren Ferguson: Doncaster boss fined £1,000 for 'shoot referees' comments. https://www.bbc.co.uk/sport/football/42887263. Cited on 22/08/18 from the World Wide Web.

[296] Ericsson, K. A., Krampe, R. Th., & Tesch-Romer, C. (1993). The role of deliberate practice in the acquisition of expert performance. *Psychological Review, 100,* 363-406.

[297] Hodges, N. J. & Starkes, J. L. (1996). Wrestling with the nature of expertise: a sport specific test of Ericsson, Krampe, and Tesch-Römer's (1993) theory of deliberate practice. *International Journal of Sport Psychology, 27,* 400-424.

[298] Premier League. (2018a). Oliver: Refs must match players for fitness. https://www.premierleague.com/news/800434. Cited on 22/08/18 from the World Wide Web.

[299] Morris, G., & O'Connor, D. (2017). Key attributes of expert NRL referees. *Journal of Sports Sciences, 35,* 852-857.

[300] Rees, P. (2018). Dan Carter: 'Seeing a psychologist allowed me to confront my demons'. *The Observer,* June 10th, 2018.

[301] Football Association, The. (2012). Respect – Four Years On. www.thefa.com/News/my-football/2012/jul/four-years-on.aspx. Cited on 11/12/12 from the World Wide Web.

[302] Samuel, R. D., Englert, C., Zhang, Q., & Basevitch, I. (2018). Hi ref, are you in control? Self-control, ego-depletion, and performance in soccer referees. *Psychology of Sport & Exercise, 38,* 167-175.

[303] Taylor, D. (2012c). Referees winning the percentage game whatever managers and media say. *The Guardian,* March 3rd, 2012.

[304] Ericsson, Krampe & Tesch-Romer, 1993

[305] MacMahon, C., Helsen, W. F., Starkes, J. L., & Weston, M. (2007). Decision-making skills and deliberate practice in elite association football referees. *Journal of Sports Sciences, 25,* 65-78.

[306] Moore, L. J., Harris, D. J., Sharpe, B. T., Vine, S. J., & Wilson, M. R. (2019). Perceptual-cognitive expertise when refereeing the scrum in rugby union. *Journal of Sports Sciences,* 1-9.

[307] Cited in Horrocks, D. E., McKenna, J., Whitehead, A. E., Taylor, P. J., Morley, A. M., & Lawrence, I. (2016). Preparation, structured deliberate practice and decision making in elite level football: The case study of Gary Neville (Manchester United FC and England). *International Journal of Sports Science & Coaching, 11,* 673-682.

[308] Samuel, R. D. (2015). A psychological preparation framework for elite soccer referees: A practitioner's perspective. *Journal of Sport Psychology in Action, 0,* 1-18.

[309] Parsons, T., & Bairner, A. (2015). You want the buzz of having done well in a game that wasn't easy: A sociological explanation of the job commitment of English football referees. *Movement & Sport Sciences, 87,* 41-52.

[310] Mallo, J., Futos, P. G., Juárez, D., & Navarro, E. (2012). Effect of positioning on the accuracy of association football top-class referees and assistant referees during competitive matches. *Journal of Sports Sciences, 30,* 1437-1445.

[311] Syed, M. (2018g). Southgate has set a whole new trend in management. *The Times,* October 17th, 2018.

[312] Burke, K. (2005). But Coach doesn't understand: Dealing with team communication quagmires. In M. B. Andersen (Ed.), *Sport Psychology in Practice* (pp.45-60). Leeds: Human Kinetics.

[313] Austin, S. (2018). Darcy Norman: the next frontier is mindset. http://trainingground.guru/articles/darcy-norman-next-frontier-is-mindset. Cited on 13/10/18 from the World Wide Web.

[314] Gladwell, M. (2009). *Outliers: The story of success.* London: Penguin.

[315] Lam, S. S. K., & Schaubroeck, J. (2000). Improving group decisions by better pooling information: A comparative advantage of group decision support systems. *Journal of Applied Psychology, 85,* 565-573 (p.565).

[316] Stasser, G., & Titus, W. (1985). Pooling of unshared information in group decision making: Biased information sampling during discussion. *Journal of Personality and Social Psychology, 48,* 1467-1478; Stasser, G., & Titus, W. (1987). Effects of information load and percentage of shared information on the dissemination of unshared information during group discussion. *Journal of Personality and Social Psychology, 53,* 81-93.

[317] Lam & Schaubroeck, 2000

[318] Thomas, L. (2018). What referee Jon Moss said to assistant Ed Smart for controversial Tottenham penalty against Liverpool. http://www.skysports.com/football/news/11661/11237166/what-referee-jon-moss-said-to-assistant-ed-smart-for-controversial-tottenham-penalty-against-liverpool. Cited on 06/02/18 from the World Wide Web.

[319] Samuel, 2015

[320] Samuel, 2015

[321] Dixon, M. & Turner, M. J. (2018). Stress appraisals of UK soccer academy coaches: an interpretive phenomenological analysis. *Qualitative Research in Sport, Exercise and Health, 10,* 620-634.

[322] Samuel (2015:p.10)

[323] Samuel, 2015

[324] Lane, A. M., Beedie, C. J., Jones, M. V., Uphill, M., & Devonport, T. J. (2012). The BASES expert statement on emotion regulation in sport. *Journal of Sports Sciences, 30,* 1189-1195.

[325] Turner, M., Carrington, S., & Miller, A. (2018). Psychological distress across sport participation groups: The mediating effects of secondary irrational beliefs on the relationship between primary irrational beliefs and symptoms of anxiety, anger, and depression. *Journal of Clinical Sport Psychology,* 1-38.

[326] Vealey, R. S. (2007). Mental skills training in sport. In G. Tenenbaum & R. C. Eklund (Eds.), *Handbook of Sport Psychology* (3rd ed., pp.287-309). Hoboken, NJ: Wiley.

[327] Dryden, W. & DiGiuseppe, R. (1990). *A primer on rational-emotive behaviour therapy.* West Sussex: Wiley.

[328] Samuel, 2015

[329] Gaoua, N., de Oliveira, R. F., & Hunter, S. (2017). Perception, action, and cognition of football referees in extreme temperatures: Impact on decision performance. *Frontiers in Psychology, 8,* 1-7.

[330] Da Silva, A. I., & Fernandez, R. (2003). Dehydration of football referees during a match. *British Journal of Sports Medicine, 37,* 502-506.

[331] Samuel, 2015

[332] BT Sport Films (2017). *Ref: Stories from the weekend.* First aired on April 4th, 2017.

[333] Hackett, K. (2018b). It looked like chaos on the Stamford Bridge touchline, but officials were ready for incident to kick off. *The Telegraph,* October 21st, 2018.

[334] Sun-Tzu, & Griffith, S. B. (1964). *The Art of War.* Oxford: Clarendon Press.

[335] Samuel, 2015

[336] Samuel, 2015

[337] Voborný, J., Zeman, T., Blahutková, M., & Václaviková, D. (2013). Factor analysis of pre-match and post-match subjective psychological experiences and mental states of football referees. *British Journal of Sports Medicine, 47,* 12.

[338] BT Sport Films (2017). *Ref: Stories from the weekend.* First aired on April 4th, 2017.

[339] Moran, A. P. (1996:p.177). *The psychology of concentration in sports performers: A cognitive analysis.* Hove: Psychology Press.

[340] Gould, D., & Udry, E. (1994). Psychological skills for enhancing performance: Arousal regulation strategies. *Medicine & Science in Sport & Exercise, 26,* 478-485.

[341] Cotterill, S., Sanders, R., & Collins, D. (2010). Developing effective pre-performance routines in golf: Why don't we ask the golfer? *Journal of Applied Sport Psychology, 22,* 51-64.

[342] Foster, D. J., Weigand, D. A., & Baines, D. (2006). The effect of removing superstitious behaviour and introducing pre-performance routine on

basketball free-throw performance. *Journal of Applied Sport Psychology, 18,* 167-171.

[343] Wrisberg, C. A., & Pein, R. C. (1992). The pre-shot interval and free throw shooting accuracy: An exploratory investigation. *The Sport Psychologist, 6,* 14-23.

[344] Hill, D. M., Hanton, S., Matthews, N., & Fleming, S. (2010). A qualitative exploration of choking in elite golf. *Journal of Clinical Sport Psychology, 4,* 221-240.

[345] Beilock, S. L., & Carr, T. H. (2001). On the fragility of skilled performance: What governs choking under pressure? *Journal of Experimental Psychology: General, 130,* 701-725.

[346] Lidor, R., & Mayan, Z. (2005). Can beginning learners benefit from pre-performance routines when serving in volleyball? *The Sport Psychologist, 19,* 343-363.

[347] Sky Sports (2017b). *The Referees: Onside with Carragher & Neville.* First aired 7th April, 2017.

[348] Lidor & Mayan, 2005

[349] See Vealey, R. S., & Greenleaf, C. A. (2010). Seeing is believing: Understanding and using imagery in sport. In J. M. Williams (Ed.) *Applied Sport Psychology: Personal Growth to Peak Performance* (pp.267-304). London: McGraw-Hill.

[350] Helsen, W. F., Gilis, B., & Weston, M. (2006). Errors in judging "offside" in association football: Test of the optical error versus the perceptual flash-lag hypothesis. *Journal of Sports Sciences, 24,* 521-528.

[351] Larkin, P., Mesagno, C., Berry, J., Spittle, M., & Harvey, J. (2018). Video-based training to improve perceptual-cognitive decision-making performance of Australian football umpires. *Journal of Sports Sciences, 36,* 239-246.

[352] Premier League. (2018b). Referees. https://www.premierleague.com/referees. Cited on 26/10/18 from the World Wide Web.

[353] Gilis, B., Helsen, W., Catteeuw, P., & Wagemans, J. (2008). Offside decisions by expert assistant referees in Association Football: Perception and recall of spatial positions in complex dynamic events. *Journal of Experimental Psychology, 14,* 21-35.

[354] Hill et al, 2010

[355] See Zinsser, N., Bunker, L., & Williams, J. M. (2010). Cognitive techniques for building confidence and enhancing performance. In J. M. Williams (Ed), *Applied Sport Psychology: Personal Growth to Peak Performance* (pp.305-335). New York: McGraw-Hill.

[356] Hardy, J., Gammage, K., & Hall, C. (2001). A descriptive study of athlete self-talk. *The Sport Psychologist, 15,* 306-318.

[357] Hanton, S., & Jones, G. (1999). The effects of a multimodel intervention program on performers: II. Training the butterflies to fly in formation. *The Sport Psychologist, 13,* 22-41.

[358] Thelwell, R., & Greenlee, I. (2003). Developing competitive endurance performance using mental skills training. *Sport Psychologist, 17,* 208-225.

[359] Tyler, J. M., & Burns, K. C. (2008). After depletion: The replenishment of the self's regulatory resources. *Self & Identity, 7,* 305-321.

[360] Samuel, 2015

361 Samuel, 2015

362 BBC Sport. (2018j). Amateur football referee attack is 'worst assault on a match on British soil'. https://www.bbc.co.uk/sport/football/44241748. Cited on 26/10/18 from the World Wide Web.

363 Wilson, J. (2018). Save our game: Referees seek talks with FA as abuse reports soar. *The Telegraph*, October 18th, 2018.

364 Morris, G., & O'Connor, D. (2017). Key attributes of expert NRL referees. *Journal of Sports Sciences, 35*, 852-857.

365 Kendall, C. (2018). Truthful & honest from referee Danny Guest: "We are normal guys...why shouldn't we have a voice!" http://thebootifulgame.co.uk/2018/10/24/truthful-honest-by-referee-danny-guest-we-are-normal-guys-why-shouldnt-we-have-a-voice/. Cited on 27/10/18 from the World Wide Web.

366 Parsons, T., & Bairner, A. (2015). You want the buzz of having done well in a game that wasn't easy: A sociological explanation of the job commitment of English football referees. *Movement & Sport Sciences, 87*, 41-52.

367 Jorm, A. F. (2000). Does old age reduce the risk of anxiety and depression? A review of epidemiological studies across the adult life span. *Psychological Medicine, 30*, 11-22.

368 Samuel, R. D. (2015). A psychological preparation framework for elite soccer referees: A practitioner's perspective. *Journal of Sport Psychology in Action, 0*, 1-18.

369 Slack, L. A., Maynard, I. W., Butt, J., & Olusoga, P. (2015). An evaluation of a mental toughness education training programme for early-career English Football League Referees. *The Sport Psychologist, 29*, 237-257.

370 BBC Sport. (2018k). Marvin Sordell calls for full-time counsellors in football clubs. https://www.bbc.co.uk/sport/football/45510063. Cited on 26/10/18 from the World Wide Web.

371 RefLIVE. (2018). How to recruit and retain more female officials: A Q&A with Sonia Denoncourt. www.reflive.com/blog/how-to-recruit-and-retain-more-female-officials/. Cited 11/10/18 from the World Wide Web.

372 MacMahon, C., Helsen, W. F., Starkes, J. L., & Weston, M. (2007). Decision-making skills and deliberate practice in elite association football referees. *Journal of Sports Sciences, 25*, 65-78.

373 Baker, J., Côté, J., & Abernethy, B. (2003). Sport-specific practice and the development of expert decision-making in team ball sports. *Journal of Applied Sport Psychology, 15*, 12-25.

374 Ziegler, M. (2018). Move to ban substitutions in injury time. *The Times*, October 26th, 2018.

375 Ziegler, M. (2019). FA to increase use of sin-bins. *The Times*, February 6th, 2019.

376 Staniforth, M. (2019). Was the referee right to award to award Manchester United's crucial penalty against PSG? https://www.independent.ie/sport/soccer/champions-league/was-the-referee-right-to-award-manchester-uniteds-crucial-penalty-against-psg-37890063.html. Cited on 08/03/19 from the World Wide Web.

377 Anderson, C., & Sally, D. (2014). *The Numbers Game: Why Everything You Know About Football is Wrong*. London: Penguin.

378 Statbunker (2019). Premier League 2018/19: Penalties awarded. https://www.statbunker.com/competitions/ForPenalty?comp_id=614. Cited on 18/03/19 from the World Wide Web.

379 BT Sport Films (2017). *Ref: Stories from the weekend*. First aired on April 4th, 2017.

380 FIFA TV (2012). *Match 64: The inside story of the 2010 Final*. https://www.youtube.com/watch?v=47yOv3MS20M. Cited on 25/06/18 from the World Wide Web.

381 Zeqiri, D. (2018). Fascinating video highlights the difficulties of being a top-flight referee – and the need for VAR. https://www.telegraph.co.uk/football/2018/08/27/fascinating-video-highlights-difficulties-top-flight-referee/. Cited on 16/09/18 from the World Wide Web.

382 Brown, A. (2018). SAIDS: Bodybuilding & rugby union report highest proportion of ADRVs. http://www.sportsintegrityinitiative.com/saids-bodybuliding-rugby-union-report-highest-proportion-of-adrvs/. Cited on 27/10/18 from the World Wide Web.

383 Souster, M. (2019). Dean Richards: England 'cheated at World Cup'. *The Times*, April 14th, 2019.

384 @officialpompeyw, 21st October, 2018

385 Holt, E. (2004). Tabloid campaign forces referee into hiding. *The Guardian*, June 30th, 2004.

386 Broadbent, R. (2018). Mason joins in the goal celebrations. *The Times*, December 10th, 2018.

387 Williams, B. (2018). The problem with chasing perfection. https://www.playersvoice.com.au/ben-williams-problem-with-chasing-perfection/. Cited on 16/11/18 from the World Wide Web.

388 Cleland, J., O'Gorman, J., & Webb, T. (2017). Respect? An investigation into the experience of referees in association football. *International Review for the Sociology of Sport*. https://doi.org/10.1177/1012690216687979

389 Fox Sports (2018). Referees planning on covering 'respect' logo on shirts after the FFA refused to sanction Mark Rudan. https://www.foxsports.com.au/football/a-league/referees-planning-on-covering-respect-logo-on-shirts-after-the-ffa-refused-to-sanction-mark-rudan/news-story/38ff1a9b59fbcf566a4f277083d21bba?nk=482e81dd80a0824e17a0f4ac8 42aaf25-1544800924. Cited on 14/12/18 from the World Wide Web.

390 Syed, M. (2018h). Why English football's reluctance to embrace 'idea sex' is stopping the game from evolving. *The Times*, April 2nd, 2018.

391 Burt, J. (2018). How Gareth Southgate fueled England's World Cup bid with inspiration from NBA, NFL and the All Blacks. *The Telegraph*, June 26th, 2018.

392 BBC News. (2018). Cricket Australia 'partly to blame' in ball-tampering scandal. https://www.bbc.co.uk/news/world-australia-46013631. Cited on 29/10/18 from the World Wide Web.

393 Leaders in Sport (2014). Tony Strudwick, Manchester United. *https://leadersinsport.com/performance/coaching-and-development/tony-strudwick-manchester-united/*. Cited on 28/01/19 from the World Wide Web.

[394] Anderson, C., & Sally, D. (2014). *The Numbers Game: Why Everything You Know About Football is Wrong*. London: Penguin.

[395] BBC Sport. (2019). Grassroots referees to meet with FA over abuse concerns. *https://www.bbc.co.uk/sport/football/46979726*. Cited on 04/02/19 from the World Wide Web.

[396] Lopez, J. A. (2019). There's a shortage of high school referees. Some feel parents are to blame. https://www.modbee.com/sports/high-school/article224522735.html. Cited on 04/09/19 from the World Wide Web.

[397] NASO. (2017). 17,487 officials had something to say. https://www.naso.org/survey/portfolio/sporting-behavior/. Cited on 04/02/19 from the World Wide Web.

[398] Sanghera, M. (2019). Liverpool v Man City: The psychology of a Premier League title race. https://www.bbc.co.uk/sport/football/47889242. Cited on 24/04/19 from the World Wide Web.

[399] Joyce, P. (2019b). Liverpool told their ballboys to hurry up. *The Times*, May 9th, 2019.

[400] Foy, C. (2019). Burnley right to be angry. *The Daily Mail*, February 4th, 2019.

[401] Laverty, R. (2019). Lewin Nyatanga: I know a lot of footballers who hate football. http://www.planetfootball.com/in-depth. Cited on 14/02/19 from the World Wide Web.

[402] Parks, T. (2003). *A Season with Verona: Travels Around Italy in Search of Illusion, National Character and Goals*. Vintage: London (p299).

[403] Hudson, M. (2019). Chelsea's Emma Hayes: Referee cost us Women's Champions League final place. *The Times*, April 29th, 2019.

[404] Wigmore, T. (2018). UK Sport ready to accept that success is about more than counting medals. https://inews.co.uk/sport/olympics/uk-sport-olympics-medal-count-mental-health-support-tokyo-2020/. Cited on 29/10/18 from the World Wide Web.

References

Abernathy, B. & Russell, D. G. (1987). Expert-novice differences in an applied selective attention task. *Journal of Sport Psychology, 9*, 326-345.

Abernathy, B. (1993). Attention. In R. N. Singer, M. Murphey, & L. K. Tennant (Eds.), *Handbook of research on sport psychology* (pp.127-170). New York: MacMillan.

Abrams, D., Randsley de Moura, G., & Travaglino, G. A. (2013). A double standard when group members behave badly: Transgression credit to ingroup leaders. *Journal of Personality & Social Psychology, 105*, 799-815.

Akawor, I. (2017). Stoke are difficult. https://www.aclsports.com/stoke-difficult-mourinho/. Cited on 10/07/19 from the World Wide Web.

Akerlof, G. A. (1997). Social distance and social decisions. Econometrica, 65, 1005-1027.

Arkelof G. A., & Kranton, R. E. (2000). Economics and identity. *The Quarterly Journal of Economics, 115*, 715-753.

Andersen, J. R. (1982). Acquisition of cognitive skill. *Psychological Review, 89*, 369-406.

Andersen, J. R. (1993). *Rules of the mind.* Hillsdale, NJ: Erlbaum.

Anderson, C., & Sally, D. (2014). The Numbers Game: Why Everything You Know About Football is Wrong. London: Penguin.

Anshel, M. H., & Weinberg, R. S. (1999). Re-examining coping among basketball referees following stressful events: Implications for coping interventions. *Journal of Sport Behaviour, 22*, 141-161.

Asch, S. E. (1955). Opinions and social pressure. *Scientific American, 5*, 31-35.

Austin, S. (2018). Darcy Norman: the next frontier is mindset. http://trainingground.guru/articles/darcy-norman-next-frontier-is-mindset. Cited on 13/10/18 from the World Wide Web.

Austin, S. (2019). Red2Blue: How to think like an All Black or a Gurkha. http://trainingground.guru/articles/red2blue-how-to-think-like-an-all-black-or-gurkha. Cited on 12/04/19 from the World Wide Web.

Baker, J., Côté, J., & Abernethy, B. (2003). Sport-specific practice and the development of expert decision-making in team ball sports. *Journal of Applied Sport Psychology, 15*, 12-25.

Balmer, N. J., Nevill, A. M., & Lane, A. M. (2005). Do judges enhance home advantage in European championship boxing? *Journal of Sports Sciences, 23*, 409-416.

Balmer, N. J., Nevill, A. M., & Williams, A. M. (2001). Home advantage in the Winter Olympics (1908-1998). *Journal of Sports Sciences, 19*, 129-139.

Barnard, P. (1968). Are we too tough on our referees? *Goal Magazine*, September 28th, 1968.

Bauman, N. J. (2016). The stigma of mental health in athletes: are mental toughness and mental health seen as contradictory in elite sport? *British Journal of Sports Medicine, 50*, 135-136.

BBC News. (2018). Cricket Australia 'partly to blame' in ball-tampering scandal. https://www.bbc.co.uk/news/world-australia-46013631. Cited on 29/10/18 from the World Wide Web.

BBC Sport. (2006). Ref Poll sent home from World Cup. http://news.bbc.co.uk/sport1/hi/football/world_cup_2006/5108722.stm. Cited on 11/06/18 from the World Wide Web.

BBC Sport. (2012b). Chelsea regret handling of Mark Clattenburg racism allegation. https://www.bbc.co.uk/sport/football/20507362. Cited on 30/07/18 from the World Wide Web.

BBC Sport. (2013). Mark Halsey fears an under-pressure official could take own life. https://www.bbc.co.uk/sport/football/24105438. Cited on 30/07/18 from the World Wide Web.

BBC Sport. (2015). Ricardo Moniz: Notts County boss says referee are 'arrogant'. https://www.bbc.co.uk/sport/football/34062441. Cited on 29/08/18 from the World Wide Web.

BBC Sport. (2018a). Mark Halsey: Former Premier League referee says player asked to be booked. https://www.bbc.co.uk/sport/football/44647718. Cited on 09/10/18 from the World Wide Web.

BBC Sport. (2018b). Neymar: PSG striker needs 'special treatment', says new boss Thomas Tuchel. https://www.bbc.co.uk/sport/football/44191348. Cited 25/05/18 from the World Wide Web.

BBC Sport. (2018c). Chelsea VAR controversy: Referee should have been told to watch video – Antonio Conte.

https://www.bbc.co.uk/sport/football/42727541. Cited on 27/06/18 from the World Wide Web.

BBC Sport. (2018d). Ellie Soutter death: Father criticises pressure on athletes. https://www.bbc.co.uk/news/uk-england-surrey-45023187. Cited on 31/07/18 from the World Wide Web.

BBC Sport. (2018e). Matt Cecchin: NRL referee quits over 'vile abuse and death threats'. https://www.bbc.co.uk/sport/rugby-league/45055588. Cited on 03/08/18 from the World Wide Web.

BBC Sport. (2018f). 'Bullets sent in post to three key figures at Italian Referees' Association'. https://www.bbc.co.uk/sport/football/43662117. Cited on 14/11/18 from the World Wide Web.

BBC Sport. (2018g). Being an amateur referee: your stories of threats and attacks, but a love of the game. https://www.bbc.co.uk/sport/football/46208857. Cited on 30/11/18 from the World Wide Web.

BBC Sport. (2018h). Amateur football referee attack is 'worst assault on a match on British soil'. https://www.bbc.co.uk/sport/football/44241748. Cited on 26/10/18 from the World Wide Web.

BBC Sport. (2018h). Russia 2018: What will happen if there is racist chanting during the World Cup? https://www.bbc.co.uk/sport/football/44405889. Cited on 07/06/18 from the World Wide Web.

BBC Sport. (2018i). Darren Ferguson: Doncaster boss fined £1,000 for 'shoot referees' comments. https://www.bbc.co.uk/sport/football/42887263. Cited on 22/08/18 from the World Wide Web.

BBC Sport. (2018j). Amateur football referee attack is 'worst assault on a match on British soil'. https://www.bbc.co.uk/sport/football/44241748. Cited on 26/10/18 from the World Wide Web.

BBC Sport. (2018k). Marvin Sordell calls for full-time counsellors in football clubs. https://www.bbc.co.uk/sport/football/45510063. Cited on 26/10/18 from the World Wide Web.

BBC Sport. (2019). Grassroots referees to meet with FA over abuse concerns. https://www.bbc.co.uk/sport/football/46979726. Cited on 04/02/19 from the World Wide Web.

Beilock, S. L., & Carr, T. H. (2001). On the fragility of skilled performance: What governs choking under pressure? *Journal of Experimental Psychology: General, 130*, 701-725.

Bense, K. (2018). 'It doesn't keep me up at night': Rory McIlroy says the hunt to win another major doesn't weigh on him. https://www.golf.com/tour-news/2018/07/05/rory-mcilroy-it-doesnt-keep-me-night-hunt-win-another-major-doesnt-weigh-him. Cited on 22/09/18 from the World Wide Web.

Bernstein, N.A. (1967). *The co-ordination and regulation of movements.* Oxford: Pergamon Press.

Biernat, M., & Vescio, T. K. (2002). She swings, she hits, she's great, she's benched: Implications of gender-based shifting standards for judgment and behaviour. *Personality & Social Psychology Bulletin, 28*, 66-77.

Bird, J. (2018). Why would anyone want to be a Sunday league referee? The love of the game. https://www.theguardian.com/football/2018/aug/30/sunday-league-referee-hackney-marshes-love-of-the-game. Cited on 30/08/18 from the World Wide Web.

Blascovich, J., & Mendes, W. B. (2000). Challenge and threat appraisals: The role of affective cues. In J. P. Forgas (ed), *Feeling and Thinking: The role of affect in social cognition* (pp.59-82). Paris: Cambridge University Press.

Boyko, R. H., Boyko, A. R., & Boyko, M. G. (2007). Referee bias contributes to home advantage in English Premiership football, *Journal of Sports Sciences, 25,* 1185-1194.

Brand, G. (2018). Referee myth-busting: How many decisions do officials get right? http://www.skysports.com/football/news/11096/10808860/referee-myth-busting-how-many-decisions-do-officials-get-right. Cited on 16/03/18 from the World Wide Web.

Brand, R. & Neß, W. (2004). Regelanwendung und Game-Management – Qualifizierende Merkmale von Schiedsrichtern in *Sportspielen. Zeitschrift für Sportpsychologie, 11(4)*, 127-136.

Broadbent, R. (2018). Mason joins in the goal celebrations. *The Times,* December 10th, 2018.

Brown, A. (2018). SAIDS: Bodybuilding & rugby union report highest proportion of ADRVs. http://www.sportsintegrityinitiative.com/saids-bodybuliding-rugby-union-report-highest-proportion-of-adrvs/. Cited on 27/10/18 from the World Wide Web.

Bruner, M. W., & Spink, K. S. (2010). Evaluating a team building intervention in a youth exercise setting. *Group Dynamics: Theory, Research & Practice, 14*, 304-317.

BT Sport (2016). Howard Webb on when to book a player. https://www.youtube.com/watch?v=nunux4SWk_E. Cited on 29/06/18 from the World Wide Web.

BT Sport Films (2017). *Ref: Stories from the weekend.* First aired on April 4th, 2017.

Buraimo, B., Forrest, D., & Simmons, R. (2010). The 12th Man?: Refereeing bias in English and German soccer. *Journal of the Royal Statistical Society: Series A, 173*, 431-449.

Burke, K. (2005). But Coach doesn't understand: Dealing with team communication quagmires. In M. B. Andersen (Ed.), *Sport Psychology in Practice* (pp.45-60). Leeds: Human Kinetics.

Burt, J. (2018). How Gareth Southgate fueled England's World Cup bid with inspiration from NBA, NFL and the All Blacks. *The Telegraph*, June 26th, 2018.

Chaiken, S. & Trope, Y. (1999). *Dual-process theories in social psychology.* New York, NY: Guilford Press.

Cleland, J., O'Gorman, J., & Webb, T. (2017). Respect? An investigation into the experience of referees in association football. International *Review for the Sociology of Sport*. https://doi.org/10.1177/1012690216687979

Cotterill, S., Sanders, R., & Collins, D. (2010). Developing effective pre-performance routines in golf: Why don't we ask the golfer? *Journal of Applied Sport Psychology, 22*, 51-64.

Coulomb-Cabagno, G., Rascle, O., & Souchon, N. (2005). Players' gender and male referees' decisions about aggression in French soccer: A preliminary study. *Sex Roles, 52,* 547-553.

Coulter, T. J., Mallett, C. J., & Gucciardi, D. F. (2010). Understanding mental toughness in Australian soccer: Perceptions of players, parents and coaches. *Journal of Sport Sciences, 28,* 699-716.

Cox, R. H. (1998). Sport Psychology: Concepts and Applications (4th Ed). New York: WCB/McGraw-Hill.

Curren, T., Hill, A. P., Hall, H. K., & Jowett, G. E. (2015). Relationships between the coach-created motivational climate and athlete engagement in youth sport. *Journal of Sport & Exercise Psychology, 37*, 193-198.

Da Silva, A. I., & Fernandez, R. (2003). Dehydration of football referees during a match. *British Journal of Sports Medicine, 37*, 502-506.

Davis, M. (2018). Sunday morning referee quits after alleged assault by player. http://www.bbc.co.uk/sport/football/43736236. Cited on 25/04/18 from the World Wide Web.

Delaney, M. (2018). Unai Emery accuses referee of Real Madrid bias after PSG's last-16 first-leg defeat. *The Independent*, February 14th, 2018.

Dixon, M. & Turner, M. J. (2018). Stress appraisals of UK soccer academy coaches: an interpretive phenomenological analysis. *Qualitative Research in Sport, Exercise and Health, 10*, 620-634.

Dohmen, T. J. (2008). The influence of social forces: Evidence from the behaviour of football referees. *Economic Inquiry, 46*, 411-424.

Dryden, W. & DiGiuseppe, R. (1990). *A primer on rational-emotive behaviour therapy*. West Sussex: Wiley.

Dryden, W. (2012). The 'ABCs' of REBT I: A preliminary study of errors and confusions in counselling and psychotherapy textbooks. *Journal of Rational-Emotive and Cognitive-Behaviour Therapy, 30*, 133-172.

Dryden, W., & Branch, R. (2008). The fundamentals of rational-emotive behavioural therapy. West Sussex: Wiley.

Duda, J. L. (2001). Goal perspective research in sport: Pushing the boundaries and clarifying some misunderstandings. In G. C. Roberts (Ed.), *Advances in motivation in sport and exercise* (pp.129-182). Champaign, IL; Human Kinetics.

Duda, J. L., & Treasure, D. C. (2010). Motivational processes and the facilitation of quality engagement in sport. In J. M. Williams (Ed.) *Applied Sport Psychology: Personal Growth to Peak Performance* (pp.267-304). London: McGraw-Hill.

Easterbrook, J. A. (1959). The effect of emotion on cue utilisation and the organisation of behaviour. *Psychological Review, 66*, 183-201.

Ellis, A. (1994). The sport of avoiding sports and exercise: A rational emotive behaviour therapy perspective. *The Sport Psychologist, 8*, 248-261.

Ellis, A., Gordon, J., Neenan, M., & Palmer, S. (1997). *Stress counselling: A rational emotive behaviour approach*. London: Cassell.

Ellis, J. (2009). David Elleray. http://metro.co.uk/2009/10/27/david-elleray-3423877/. Cited on 30/04/18 from the World Wide Web.

Endler, N. S. (1978). The interaction model of anxiety: Some possible implications. In D. M. Landers & R. W. Christina (Eds.), *Psychology of motor behaviour in sport – 1977* (pp.332-351). Champaign, IL: Human Kinetics.

Endler, N. S. (1996). Stress, anxiety and coping: The multidimensional interaction model. *Canadian Psychology, 38*, 136-153.

Ericsson, K. A., Krampe, R. Th., & Tesch-Romer, C. (1993). The role of deliberate practice in the acquisition of expert performance. *Psychological Review, 100*, 363-406.

ESPN. (2018). Referee suspended, apologies for tripping Nantes player in PSG game. http://www.espn.co.uk/football/nantes/story/3349068/referee-suspended-apologises-for-tripping-nantes-player-in-psg-game. Cited on 11/10/18 from the World Wide Web.

Eurosport. (2014). Thierry Henry retires: Why France will never love its record scorer. https://www.eurosport.com/football/thierry-henry-retires-why-france-will-never-love-its-record-scorer_sto4718482/story.shtml. Cited on 21/09/18 from the World Wide Web.

FIFA TV (2012). *Match 64: The inside story of the 2010 Final.* https://www.youtube.com/watch?v=47yOv3MS20M. Cited on 25/06/18 from the World Wide Web.

Fifield, D. (2010). World Cup final: Howard Webb's dream job descends into nightmare. https://www.theguardian.com/football/2010/jul/12/howard-webb-final-nightmare-yellow-cards. Cited on 29/06/18 from the World Wide Web.

Fifield, D. (2015). Jose Mourinho: referee was 'weak and naïve' in Chelsea's draw at Dynamo Kyiv. https://www.theguardian.com/football/2015/oct/20/dynamo-kyiv-chelsea-champions-league-match-report. Cited on 06/06/18 from the World Wide Web.

Findlay, L. C., & Ste-Marie, D. M. A. (2004). Reputation bias in figure skating judging. *Journal of Sport & Exercise Psychology, 26*, 154-166.

Fischer, A. H., Manstead, A. S. R., Evers, C., Timmers, M., & Valk, G. (2004). Motives and norms underlying emotion regulation. In P. Philoppot & R. S. Feldman (Eds.), *The regulation of emotion* (pp.187-210). Mahwah, NJ: Lawrence Erlbaum.

Fiske, S. T., & Taylor, S. E. (1991). *Social cognition*. Reading, MA: Addison-Wesley.

Fiske, S. T., Neuberg, S. L., Beattie, A. E., & Milberg, S. J. (1987). Category-based and attribute-based reactions to others: Some informational conditions of stereotyping and individuating processes. *Journal of Experimental Social Psychology, 23*, 399-427.

Fitts, P. M., & Posner, M. I. (1967). *Human Performance*. Belmont: Brooks/Cole.

Folkesson, P., Nyberg, C., Archer, T., & Norlander, T. (2002). Soccer referees' experience of threat and aggression: Effects of age, experience, and life orientation on outcome of coping strategy. *Aggressive Behaviour, 28*, 317-327.

Football Association, The. (2012). Respect – Four Years On. www.thefa.com/News/my-football/2012/jul/four-years-on.aspx. Cited on 11/12/12 from the World Wide Web.

Football Association, The. (2018). Law 5: The Referee. www.thefa.com/football-rules-governance/lawsandrules. Cited on 16/03/18 from the World Wide Web.

Foster, D. J., Weigand, D. A., & Baines, D. (2006). The effect of removing superstitious behaviour and introducing pre-performance routine on basketball free-throw performance. *Journal of Applied Sport Psychology, 18*, 167-171.

FourFourTwo Australia (2016). How important is the 12th man? January 1st, 2016.

Fox Sports (2018). Referees planning on covering 'respect' logo on shirts after the FFA refused to sanction Mark Rudan. https://www.foxsports.com.au/football/a-league/referees-planning-on-covering-respect-logo-on-shirts-after-the-ffa-refused-to-sanction-mark-rudan/news-story/38ff1a9b59fbcf566a4f277083d21bba?nk=482e81dd80a0824e17a0f4ac842aaf25-1544800924. Cited on 14/12/18 from the World Wide Web.

Foy, C. (2019). Burnley right to be angry. *The Daily Mail*, February 4th, 2019.

Fraser, S. (2018). Johanna Konta delivers angry outburst and storms off after defeat in Nottingham final. https://www.thetimes.co.uk/article/johanna-konta-delivers-angry-outburst-and-storms-off-after-defeat-in-nottingham-final-8ll8tgl30. Cited on 18/06/18 from the World Wide Web.

Fuller, C. W., Junge, A., & Dvorak, J. (2004): An assessment of football referees' decisions in incidents leading to player injuries. *The American Journal of Sports Medicine, 32*, 17-22.

Gaoua, N., de Oliveira, R. F., & Hunter, S. (2017). Perception, action, and cognition of football referees in extreme temperatures: Impact on decision performance. *Frontiers in Psychology, 8*, 1-7.

Gibson, J. L., & Gore, J. S. (2016). Is he a hero or a weirdo? How norm violations influence the Halo Effect. *Gender Issues, 33*, 299-310.

Gilis, B., Helsen, W., Catteeuw, P., & Wagemans, J. (2008). Offside decisions by expert assistant referees in Association Football: Perception and recall of spatial positions in complex dynamic events. *Journal of Experimental Psychology, 14*, 21-35.

Gladwell, M. (2009). *Outliers: The story of success*. London: Penguin.

Gleeson, S., & Brady, E. (2017). When athletes share their battles with mental illness. https://eu.usatoday.com/story/sports/2017/08/30/michael-phelps-brandon-marshall-mental-health-battles-royce-white-jerry-west/596857001/. Cited on 06/08/18 from the World Wide Web.

Gohm, C. L. (2003). Mood regulation and emotional intelligence: Individual differences. *Journal of Personality & Social Psychology, 84*, 594-607.

Goldfried, M. R., & Sobocinski, D. (1975:p.509). Effect of irrational beliefs on emotional arousal. *Journal of Consulting & Clinical Psychology, 43*, 504-510.

Gould, D., & Udry, E. (1994). Psychological skills for enhancing performance: Arousal regulation strategies. *Medicine & Science in Sport & Exercise, 26*, 478-485.

Goumas, C. (2014). Home advantage and referee bias in European football. *European Journal of Sports Science, 14*, 243-249.

Greenwald, A. G., McGhee, D. E., & Schwartz, J. L. K. (1998). Measuring Individual Differences in Implicit Cognition: The Implicit Association Test. *Journal of Personality & Social Psychology, 34*, 1464-1480.

Gross, J. J. & Thompson, R. A. (2007). Emotion Regulation: Conceptual Foundations. In J. J. Gross (Ed.*), Handbook of Emotion Regulation* (pp.3-24). New York: Guilford Press.

Guardian, The. (2018). Manchester City fended off a brief West Ham revival to win 4-1 at the London Stadium and continue David Moyes's relegation concerns. https://www.theguardian.com/football/live/2018/apr/29/west-ham-v-manchester-city-premier-league-live. Cited on 30/04/18 from the World Wide Web.

Guillen, F., & Feltz, D. (2011). A conceptual model of referee efficacy. *Frontiers in Psychology, 2*, 1-5.

Hackett, K. (2018a). Referees – Being confident not arrogant earns respect. https://www.soccertoday.com/referees-being-confident-not-arrogant-earns-respect/. Cited on 09/10/18 from the World Wide Web.

Hackett, K. (2018b). Referees need to display presence. https://www.soccertoday.com/referees-need-to-display-presence/. Cited on 23/12/18 from the World Wide Web.

Hackett, K. (2018c). It looked like chaos on the Stamford Bridge touchline, but officials were ready for incident to kick off. *The Telegraph*, October 21st, 2018.

Hackett, K. (2019). Card-happy Mike Dean should try a quiet word rather than going to war with misbehaving players. https://www.telegraph.co.uk/football/2019/02/04/card-happy-mike-dean-should-try-quiet-word-rather-going-war/. Cited on 06/02/19 from the World Wide Web.

Hagemann, N., Strauss, B., & Leißing, J. (2008). When the referee sees red... *Psychological Science, 19*, 769- 771.

Hanin, Y. L. (Ed., 2000). *Emotions in sport*. Champaign, IL: Human Kinetics.

Hanton, S., & Jones, G. (1999). The effects of a multimodel intervention program on performers: II. Training the butterflies to fly in formation. *The Sport Psychologist, 13*, 22-41.

Hardy, J., Gammage, K., & Hall, C. (2001). A descriptive study of athlete self-talk. *The Sport Psychologist, 15*, 306-318.

Haselton, M. G., & Nettle, D. The paranoid optimist: An integrative evolutionary model of cognitive biases. *Personality & Social Psychology Review, 10*, 47-66.

Helsen, W. F., Gilis, B., & Weston, M. (2006). Errors in judging "offside" in association football: Test of the optical error versus the perceptual flash-lag hypothesis. *Journal of Sports Sciences, 24*, 521-528.

Hermansson, G., & Hodge, K. (2012:p.128). Uncontrollable outcomes: Managing expectations at the Olympics. *Journal of Sport Psychology in Action, 3*, 127-138.

Hill, D. M., Hanton, S., Matthews, N., & Fleming, S. (2010). A qualitative exploration of choking in elite golf. *Journal of Clinical Sport Psychology, 4*, 221-240.

Hodges, N. J. & Starkes, J. L. (1996). Wrestling with the nature of expertise: a sport specific test of Ericsson, Krampe, and Tesch-Römer's (1993) theory of deliberate practice. *International Journal of Sport Psychology, 27*, 400-424.

Holt, E. (2004). Tabloid campaign forces referee into hiding. *The Guardian*, June 30th, 2004.

Horrocks, D. E., McKenna, J., Whitehead, A. E., Taylor, P. J., Morley, A. M., & Lawrence, I. (2016). Preparation, structured deliberate practice and decision making in elite level football: The case study of Gary Neville (Manchester United FC and England). *International Journal of Sports Science & Coaching, 11*, 673-682.

Hudson, M. (2019). Chelsea's Emma Hayes: Referee cost us Women's Champions League final place. *The Times*, April 29th, 2019.

Hull, C. L. (1943). *Principles of behaviour*. New York: Appleton Century.

Hunt, S. (2017). 'He's probably the most arrogant man I've met on a football pitch': Stephen Hunt on Premier League referee Mike Dean. https://www.independent.ie/sport/soccer/premier-league/hes-probably-the-most-arrogant-man-ive-met-on-a-football-pitch-stephen-hunt-on-premier-league-referee-mike-dean-35333847.html. Cited on 29/08/18 from the World Wide Web.

Hytner, D. (2018). Chris Kirkland: 'I didn't want to wake up in the morning. It just starts again.' *The Guardian*, October 11th, 2017.

Idessane, K. (2018). Scottish referees: 'Abuse culture' needs to stop, says John Mckendrick. https://www.bbc.co.uk/sport/football/46513470. Cited on 12/12/18 from the World Wide Web.

ITV (2006). *The Truth About Referees*. First aired March 7th, 2006.

Jacob, G. (2018). Rule change allows managers to watch TV replays during matches. https://www.thetimes.co.uk/article/rule-change-allows-managers-to-watch-tv-replays-during-matches-b8sxh036s. Cited on 02/08/18 from the World Wide Web.

Jacobs, J. E., & Eccles, J. S. (1992). The impact of mothers' gender-role stereotypic beliefs on mothers' and children's ability perceptions. *Journal of Personality & Social Psychology, 63*, 932-944.

Jamieson, J. P. (2010). The home field advantage in athletics: A meta-analysis. *Journal of Applied Social Psychology, 40*, 1819-1848.

Johansen, B. T. (2015). Reasons for officiating soccer: the role of passion-based motivations among Norwegian elite and non-elite referees. *Movement & Sport Sciences, 87*, 23-30.

Jones, M. V., Paull, G. C., & Erskine, J. (2002). The impact of a team's aggressive reputation on the decision of association football referees. *Journal of Sports Science, 20*, 991-1000.

Jordet, G. (2009). When superstars flop: Public status and choking under pressure in international soccer penalty shootouts. *Journal of Applied Sport Psychology, 21*, 125-130.

Jorm, A. F. (2000). Does old age reduce the risk of anxiety and depression? A review of epidemiological studies across the adult life span. *Psychological Medicine, 30*, 11-22.

Joyce, P. (2019a). Klopp facing charge over claim of referee bias. *The Times*, February 6th, 2019.

Joyce, P. (2019b). Liverpool told their ballboys to hurry up. *The Times*, May 9th, 2019.

Kahneman, D. (1973). *Attention and effort*. Englewood Cliffs, NJ: Prentice Hall.

Kay, O. (2019). No wonder referees live in fear when players' abuse goes unpunished. *The Times*, February 9th, 2019.

Kaya, A. (2014). Decision making by coaches and athletes in sport. *Social & Behavioural Sciences, 152*, 333-338.

Kelner, M. (2018). Danny Rose open up about depression after tragedy and tough year at Spurs. *The Guardian*, June 6th, 2018.

Kelso, P. (2013). West Ham manager Sam Allardyce charged by FA over comments after Manchester United defeat. https://www.telegraph.co.uk/sport/football/teams/west-ham/9812243/West-Ham-manager-Sam-Allardyce-charged-by-FA-over-comments-after-Manchester-United-defeat.html. Cited on 02/09/18 from the World Wide Web.

Kendall, C. (2018). Truthful & honest from referee Danny Guest: "We are normal guys…why shouldn't we have a voice!" http://thebootifulgame.co.uk/2018/10/24/truthful-honest-by-referee-danny-guest-we-are-normal-guys-why-shouldnt-we-have-a-voice/. Cited on 27/10/18 from the World Wide Web.

Kuper, S. & Szymanski, S. (2009). Why England Lose & Other Curious Football Phenomena Explained. London: Harper Collins.

Lam, S. S. K., & Schaubroeck, J. (2000). Improving group decisions by better pooling information: A comparative advantage of group decision support systems. *Journal of Applied Psychology, 85*, 565-573.

Landin, D. (1994). The role of verbal cues in skill learning. *Quest, 46*, 299-313 (p299).

Lane, A. M., Beedie, C. J., Jones, M. V., Uphill, M., & Devonport, T. J. (2012). The BASES expert statement on emotion regulation in sport. *Journal of Sports Sciences, 30*, 1189-1195.

Larkin, P., Mesagno, C., Berry, J., Spittle, M., & Harvey, J. (2018). Video-based training to improve perceptual-cognitive decision-making performance of Australian football umpires. *Journal of Sports Sciences, 36*, 239-246.

Laverty, R. (2019). Lewin Nyatanga: I know a lot of footballers who hate football. http://www.planetfootball.com/in-depth. Cited on 14/02/19 from the World Wide Web.

Law, M. (2015). Leicester City news: Nigel Pearson blasts referee Mike Dean as 'arrogant' after penalty decision. https://www.telegraph.co.uk/sport/football/teams/leicester-city/11487920/Leicester-City-news-Nigel-Pearson-blasts-referee-Mike-Dean-as-arrogant-after-penalty-decision.html. Cited on 06/06/18 from the World Wide Web.

Lazarus, R. S. (1993). From psychological stress to the emotions: A history of changing outlooks. *Annual Review of Psychology, 44*, 1-21.

Lazarus, R. S. (1999). *Stress and emotion: A new synthesis*. London: Free Association.

Lazarus, R. S. (2000). How emotions influence performance in competitive sports. *The Sport Psychologist, 14*, 229-252.

Lazarus, R.S. & Folkman, S. (1984). *Stress, appraisal, and coping*. New York: Springer.

Leaders in Sport (2014). Tony Strudwick, Manchester United. https://leadersinsport.com/performance/coaching-and-development/tony-strudwick-manchester-united/. Cited on 28/01/19 from the World Wide Web.

Lex, H., Pizzera, A., Kurtes, M., & Schack, T. (2014). Influence of players' vocalisations on soccer referees' decisions. *European Journal of Sport Science, 5*, 424-428.

Lidor, R., & Mayan, Z. (2005). Can beginning learners benefit from pre-performance routines when serving in volleyball? *The Sport Psychologist, 19*, 343-363.

Loftus, E. F. & Palmer, J. C. (1974). Reconstruction of automobile destruction: An example of the interaction between language and memory. *Journal of verbal learning and verbal behaviour, 13*, 585-589.

Lopez, J. A. (2019). There's a shortage of high school referees. Some feel parents are to blame. https://www.modbee.com/sports/high-school/article224522735.html. Cited on 04/09/19 from the World Wide Web.

MacInnes, P. (2016). West Ham feeling far from home after London Stadium teething problems. *The Guardian*, September 11th, 2016.

MacMahon, C. & Mildenhall, B. (2012). A practical perspective on decision making influences in sports officiating. *International Journal of Sports Science & Coaching, 7*, 153-165.

MacMahon, C., Helsen, W. F., Starkes, J. L., & Weston, M. (2007). Decision-making skills and deliberate practice in elite association football referees. *Journal of Sports Sciences, 25,* 65-78.

Magee, W. (2018). 'Why do you want more time?' Fourth official could not believe Arsene Wenger wanted no end to League Cup suffering. *The Telegraph,* February 25th, 2018.

Mallo, J., Futos, P. G., Juárez, D., & Navarro, E. (2012). Effect of positioning on the accuracy of association football top-class referees and assistant referees during competitive matches. *Journal of Sports Sciences, 30,* 1437-1445.

Mann, D. T. Y., Williams, A. M., Ward, P., & Janelle, C. M. (2007). Perceptual-cognitive expertise in sport: A meta-analysis. *Journal of Sport & Exercise Psychology, 29,* 457-478.

Masters, R. S. W., Lo, C. Y., Maxwell, J. P., & Patil, N. G. (2008). Implicit motor learning in surgery: Implications for multi-tasking. *Surgery, 14,* 140-145

Masters, R. S. W., Poolton, J. M., & Maxwell, J. P. (2008). Stable implicit motor processes despite aerobic locomotor fatigue. *Consciousness and Cognition, 17,* 335-338

McClelland, D. C., Atkinson, J. W., Clark, R. W., & Lowell, E. L. (1953). *The achievement motive.* New York: Appleton-Century-Crofts.

McFee, G. (2013). Officiating in aesthetic sports. *Journal of the Philosophy of Sport, 40,* 1-17.

Mellick, M. C., Fleming, S., Bull, P., & Laugharne, E. J. (2005). Identifying best practice for referee decision communication in association and rugby union football. *Football Studies, 8,* 42-57.

Men in Blazers. (2017). Mark Clattenburg podcast special. https://soundcloud.com/meninblazers/men-in-blazers-120117-mark-clattenburg-pod-special. Cited on 24/08/18 from the World Wide Web.

Metro News (2018). Manchester United fans demand Pep Guardiola ban following Jose Mourinho's suspension for kicking water bottle. https://metro.co.uk/2018/02/20/manchester-united-fans-demand-pep-guardiola-ban-following-jose-mourinhos-suspension-kicking-water-bottle-7326556/. Cited 18/05/18 from the World Wide Web.

Moore, L. J., Harris, D. J., Sharpe, B. T., Vine, S. J., & Wilson, M. R. (2019). Perceptual-cognitive expertise when refereeing the scrum in rugby union. *Journal of Sports Sciences,* 1-9.

Moran, A. P. (1996). The psychology of concentration in sports performers: A cognitive analysis. Hove: Psychology Press.

Morris, G., & O'Connor, D. (2017). Key attributes of expert NRL referees. *Journal of Sports Sciences, 35,* 852-857.

Moskowitz, G. B. & Carter, D. (2018). Confirmation bias and the stereotype of the black athlete. *Psychology of Sport & Exercise, 36,* 139-146.

Nakrani, S. (2019). Paul Pogba's 'pace and power' stresses need for rethink over BAME coverage. *The Guardian,* January 21st, 2019.

NASO. (2017). 17,487 officials had something to say. https://www.naso.org/survey/portfolio/sporting-behavior/. Cited on 04/02/19 from the World Wide Web.

Neil, R., Bayston, P., Hanton, S., & Wilson, K. (2013). The influence of stress and emotions on association football referees' decision-making. *Sport & Exercise Psychology Review, 9,* 22-41.

Nevill, A. M., Balmer, N. J., & Williams, A. M. (2002). The influence of crowd noise and experience upon refereeing decisions in football. *Psychology of Sport & Exercise, 3,* 261-272.

New Zealand Institute of Health & Fitness (2018). Personal Training Attribution Theory. https://nzihf.ac.nz/personal-training/attribution-theory/. Cited on 04/05/18 from the World Wide Web.

Nicholls, J. (1989). *The competitive ethos and democratic education.* Cambridge, MA: Harvard University Press.

Nideffer, R. N. (1981). The ethics and practice of applied sport psychology. Ithaca, NY: Mouvement.

Nideffer, R. N. (1993). Attention control training. In R. N. Singer, M. Murphey, & L. K. Tennant (Eds.), *Handbook of research on sport psychology* (pp.542-556). New York: MacMillan.

Ogden, J. (2010). The Psychology of Eating: From Health to Disordered Behaviour (2nd Ed). New Jersey: Wiley-Blakwell.

Page, K., & Page, L. (2010). Alone against the crowd: Individual differences in referees' ability to cope under pressure. *Journal of Economic Psychology, 31,* 192-199.

Palmer, K. (2018). Exclusive: Former referee accuses Anthony Taylor of 'weakness' after FA Cup chaos at Wigan. www.uk.sports.yahoo.com/news. Cited on 26/03/18 from the World Wide Web.

Papineau, D. (2017). Knowing the Score: How sport teaches us about philosophy (and philosophy about sport). London: Constable.

Parks, T. (2003). A Season with Verona: Travels Around Italy in Search of Illusion, National Character and Goals. London: Vintage.

Parsons, T., & Bairner, A. (2015). You want the buzz of having done well in a game that wasn't easy: A sociological explanation of the job commitment of English football referees. *Movement & Sport Sciences, 87,* 41-52.

Peach, S. (2014). Kelvin Davis defends Adam Lallana over Mark Clattenburg referee complaint. https://www.independent.co.uk/sport/football/premier-league/kelvin-davis-defends-adam-lallana-over-mark-clattenburg-referee-complaint-9052748.html. Cited on 08/12/18 from the World Wide Web.

Phillipe, F. L., Vallerand, R. J., Andrianarisoa, J., & Brunel, P. (2009). Passion in referees: Examining their affective and cognitive experiences in sport situations. *Journal of Sport & Exercise Psychology, 31,* 77-96.

Pinker, S. (1999). *How the Mind Works.* London: Penguin.

Pitchford, A. (2005). Referee training & development in England: A report for The Football Association. Unpublished MSc thesis, Gloucester: University of Gloucestershire.

Plessner, H. & Betsch, T. (2001). Sequential effects in important referee decisions: The case of penalties in soccer. *Journal of Sport & Exercise Psychology, 23,* 254-259.

Plessner, H. & Haar, T. (2006). Sports performance judgments from a social cognitive perspective. *Psychology of Sport & Exercise, 7,* 555-575.

Plessner, H. (1999). Expectation biases in gymnastics judging. *Journal of Sport & Exercise Psychology, 21,* 131-144.

Pollard, R. (2006). Worldwide regional variations in home advantage in association football. *Journal of Sports Sciences, 24,* 231-240.

Poolton, J. M., Masters, R. S. W., & Maxwell, J. P. (2007). Passing thoughts on the evolutionary stability of implicit motor behaviour: Performance retention under physiological fatigue. *Consciousness and Cognition, 16,* 456-468.

Premier League. (2018a). Oliver: Refs must match players for fitness. https://www.premierleague.com/news/800434. Cited on 22/08/18 from the World Wide Web.

Premier League. (2018b). Referees. https://www.premierleague.com/referees. Cited on 26/10/18 from the World Wide Web.

Prenderville, L. (2018). Graham Poll hails Michael Oliver's "courage" over Real Madrid penalty – 'it's a pity he isn't going to the World Cup'. *The Mirror*, April 12th, 2018.

Pritchard, C. (2012). Fergie time: Does it really exist? www.bbc.co.uk/news/magazine-20464371. Cited on 28/02/18 from the World Wide Web.

PsychRef. (2019). The referee as game-manager. http://www.psychref.org/2018/01/the-referee-as-game-manager.html. Cited on 06/02/19 from the World Wide Web.

Rada, J. (1996). Color blind-sided: Racial bias in network television's coverage of professional football games. *The Howard Journal of Communications, 7*, 231-240.

Raghunathan, R., & Pham, M. T. (1999). All negative moods are not equal: Motivational influences of anxiety and sadness on decision making. *Organisational Behaviour & Human Decision Processes, 79*, 56-77.

Ready to Go (2010). Owen Coyle – f**king nob. https://www.readytogo.net/smb/threads/owen-coyle-f-ing-nob.550109/. Cited on 14/05/18 from the World Wide Web.

Rees, P. (2018). Dan Carter: 'Seeing a psychologist allowed me to confront my demons'. *The Observer,* June 10th, 2018.

Referees' Association. (2012a). Background and Formation. www.refereesassociation.co.uk/index.asp?page=become-a-referee. Cited 08/08/18 from the World Wide Web.

Referees' Association. (2012b). Background and Formation. www.refereesassociation.co.uk/index.asp?page=ra-history. Cited 08/08/18 from the World Wide Web.

RefLIVE. (2018). How to recruit and retain more female officials: A Q&A with Sonia Denoncourt. www.reflive.com/blog/how-to-recruit-and-retain-more-female-officials/. Cited 11/10/18 from the World Wide Web.

Rejer, P. (2018). Geiger deserves much praise. https://theref.online/paul-rejer-geiger-deserves-much-praise/. Cited on 25/07/18 from the World Wide Web.

Riedl, D., Strauss, B., Heuer, A., & Rubner, O. (2015). Finale furioso: referee-biased injury times and their effects on home advantage in football. *Journal of Sports Sciences, 33*, 327-336.

Roan, D. (2018). How big a problem is football facing? And what is being done? https://www.bbc.co.uk/sport/football/45135228. Cited on 10/08/18 from the World Wide Web.

Roohafza, H. R., Afshar, H., Keshteli, A. H., Mohammadi, N., Feizi, A., Taslimi, M., & Adibi, P. (2014). What's the role of perceived social support and coping styles in depression and anxiety? *Journal of Research in Medical Sciences, 19*, 944-949.

Rudd, A. (2018). Clinical Manchester City leave West Ham in trouble. *The Times*, April 30th, 2018.

Runciman, D. (2008). Home sweet home? *The Guardian*, February 3rd, 2008.

Samuel, R. D. (2015). A psychological preparation framework for elite soccer referees: A practitioner's perspective. *Journal of Sport Psychology in Action, 0*, 1-18.

Samuel, R. D., Englert, C., Zhang, Q., & Basevitch, I. (2018). Hi ref, are you in control? Self-control, ego-depletion, and performance in soccer referees. *Psychology of Sport & Exercise, 38*, 167-175.

Sanghera, M. (2019). Liverpool v Man City: The psychology of a Premier League title race. https://www.bbc.co.uk/sport/football/47889242. Cited on 24/04/19 from the World Wide Web.

Schmidt, R. A. (2003). Motor Schema Theory after 27 years: Reflections and implications for a new theory. *Research Quarterly for Exercise and Sport, 74*, 366-375.

Schwarz, N., & Bless, H. (1992). Constructing realities and its alternatives: Assimilation and contrast effects in social judgment. In L. L. Martin & A. Tesser (Eds.), *The Construction of Social Judgment* (pp.217-245). Hillsdale, NJ: Erlbaum.

Seyle, H. (1950). *Stress*. Montreal: Acta.

Sharpe, J. (2017). How good a signing is Harry Maguire for Leicester City? https://www.hinckleytimes.net/sport/football/how-good-signing-harry-maguire-13194288. Cited on 23/05/18 from the World Wide Web.

Sheldon, W. H. (1954). Atlas of Men: A Guide for Somatotyping the Male at All Ages. New York: Harper.

Sky Sports (2017a). Remembering Sergio Aguero's Man City title-winning goal, five years on. www.skysports.com/football/news/11679/10871583. Cited on 28/2/18 from the World Wide Web.

Sky Sports (2017b). *The Referees: Onside with Carragher & Neville*. First aired 7th April, 2017.

Sky Sports (2017c). Clattenburg: I let Spurs self-destruct against Chelsea at Stamford Bridge in 2016. http://www.skysports.com/football/news/11661/11156272/mark-clattenburg-let-tottenham-self-destruct-against-chelsea-at-stamford-bridge-in-2016. Cited on 04/12/17 from the World Wide Web.

Sky Sports (2017d). Mark Clattenburg game-plan comments are 'nonsense', says Dermot Gallagher. http://www.skysports.com/football/news/11095/11157862/mark-clattenburg-game-plan-comments-are-nonsense-says-dermot-gallagher. Cited on 06/12/17 from the World Wide Web.

Sky Sports (2018a). Ref Watch: Dermot Gallagher's verdict on Tottenham's penalties. www.skysports.com/football/news/11661. Cited on 16/2/18 from the World Wide Web.

Sky Sports (2018b). Bournemouth v Everton live. www.skysports.com/football/bmouth-vs-everton/live/390778. Cited on 25/08/18.

Sky Sports (2018c). Pierluigi Collina says World Cup VAR has proved successful. http://www.skysports.com/football/news/12098/11421135/pierluigi-collina-says-world-cup-var-has-proved-successful. Cited on 13/08/18 from the World Wide Web.

Sky Sports (2019). Hugo Lloris says Tottenham must win remaining Premier League games in top-four bid. https://www.skysports.com/football/news/11675/11661639/hugo-lloris-says-tottenham-must-win-remaining-premier-league-games-in-top-four-bid. Cited on 13/05/19 from the World Wide Web.

Slack, L. A., Maynard, I. W., Butt, J. & Olusoga, P. (2013). Factors underpinning football officiating excellence: Perceptions of English football referees. *Journal of Applied Sport Psychology, 25*, 298-315.

Slack, L. A., Maynard, I. W., Butt, J., & Olusoga, P. (2015). An evaluation of a mental toughness education training programme for early-career English Football League Referees. *The Sport Psychologist, 29*, 237-257.

Slater, M. J., Haslam, S. A., & Steffens, N. K. (2018). Singing it for "us": Team passion displayed during national anthems is associated with subsequent success. *European Journal of Sport Science, 18*, 541-549.

Souster, M. (2019). Dean Richards: England 'cheated at World Cup'. The Times, April 14th, 2019.

Spence, J. T., & Spence, K. W. (1966). The motivational components of manifest anxiety: Drive and drive stimuli. In C. D. Spielberger (Ed.), *Anxiety and Behaviour* (pp.291-326). New York: Academic Press.

Sports Law Scotland. (2018). A look at the relationship between referees and governing bodies. http://www.sportslawscotland.co.uk/2018/11/referees-appointment-management-and.html#.XAmMyWZ1TIU. Cited on 06/12/18 from the World Wide Web.

Staffieri, J. R. (1967). A study of social stereotype of body image in children. *Journal of Personality and Social Psychology, 7*, 101-104.

Staniforth, M. (2019). Was the referee right to award to award Manchester United's crucial penalty against PSG? https://www.independent.ie/sport/soccer/champions-league/was-the-referee-right-to-award-manchester-uniteds-crucial-penalty-against-psg-37890063.html. Cited on 08/03/19 from the World Wide Web.

Stapel, D. A., & Winkielman, P. (1998). Assimilation and contrast as a function of context-target similarity, distinctness, and dimensional relevance. *Personality & Social Psychology Bulletin, 24*, 634-646.

Stasser, G., & Titus, W. (1985). Pooling of unshared information in group decision making: Biased information sampling during discussion. *Journal of Personality and Social Psychology, 48*, 1467-1478.

Stasser, G., & Titus, W. (1987). Effects of information load and percentage of shared information on the dissemination of unshared information during group discussion. *Journal of Personality and Social Psychology, 53*, 81-93.

Statbunker (2019). Premier League 2018/19: Penalties awarded. https://www.statbunker.com/competitions/ForPenalty?comp_id=614 . Cited on 18/03/19 from the World Wide Web.

Steinberg, J. (2016). Nine decades of memories of Upton Park as West Ham prepare to depart. *The Guardian*, May 7th, 2016.

Steinfeldt, J. A., Foltz, B. D., Mungro, J., Speight, Q. L., Wong, Y. J., & Blumberg, J. (2011). Masculinity socialisation in sports: Influence of college football coaches. *Psychology of Men & Masculinity, 12*, 247-259.

Sun-Tzu, & Griffith, S. B. (1964). *The Art of War*. Oxford: Clarendon Press.

Surujlal, J., & Dhurup, M. (2012). Athlete preference of a coach's leadership style. *African Journal for Physical, Health Education, Recreation & Dance, 18*, 111-121.

Sutcliffe, S. (2019). Mistakes, abuse and VAR: What are the pressures like on a Premier League referee? https://www.bbc.co.uk/sport/football/47690634. Cited on 24/04/19 from the World Wide Web.

Sutter, M. & Kocher, M. G. (2004). Favouritism of agents – the case of referees' home bias. *Journal of Economic Psychology, 25* (4), 461-469.

Syed, M. (2016). Black Box Thinking: Marginal Gains and the Secrets of High Performance. London: John Murray.

Syed, M. (2018a). Why an ancient need to defend territory gives home team a sporting advantage. *The Times*, April 9th, 2018.

Syed, M. (2018b). Sir Alex Ferguson and José Mourinho helped nurture shameful idea that referees are biased. *The Times*, April 16th, 2018.

Syed, M. (2018c). Mark Clattenburg: 'People say my tattoos mean I'm an egotist. Why should they tell me how to live my life?' *The Times*, May 12th, 2018.

Syed, M. (2018d). Why Pep Guardiola gets an easier ride than Jose Mourinho. *The Times*, February 21st, 2018.

Syed, M. (2018e). Referee intoxicated by power – like a nightclub bouncer. *The Times*, April 2nd, 2018.

Syed, M. (2018f). Karius was too focused to think clearly. *The Times*, May 30th, 2018.

Syed, M. (2018g). Southgate has set a whole new trend in management. *The Times*, October 17th, 2018.

Syed, M. (2018h). Why English football's reluctance to embrace 'idea sex' is stopping the game from evolving. *The Times*, April 2nd, 2018.

Szczepanik, N. (2009). Ancelotti enjoys warm glow of a Cole-fired performance. *The Times*, October 26th, 2009.

Tamir, M. (2016). Why do people regulate their emotions? A taxonomy of motives in emotion regulation. *Personality & Social Psychology Review*, 20, 199-222.

Tayeb, M. (2013). Geert Hofstede. In M. Witzel & M. Warner (Eds.), *The Oxford Handbook of Management Theorists* (pp.427-447). Oxford: Oxford University Press.

Taylor, D. (2012a). Referee Mike Dean demoted after Manchester United v Chelsea errors. *The Guardian*, April 7th, 2010.

Taylor, D. (2012b). Michael Carrick: 'Depression over a game sounds extreme but I felt in a very dark place'. *The Guardian*, October 12th, 2018.

Taylor, D. (2012c). Referees winning the percentage game whatever managers and media say. *The Guardian*, March 3rd, 2012.

Thakare, A. E., Mehrotra, R., & Singh, A. (2017). Effect of music tempo on exercise performance and heart rate among young adults. *International Journal of Physiology, Pathophysiology and Pharmacology*, 9, 35-39.

Thelwell, R., & Greenlee, I. (2003). Developing competitive endurance performance using mental skills training. *Sport Psychologist*, 17, 208-225.

Thomas, L. (2018). What referee Jon Moss said to assistant Ed Smart for controversial Tottenham penalty against Liverpool. http://www.skysports.com/football/news/11661/11237166/what-referee-jon-moss-said-to-assistant-ed-smart-for-controversial-tottenham-penalty-against-liverpool. Cited on 06/02/18 from the World Wide Web.

Thorndike, E. L. (1920). A constant error in psychological ratings. *Journal of Applied Psychology, 4*, 25-29.

Transfermarkt.com (2018). Average UEFA attendances 16/17. www.transfermarkt.com/uefa-champions-league/besucherzahlen/pokalwettbewerb/CL/plus/0/galerie/0?saison_id=2016. Cited on 28/11/18 from the World Wide Web.

Turner, M., Carrington, S., & Miller, A. (2018). Psychological distress across sport participation groups: The mediating effects of secondary irrational beliefs on the relationship between primary irrational beliefs and symptoms of anxiety, anger, and depression. *Journal of Clinical Sport Psychology*, 1-38.

Tyler, J. M., & Burns, K. C. (2008). After depletion: The replenishment of the self's regulatory resources. *Self & Identity, 7*, 305-321.

Unkelbach, C. & Memmert, D. (2010). Crowd noise as a cue in referee decisions contributes to the home advantage. *Journal of Sport & Exercise Psychology, 32*, 483-498.

Vallerand, R. J., Blanchard, C. M., Mageau, G. A., Koestner, R., Ratelle, C., Léonard, M., Gagne, M., Marsolais, J. (2003). Les passions de l'âme: On obsessive and harmonious passion. *Journal of Personality & Social Psychology, 85*, 756-767.

Van Kleef, G. A., De Dreu, C. K. W., & Manstead, A. S. R. (2004). The interpersonal effects of anger and happiness in negotiations. *Journal of Personality & Social Psychology, 86*, 57-76.

Van Quaquebeke, N., & Giessner, S. R. (2010). How embodied cognitions affect judgments: Height related attribution bias in football foul calls. *Journal of Sport & Exercise Psychology, 32*, 3-22.

Vargas, T. M., & Short, S. E. (2011). Athletes' perceptions of the psychological, emotional, and performance effects of coaches' pre-game speeches. *International Journal of Coaching Science, 5*, 27-43.

Vealey, R. S. (2007). Mental skills training in sport. In G. Tenenbaum & R. C. Eklund (Eds.), *Handbook of Sport Psychology* (3rd ed., pp.287-309). Hoboken, NJ: Wiley.

Vealey, R. S., & Greenleaf, C. A. (2010). Seeing is believing: Understanding and using imagery in sport. In J. M. Williams (Ed.) *Applied Sport Psychology: Personal Growth to Peak Performance* (pp.267-304). London: McGraw-Hill.

Voborný, J., Zeman, T., Blahutková, M., & Václaviková, D. (2013). Factor analysis of pre-match and post-match subjective psychological experiences and mental states of football referees. *British Journal of Sports Medicine, 47*, 12.

Webb, T. (2016). 'Knight of the Whistle': W.P. Harper and the impact of the media on an Association Football referee. The International *Journal of the History of Sport, 33*, 306-324.

Webb, T. (2017). Elite Soccer Referees: Officiating in the Premier League, La Liga and Serie A. London: Routledge.

Webb, T. (2019). How to improve your officiating association. http://reflive.com/blog/tom-webb-interview. Cited on 25/01/19 from the World Wide Web.

Weiner, B. (1972). Attribution theory, achievement motivation, and the educational process. *Review of educational research, 42*, 203-215.

Wigmore, T. (2018). UK Sport ready to accept that success is about more than counting medals. https://inews.co.uk/sport/olympics/uk-sport-olympics-medal-count-mental-health-support-tokyo-2020/. Cited on 29/10/18 from the World Wide Web.

Williams, B. (2018). The problem with chasing perfection. https://www.playersvoice.com.au/ben-williams-problem-with-chasing-perfection/. Cited on 16/11/18 from the World Wide Web.

Williams, J. M., Nideffer, R. M., Wilson, V. E., Sagal, M., & Peper, E. (2010). Concentration and strategies for controlling it. In J. M. Williams (Ed), *Applied Sport Psychology: Personal Growth to Peak Performance* (pp.336-360). New York: McGraw-Hill.

Williams, O. (2010). Let's choose the music and dance. www.bbc.co.uk/blogs/olliewilliams/2010/02/ice_dance_music.shtml. Cited on 05/02/18 from the World Wide Web.

Wilson, J. (2017). FA relaunches Respect campaign amid referee strike threat over increasing abuse at grassroots. https://www.telegraph.co.uk/football/2017/01/17/referee-strike-threat-triggers-fa-action-abuse-grassroots-match/. Cited on 13/08/18 from the World Wide Web.

Wilson, J. (2018). Save our game: Referees seek talks with FA as abuse reports soar. *The Telegraph*, October 18th, 2018.

Wilson, J. (2019). Referees charity calls on FA to reboot Respect campaign after rise in reports of abuse of officials. http://www.telegraph.co.uk/football/2019/01/23/referee-reports. Cited on 28/01/19 from the World Wide Web.

Wilson, J. (2019b). Exclusive: FA wants threat of prison sentences for referee assaults. https://www.telegraph.co.uk/football/2019/06/18/exclusive-fa-wants-threat-prison-sentences-referee-assaults/. Cited on 19/06/19 from the World Wide Web.

Winter, J. (2006). Who's the B*****d in the Black?: Confessions of a Premiership Referee. London: Ebury Press.

Wolfson, S. & Neave, N. (2007). Coping under pressure: Cognitive strategies for maintaining confidence among soccer referees. *Journal of Sport Behaviour, 30,* 232-247.

World Football. (2018). Premier League 2016/17 attendance. www.worldfootball.net/attendance/eng-premierleague. Cited on 15/2/18 from the World Wide Web.

Wrisberg, C. A. (1993). Levels of performance skill. In R. N. Singer, M. Murphey, & L. K. Tennant (Eds.), *Handbook of research on sport psychology* (pp.61-72). New York: MacMillan.

Wrisberg, C. A., & Pein, R. C. (1992). The pre-shot interval and free throw shooting accuracy: An exploratory investigation. *The Sport Psychologist, 6,* 14-23.

Zeqiri, D. (2018). Fascinating video highlights the difficulties of being a top-flight referee – and the need for VAR. https://www.telegraph.co.uk/football/2018/08/27/fascinating-video-highlights-difficulties-top-flight-referee/. Cited on 16/09/18 from the World Wide Web.

Ziegler, M. (2018). Move to ban substitutions in injury time. *The Times,* October 26th, 2018.

Ziegler, M. (2019). FA to increase use of sin-bins. *The Times,* February 6th, 2019.

Zinsser, N., Bunker, L., & Williams, J. M. (2010). Cognitive techniques for building confidence and enhancing performance. In J. M. Williams (Ed), *Applied Sport Psychology: Personal Growth to Peak Performance* (pp.305-335). New York: McGraw-Hill.

Other Books from Bennion Kearny

Tipping The Balance: The Mental Skills Handbook For Athletes

Many athletes grow up with the philosophy that their mental approach to performance is fixed. They do the same things over and over again and expect excellence. But we know that mental approaches are not fixed. They are extremely changeable and adaptable, and therefore the greatest athletes can develop their mental approaches to fulfil their potential. Athletes who can deal with pressure enjoy their sport more, achieve excellence and are resilient to the demands of competition and training. *Tipping The Balance* offers contemporary evidence-based and highly practical mental strategies to help an athlete to develop the crucial mental skills that enable them to thrive under pressure, perform consistently when it matters most, and enjoy the challenge of the big event.

Togetherness:
How to Build a Winning Team

Togetherness is a powerful state of connection between individuals that can lead to amazing triumphs. In sport, teams win matches, but teams with togetherness win championships and make history.

If you want the individuals on your team to develop their skills and reach their potential, get them 'together'. The key to this, is to understand your players' group memberships and how to harness them, to create a unique team identity that is special to "us".

This concise and practical book – from Dr. Matt Slater, a world authority on togetherness – shows you how you can develop togetherness in your team. The journey starts with an understanding of what underpins togetherness and how it can drive high performance and well-being simultaneously. It then moves onto practical tips and activities based on the 3R model (Reflect, Represent, Realise) that you can learn and complete with your team to unlock their togetherness.

The 3R model provides you with a framework to take your team on a journey from "me" to "we".

With memorable stories from the world of high-performance sport, and a robust evidence-base, this book will help you to create and maintain togetherness in your team – whether in sport or other fields such as business or voluntary sectors – simply and effectively.

Achieve the impossible with your team… through togetherness.